Modeling Aggregate Behavior and Fluctuations in Economics

This book has two components: stochastic dynamics and stochastic random combinatorial analysis. The first discusses evolving patterns of interactions of a large but finite number of agents of several types. Changes of agent types or their choices or decisions over time are formulated as jump Markov processes with suitably specified transition rates: Optimizations by agents make these rates generally endogenous. Probabilistic equilibrium selection rules are also discussed, together with the distributions of relative sizes of the basin of attraction. As the number of agents approaches infinity, we recover deterministic macroeconomic relations of more conventional economic models. The second component analyzes how agents form clusters of various sizes. This has applications for discussing sizes or shares of markets by several types of agents, which involves some combinatorial analysis patterned after the population genetics literature. These are shown to be relevant to distributions of returns to assets, volatility of returns, and power laws.

Masanao Aoki is Professor Emeritus in the Department of Economics at the University of California, Los Angeles. He has held professorial appointments at the Institute for Social and Economic Research at Osaka University, Tokyo Institute of Technology, and the University of Illinois. Professor Aoki is a past President of the Society for Economic Dynamics and Control, a Fellow of the Econometric Society, and a Fellow of the IEEE Control Systems Society. Currently Associate Editor of the journal *Macroeconomic Dynamics*, published by Cambridge University Press, he also served as Editor of the *Journal of Economic Dynamics and Control* and the *International Economic Review* and as Associate Editor of the IEEE's *Transactions of Automatic Control, Information Sciences*, and the *Journal of Mathematical Analysis and Application*. Professor Aoki is the author or editor of a dozen books, including *New Approaches to Macroeconomic Modeling: Evolutionary Stochastic Dynamics, Multiple Equilibria, and Externalities as Field Effects* (Cambridge University Press, 1996).

Modeling Aggregate Behavior and Fluctuations in Economics

Stochastic Views of Interacting Agents

MASANAO AOKI
University of California, Los Angeles

 CAMBRIDGE
UNIVERSITY PRESS

CAMBRIDGE
UNIVERSITY PRESS

32 Avenue of the Americas, New York NY 10013-2473, USA

Cambridge University Press is part of the University of Cambridge.

It furthers the University's mission by disseminating knowledge in the pursuit of
education, learning and research at the highest international levels of excellence.

www.cambridge.org
Information on this title: www.cambridge.org/9780521606196

First published 2002
First paperback edition 2004

A catalogue record for this publication is available from the British Library

Library of Congress Cataloguing in Publication data
Aoki, Masanao.
Modeling aggregate behavior and fluctuations in economics : stochastic views of
interacting agents / Masanao Aoki.
p. cm.
Includes bibliographical references and index.
ISBN 0-521-78126-4
1. Demand (Economic theory) – Mathematical models. 2. Supply and demand –
Mathematical models. 3. Consumption (Economics) – Mathematical models.
4. Business cycles – Mathematical models. 5. Statics and dynamics (Social sciences) –
Mathematical models. 6. Stochastic processes – Mathematical models. I. Title.
HB842 .A57 2001
338.5212 – dc21   2001025596

ISBN 978-0-521-60619-6 Paperback

To My Late Father

CONTENTS

PREFACE

This book is a sequel to Aoki (1996) in the loose sense that it is motivated by a similar set of considerations to its predecessor and shares some of the same objectives. It records my efforts, since the publication of that book, at evaluating and reformulating macroeconomic models that are employed by the mainstream economic profession. In this book, a stochastic point of view is taken to construct models for finite numbers of interacting agents. In other words, the book emphasizes models that focus on economic phenomena that involve stochastic laws, or stochastic regularities that govern economic phenomena.

To make this book more readily accessible to traditionally trained economists and graduate students in economics, it is more narrowly focused than my previous one, and it attempts to establish better links with some well-known models in the macroeconomic literature. This book is motivated by my strong desire to persuade some traditionally trained economists to phrase their questions in stochastic ways and apply some of the methods presented in it to their work.

Mainstream economists and graduate students of economics may wonder why to use stochastic models or what additional or new insights they yield or, if stochastic laws in economics are so useful, why they have not heard of them before. A short answer is that models with finite numbers of agents in appropriate stochastic contexts reveal interesting economic phenomena that are invisible in deterministic models with infinite numbers of (representative) agents. Traditional models wash out some important information about economies, but one would not know them. This finitary and stochastic approach provides more information about the economy than deterministic economic laws permit.

There are many areas of economics to which my approach applies. In speaking of inflation and unemployment, Tobin, in his presidential address at the American Economic Association Meeting in 1971, came close to describing stochastic laws and aggregate dynamics and fluctuations (in terms of Fokker–Planck equations, say), according to my way of modeling, when he said, "... stochastic macro-equilibrium, stochastic, because random intersectoral shocks keep individual labor markets in diverse states of disequilibrium;

macro-equilibrium, because the perpetual flux of particular markets produces fairly definite aggregate outcomes of unemployment and wages . . . ."

Another major class of examples is building business-cycle models. All kinds of theories are found in the literature, and new theories keep cropping up. The real business cycle (RBC) theory by Kydland and Prescott (1982) may arguably be the most influential current theory among mainstream economists. As typified by the RBC, a natural research strategy to study business cycles is to explain fluctuations as a direct outcome of the behavior of *individual agents*. The more strongly one wishes to interpret aggregate fluctuations as something "rational" or "optimal," the more one is led to this essentially microeconomic approach. The mission of this approach is to explain fluctuations as responses of individual agents to changes in their economic environments. The consumer's intertemporal substitution, for example, is a device to achieve this goal. This has been the standard approach in the mainstream economics in the last twenty years or so.

Surely, we would like to know the distribution of durations of "good" times and "bad" times. When models admit multiple equilibria, which equilibrium, if any, will the model settle in? How long can the system be expected to stay in one basin of attraction before it moves to another? And so on. This book presents a different approach to fluctuations. This alternative approach is based on the fact that economy consists of a large number of agents or sectors. (The population of a large industrialized economy, for example, contains of the order of 10^8 agents.) Even if agents intertemporally maximize their respective objective functions, their environments or constraints all differ and are always subject to idiosyncratic shocks. Our alternative approach emphasizes that an outcome of interactions of a large number of agents facing such incessant idiosyncratic shocks cannot be described by a response of the representative agent and calls for a model of stochastic processes. In a seminal work, Slutzky (1937) proposed a stochastic approach. We follow his lead in this book to build a stochastic model of fluctuations and growth.

Although studies of macroeconomy with many heterogeneous agents are not new, dynamic behavior of economies in disequilibrium is not satisfactorily analyzed. The traditional Walrasian economy is the egregious example. It focuses on price adjustment with the help of nonexistent auctioneer.

In a nutshell, this book formulates and analyzes a large but finite number of interacting economic agents as continous-time Markov chains with discrete state spaces. Dynamics are described in terms of the backward Chapman–Kolomogorov equations, also known as the master equations. We are interested in such questions as the existence of stationary probability distributions for some variables, of critical points of aggregate dynamics, and of fluctuations about locally stable equilibria, and in the distributions of relative sizes of the basins of attraction and associated probabilities, how they relate to the lengths of business cycles, and so forth. The agents are assumed to be exchangeable rather than representative and have either a finite or countably infinite number of decisions to choose from, or they belong to a finite or countably infinite number of types or categories.

Unlike the jump Markov processes treated in standard textbooks on probability or stochastic processes, the transition rates of the processes in this book are endogenously determined via the value maximizations by the agents in the model. Using this framework, we take fresh looks at some well-known search models, such as the Diamond model and disequilibrium quantity adjustment models, as well as models for diffusions of innovations and endogenous growth. Formulations involving a few large clusters of agents in markets, and the implications for the volatility of returns on financial-asset markets, which may develop from interaction of many agents, are also examined using random combinatorial analysis. Such investigations lead to results not usually discussed in the traditional macroeconomic literature, such as the existence of power laws for some variables of interest, discoveries that some common laws apply to seemingly unrelated areas, and so on.

This book is aimed at advanced graduate students and practicing professionals in economics, as well as in some related areas, such as the recently formed area of econophysics. Some of the topics have been discussed in my graduate courses at UCLA and at Keio University, Tokyo, and at several conferences, workshops, and seminars. I wish to express appreciation to Professors R. Craine, K. Kawamata, A. Kirman, M. Marchesi, T. Lux, W. Semmler, H. Yoshikawa, and J.-B. Zimmermann for opportunities for presenting talks, and to Professors Y. Shirai, D. Costantini, U. Garibaldi, and D. Sornette for their useful comments on some parts of the topics in the book. I am particularly indebted to Professors Yoshikawa, Costantini, and Garibaldi for their help and guidance in overcoming my ignorance and misunderstandings. Simulations reported in this book were programmed by a former and a current graduate student at UCLA, J. Nagamine and R. Singh. I thank them for their help.

Some of my research activities reported here were supported in part by grants from the Academic Senate of the University of California, Los Angeles.

CHAPTER 1

Overviews

1.1   Our objectives and approaches

This book is about modeling a large collection of interacting agents, and examining aggregate (deterministic) dynamics and associated stochastic fluctuations.

There are two aspects or components in carrying out these objectives: dynamics, and random combinatorial analysis. The former is more or less self-explanatory and familiar to economists, although some of the techniques that are presented in this book may be new to them. The latter involves some facts or results that are rather new in economics, such as obtaining statistical distributions for cluster sizes of agents by types. More will be said on types later.

We regard economic processes as jump Markov processes, that is, continuous-time Markov processes with at most countable state spaces, and analyze formations of subgroups or clusters of agents by types. Jump Markov processes allow us to model group sentiments or pressure, such as fashion, fads, bandwagon effects, and the like. A cluster is formed by agents who use the same choices or decisions. Agents are thus identified with the rules they use at that point in time. Agents generally change their minds – that is, types – over time. This aspect is captured by specifying a set of transition rates in the jump Markov processes. Distributions of cluster sizes matter, because a few of the larger clusters, if and when formed, approximately determine the market excess demands for whatever goods are in the markets. There are some new approaches to firm size distributions as well.

Dynamics are represented by the master equations (the backward Chapman–Kolmogorov equations) for the joint probability distributions of suitably defined states of the collection of agents. The solutions of the master equations give us stationary or equilibrium behavior of the model and some fluctuations about them, obtained by solving the associated Fokker–Planck equations. Nonstationary solutions give us information on the time profiles of interactions, and how industries or sectors of economies mature or grow with time. These solutions may require some approximations, such as expansion of the master equations in some inverse powers of a parameter that represents the size of the model. In discussing multiple equilibria, we introduce a new equilibrium selection criterion, and consider distributions of the sizes of the associated basins of attractions in some random mapping contexts.

To fulfill our objectives, we use concepts such as partition vectors as state vectors, which arise in examining patterns formed by partitions of agents by types; Stirling numbers of the first and second kind, which have roots in combinatorial analysis; and distributions such as the Poisson–Dirichlet distributions and the multivariate Ewens distribution. All of these are unfamiliar to traditionally trained economists and graduate students of economics. We therefore present these as well as some others, as needs arise, to advance and support our modeling tasks and views proposed in this book.

Our approach is finitary. We start with a finite number of agents, each of whom is assumed to have a **choice set** – a set of at most countably many decision rules or behavioral rules. We define a demographic profile of agents composed of fractions of agents of the same type, with a finite number of total agents. We may let the number of agents go to infinity later, but we do not start with fractions of uncountably many agents arranged in a unit interval, for example (a typical starting point of some models in the economic literature). Our finitary approach is more work, but we reap a greater harvest of results. We may obtain more information on the natures of fluctuations, and more insight into dynamics, which get lost in the conventional approach.

Here is our approach in a nutshell. We start with a collection of a large, but finite, number of microeconomic agents in some economic context. We first specify a set of transition rates in some state space to model agent interactions stochastically. Agents may be households, firms, or countries, depending on the context of the models. Unlike examples in textbooks in probability, chemistry, or ecology, the reader will recognize that our transition rates are endogenously determined by considerations of value-function maximization associated with evaluations of alternative choices that confront agents.

Then we analyze the master equations that incorporate specified transition rates. Their size effects may be important in approximate analysis of the master equations. Stationary or nonstationary solutions of the master equations are then examined to draw their economic implications.

In models that focus on the decomposable random combinatorial aspects, distributions of a few of the largest order statistics of the cluster size distributions are examined to examine their economic consequences.

1.2   Partial list of applications

A number of models, mostly elementary or simple, are presented in Chapters 4 through 11 to illustrate the methods and potential usefulness of the proposed approaches. Some more elaborate models are found in parts of

Chapters 8 through 11, with some additional supporting material for them in Chapter 10.

One of the important consequences of our efforts is the derivation of aggregate, or emergent, or evolutionary patterns of behavior of large collections of agents. We deduce macroeconomic or sectoral properties or behavior of the microeconomic agents, starting from probabilistic descriptions of individual agents. Thus, we go part way from the microeconomic specifications of models to macroeconomic models, a level of models called **mesoscopic** by van Kampen (1992). By mesoscopic, we mean that we can deduce (nearly) deterministic average behavior and associated fluctuations. For example, we may think of building sectoral models composed of a large number of firms as mesoscopic models. Several or many such mesoscopic models may then be connected, or aggregated, as macroeconomic models.

We examine with fresh and different views processes for diffusion of new ideas or practices among firms in an industry, due to innovation, changing economic and social environments, disturbances, or the appearance and spread of new products among firms of an industrial sector, such as new manufacturing processes, new inventions, new employment policies, and technical improvements. We also examine a well-known model in the search literature, due to Diamond (1982), from our finitary perspectives in Chapter 9. In taking a new look at the Diamond model, we show a new probabilistic equilibrium selection criterion. In evaluating the Kiyotaki–Wright model (Kiyotaki and Wright 1993), which has similar dynamic structure to the Diamond model, we provide more dynamic analysis, and respecify their model so that money traders hold several units of money. Here, we show how partition vectors may be applied.

There are obviously many new results we can obtain in the area of industrial organization, such as entry and exit problems, changing market shares (Herfindahl index), or distributions of firm sizes or growth-rate distributions.

We also present, in Chapter 11, a simplified account of power laws that govern distributions of large price differences or returns in prices of some financial assets, and explanations of volatility switchings observed in financial time series, by examining conditions under which two large subgroups of agents with two opposing strategies form such that they largely determine the market excess demands for some financial assets.

1.3   States: Vectors of fractions of types and partition vectors

Levels of detail in describing behavior of a large collection of agents of several (or countably many) types dictate our choice of state variables.

Models are depicted in terms of **configurations**, namely patterns, or **states**, in more technical terms, and how they or some functions of them evolve with time. If we start our modeling task by specifying how sets of interacting agents behave at the level of microeconomics, then we may next inquire how some subsets or subgroups of microeconomic agents behave by attempting to describe their behavior in terms of less detailed state variables. These more **aggregated** state variables, or variables averaged over some larger subsets of agents than the original configurations, refer to model behavior at the aggregated, or more macroeconomic, levels of description. We use rather less detailed, or less probabilistic, specifications of states. Indeed, one of the insights we gain after many model-building exercises is that some of the very detailed microeconomic description found in some of the economic literature disappears, or matters less, as we describe agent behaviors averaged over larger sets of microeconomic configurations.

At the highest level of aggregation we have macroeconomic models in terms of macroeconomic variables. At a less aggregated level, we may have sectoral models described in terms of sectoral variables, which are less aggregated than the macroeconomic variables, but are more aggregated than microeconomic variables.[1] Stochastic description in terms of macroeconomic variables imply deterministic laws and the fluctuations about them (van Kampen 1992, p. 57).

We seek to link models for collections of microeconomic agents, whose behavior are described or stated by microeconomic specifications, with the aggregate or global behavior, which corresponds to mesoscopic or macroeconomic description.

1.3.1   Vectors of fractions

In this book, we use discrete states and models with finite or at most countable state spaces. This choice of state spaces is based on the way we describe microeconomic models and the details with which we describe behavior of agents – or, more pertinently, the decisions or choices they make, or the way we aggregate or incorporate microeconomic agents into macroeconomic models.

An example may help to clarify what we have in mind. At this preliminary stage of our explanation, let us suppose that agents have binary choices, or there are two types of agents, if we associate types with choices. The binary choices may be to participate or not in some joint projects, or to buy or not to buy some commodity or stocks at this point in time, etc. The nature of choices varies from model to model and from context to context. Here, we merely illustrate abstractly the ways states may be introduced. The two choices may be labeled or represented by 1 and 0, say. Then the state of n agents could be $\mathbf{s} = (s_1, s_2, \ldots, s_n)$, where $s_i = 1$ or $s_i = 0$, $i = 1, 2, \ldots, n$.

---

[1] To refer to variables at these intermediate levels we borrow a term from van Kampen (1992, p. 185) and call them **mesoscopic** variables for mesoscopic models. According to him, a mesoscopic quantity is a functional of the probability distribution (of states). He distinguishes mesoscopic variable from macro-variables.

This vector gives us a complete picture of who has chosen what. Thus, with regard to the information on the choice patterns by n agents, we don't need, nor can we have, more detail than that provided by this state vector. This is the microeconomic state at a point in time. We may then proceed to incorporate mechanisms or interaction patterns that determine how they may revise their choices over time, by specifying reward or cost structures and particulars on externalities among agents.

In some cases, we may decide not to model the collection of agents with that much detail. For example, identities of agents who have chosen 1 may not be relevant to our objectives of constructing models. We may care merely about the fraction of agents with choice 1, for example. Then, $\sum_i s_i / n$ is the information we need. Then we may proceed to specify how this **demographic** or fractional compositional information of agents evolves with time. At this level of completeness of describing the collection of a set of agents, the vector (n_1, n_2), where n_i is the number of agents with choice $i = 1, 2$, is a state vector. So is the vector made of fractions of each type of agents. This vector is related to the notion of empirical distribution in statistics. If the total number of agents is fixed, then the scalar variable n_1 or $f_1 = n_1/(n_1 + n_2)$ serves as the state variable.

With K choices or types, where K is larger than 2, detailed information on the choice pattern is provided by the vector **s**, where s_i now takes on one of K possible values, and choice patterns may be represented by the vector of demographic fractions, or by a vector $\mathbf{n} = (n_1, n_2, \ldots, n_K)$, where n_j is the total number of agents making the jth choice.

1.3.2   Partition vectors

This choice of state vector may look natural. There is, however, another possibility. To understand this, let us borrow the language of the occupancy problem in probability, and think of K unmarked or indistinguishable boxes into which agents with the same choices (identical-looking balls) are placed. Let a_i be the number of boxes with i agents in them. With n agents distributed into K boxes, we have $\sum_{j=1}^n j a_j = n$, and $\sum_{j=1}^n a_j := K_n \le K$. The first equation counts the number of agents, and the second the number of occupied boxes.

The vector with these as as components is a state vector for some purposes. In dealing with demographic distributions such as the number of firms in various size classes, the numbers of employees, the amount of sales per month, and so on, we are not interested in the identities of firms but in the number of firms each size class, as in the histogram representations of the numbers of firms of given characteristics or categories.

In some applications, we are faced with the problem of describing sets of partitions of agents of the type called exchangeable random partitions by

Kingman (1978a,b). The notion of partition vectors, in Zabell (1992), is just the right notion for discussing models in which some types of agents play a dominant role in determining market demands. This notion is discussed in detail in Chapter 3, and applied in Chapter 11 among many places.

We have briefly mentioned two alternative choices for state vectors. One of them is in terms of fractions of agents of each type or category. Instead of this more obvious choice of state variables, Watterson (1976) has proposed another way of describing states, which is less detailed than the one above using **n**. A level of disaggregation, or a way of describing the delabeled composition of a population of agents, is proposed that is suitable in circumstances in which new types of agents appear continually and there is no theoretical upper limit to the number of possible types. This is the so-called sampling-of-species problem in statistics (see Zabell 1993). The state of a population is described by the (unordered) set of type frequencies, i.e., fractions or proportions of different types, without stating which frequency belongs to which type. In the context of economic modeling, this way of description does not require model builders to know in advance how many or what types of agents are in the population. It is merely necessary to recognize that there are k distinct types in his sample of size n, and that there are a_j types with j agents or representatives in the sample. Compositions of samples and populations at this level are given by vectors **a** and **b** with components a_j and b_j, respectively, such that

$$\sum_{j=1}^{n} j a_j = n, \qquad \sum_{j=1}^{n} a_j = k,$$

and

$$\sum_{j=1}^{n} j b_j = n, \qquad \sum_{j=1}^{n} b_j = K$$

in the population, where N is the number of agents in the population, and K the number of distinct types, categories, or choices in the population, both being possibly infinite.

1.4   Jump Markov processes

By associating types with the decisions or choices, we may think of groups in which each agent has several alternative decisions to choose from. Agents may change their types when types are associated with their decisions, actions, or choices. In open models, agents of various types may, in addition, enter or leave the group or collection. These changes of fractions may occur at any time, not necessarily at the equally spaced discrete points of discrete dynamics. They are therefore modeled by continous-time (jump) Markov processes with finite or countable state spaces. See Norris (1997).

Among Markov processes we use those with a finite or at most countable states, and time running continuously. They are called jump or pure jump Markov processes in the probability literature.

1.5   The master equation

Once states have been assigned to a collection of economic agents, their behavior over time is specified by the dynamics for the joint probabilities of the states. Dynamics are set up by taking account of the probability fluxes into and out of a specified state over a small interval of time. We use the backward Chapman–Kolmogorov equation to do this accounting. We adopt the shorter name that is used in the physics and ecology literature and call the dynamic equation the **master equation**. This is an appropriate name because everything of importance we need to know about the dynamic behavior can be deduced from this equation. In particular we derive the dynamics for aggregate variables, which we call the **aggregate** dynamics (roughly corresponding to macroeconomic dynamics) and the dynamics for the fluctuations of state variables about the mean, or aggregate, values. The latter is called the Fokker–Planck equation.

It should be emphasized that the master equation describes the time evolution of the probability distribution of states, not the time evolution of the states themselves. This distinction may seem unimportant to the reader, but it is a crucial one and helps to avoid some technical difficulties. For example, in a model with two types of agents of a fixed total number, the fraction of one type of agents is often used as the state. The master equation describes how the probability for the fraction of one type evolves with time, not the time evolution of the fraction itself. The latter may exhibit some abnormal behavior at the extreme values of zero and one, but the probability distribution cannot.

When the master equations admit stationary solutions, as some models in this book do, we can deduce much from those distributions. Some nonstationary distributions may be obtained by the method of probability generating functions, or information on moments derived from cumulant generating functions. These are discussed in Chapters 3 and 4.

In general, we use Taylor series expansion in inverse powers of some measure of the model size, such as the number of agents in the model. We can show that in the limit of an infinite number of agents we recover traditional macroeconomic results. This is illustrated by reworking the well-known Diamond (1982) model in our framework in Chapter 9.

1.6   Decomposable random combinatorial structures

How do agents cluster or form subgroups in a market? What are the distributions of fractions on (high-dimensional) simplexes? These questions essentially have to do with random combinatorial structures such as random partitions. We borrow from Watterson (1976), Watterson and Guess (1977), and, more recently, Arratia (1992) and others to deal with the questions of multiplicities of micro-economic states compatible with a set of observations of (macroeconomic or mesoscopic) variables. In the second longest chapter of this book, Chapter 10, we connect three types of transition rates with three types of distributions, and discuss dynamics of clusters. Some of the results are then applied in Chapter 11, in which the two largest groups are on the opposite sides of the market and their excess demands drive the price dynamics of the shares.

1.7   Sizes and limit behavior of large fractions

We use order statistics of the fractions in some of the later chapters of this book. These have a well-defined limit distribution, called the Poisson–Dirichlet distribution, as the number of agents goes to infinity. The probability density of the first few of the fractions is later used in our discussion of approximations of market excess demands by a few dominant fractions in Chapters 10 and 11.

CHAPTER 2

Setting up dynamic models

This book is about setting up and analyzing economic models for large collections of interacting agents. We describe models in terms of states: as stationary distribution of states, or dynamics for time evolution of states. We may speak informally also of patterns of partitions of the set of agents by types or categories, or configurations, and how they or some functions of them evolve with time. Our models are usually specified as jump Markov processes, that is, Markov processes with a finite or at most countable number of states, and time running continuously.

In setting up a stochastic model for a collection of agents, then, we first choose a set of variables as a state vector for the model. The state vector should carry enough information about the model for the purpose at hand, so that we can, in principle, calculate the conditional distributions of future state vectors, given the current one.[1] Put differently, we must be able to calculate the conditional probability distributions of the model state vector at least for a small step forward in time, given current values of the state vector and time paths of exogenous variables.

This dynamic aspect of the model is described by the master equation, which is introduced in Chapter 3. Briefly, the master equation is the differential (or difference) equation that indicates how the probability of the model being at some specific state at a point in time is changed by the inflows and outflows of the probability fluxes. The name originates in the physics literature; see van Kampen (1992, p. 97).

The master equation is specified once the relevant set of transition rates for the model states is determined. Specifying these transition rates replaces the usual microeconomic specification of models.

---

[1] Strictly speaking, states should be (conditional) probability distributions, as pointed out by Bellman (1949). Informally and for convenience, however, we speak of a state vector even when we should speak of the distribution of the vector as the state.

In this chapter, we mention two basic types of state vectors we use in this book.

2.1   Two kinds of state vectors

Here, we begin by introducing two types of state vectors, called empirical distributions (frequencies) and partition vectors. Since the latter type is not used in the economic literature, we discuss it here and indicate why it is needed.

With K choices or types, where K is larger than 2, detailed information on the choices by individual agents is provided by the vector $\mathbf{s}$, where s_i now takes on one of K possible values, and choice patterns may be represented by the vector of demographic fractions, or by $(n_1, n_2, \ldots, n_K)$, where n_j is the total number of agents making the jth choice.

As touched on in Section 1.2, there is, however, another possibility when types or choices do not have any inherent labels. The key is whether agents or categories are distinguishable or not. Do labels carry intrinsic information, or do they serve as mere labeling? The situation is exactly the same as that of the occupancy problem in which distinguishable or indistinguishable balls are to be placed in distinguishable or indistinguishable boxes. With identical-looking balls in boxes with no labels or distinguishing marks, how do we count the number of possible patterns of ball placements?

Suppose that K boxes, into which agents with the same choices are allocated, are indistinguishable. Let a_i be the number of boxes with i agents in them. With n agents distributed into K boxes, we have $\sum_{j=1}^{n} j a_j = n$ and $\sum_{j=1}^{n} a_j = K$. The first equation counts the number of agents, and the second the number of boxes. In Section 1.2 we introduced the partition vector. The partition vector $\mathbf{a}$ with these a's as components is a state vector for some purposes. It is called the partition vector by Zabell (1992) in the statistics literature, and is called the allelic vector by Kingman (1980) in the population-genetics literature. Sachkov (1996, p. 82) refers to it as the secondary specification of states. We give several examples in later chapters.

In other examples our interest in modeling lies not so much in the manner n agents are partitioned or clustered among different groups or types, which is captured by the frequencies, as in some structural properties of the patterns of partitions, for example, in the patterns of frequency variations. These are what are called frequencies of frequencies in the literature of ecology or population genetics.

We use probabilities that are invariant with respect to permutations of agents, because we regard agents as interchangeable. Empirical distributions are invariant under permutations of agents. Random partitions are equiprobable when their partition vectors are the same. These matters will be taken up in this chapter, as well as some technical points on the existence of stationary or equilibrium distributions for the master equations.

2.2 Empirical distributions

When models have no dynamics, the states of agents are the same as the choices they make. We keep track of the population composition of agents by types, which are the same as the decisions they make, namely, the demography of the population of n agents according to their decisions. For this purpose we use the empirical distributions. We denote the set of states by $S = \{c_1, c_2, \ldots, c_K\}$. There are n agents in the model, and we denote their joint states by $\mathbf{x} = (x_1, x_2, \ldots, x_n) \in S^n$. The set of population compositions by types or demography is in one-to-one correspondance with that of configurations of balls in allocating n indistinguishable balls into K distinguishable boxes. Among n agents, $n(s_i | \mathbf{x})$ is the number of agents making choice i, i.e., in state s_i. The fraction of agents making choice i is found by dividing this number by n. In the analogy with balls and boxes, the fractions are the percentages of the total balls in the K boxes.

Let X_i, $i = 1, 2, \ldots, n$, be i.i.d. random variables taking values in S with probabilities q_i, $i = 1, 2, \ldots, K$. We denote the (discrete) probability distribution on S by Q, that is, we let $Q(i) = q_i$, $i = 1, 2, \ldots, K$. We simplify notation without loss of generality by taking the set S to be $\{1, 2, \ldots, K\}$, and write $Q(i)$ for $Q(s_i)$, and similarly $n(i | \mathbf{x})$ for $n(s_i | \mathbf{x})$.

Under the probability distribution Q, the joint probability of a state $\mathbf{x}$ is denoted by

$$Q^n(\mathbf{x}) := \Pr(X_1 = x_1, \ldots, X_n = x_n).$$

Given $\mathbf{x}$, its empirical distribution is defined by

$$P_\mathbf{x} := \{P_\mathbf{x}(1), P_\mathbf{x}(2), \ldots, P_\mathbf{x}(K)\},$$

where we define the components by

$$P_\mathbf{x}(i) := \frac{1}{n} \sum_{j=1}^{n} I_{(X_j = i)} = \frac{n(i | \mathbf{x})}{n},$$

where I is the indicator function. Empirical distributions thus give the frequencies with which each j occurs in the states, $j = 1, 2, \ldots, K$. By definition, P_i is one of $\{0/n, 1/n, \ldots, n/n\}$.

2.3   Exchangeable random sequences

Let $X_1, X_2, \ldots$ be an infinite sequence of random variables taking on K distinct values, $c_1, c_2, \ldots, c_K$, say. These may correspond to possible categories or types of decisions or choices by agents; they correspond to cells in the literature on occupancy numbers in probability theory.

The sequence is said to be exchangeable if all cylinder set the probabilities

$$\Pr(X_1 = c_1, X_2 = c_2, \ldots, X_n = c_n) = \Pr(c_1, c_2, \ldots, c_n)$$

are invariant under all possible permutations of the subscripts of Xs.[2] In other words, two sequences have the same probability if one is a rearrangement of the other.

Let n_i denote the number of times the ith type occurs in the sequence. The vector $\mathbf{n} = (n_1, n_2, \ldots, n_K)$ is the state vector. The vector $\mathbf{n}/\sum_1^K n_i$ is the empirical distribution discussed in the previous section in this book. Note that given any two sequences, one can be obtained from the other by rearrangement if and only if the two sequences have the same frequency vector or empirical distribution.

Definition.   We call two vectors $\mathbf{x}$ and $\mathbf{y}$ **exchangeable** if the empirical distribution of the two vectors are the same.

For more detail, see Zabell (1992).

By definition, each of the exchangeable sequences having the same frequency vector is equally probable. There are $n!/n_1!n_2! \cdots n_K!$ such sequences, and if they are given equal probability,

$$\Pr(X_1, X_2, \ldots, X_n|\mathbf{n}) = \frac{n_1!n_2! \cdots n_K!}{n!},$$

where $n = n_1 + n_2 + \cdots + n_K$. The observed frequency counts $n_j = n_j(X_1, X_2, \ldots, X_n)$ are **sufficient statistics**, in the language of statistics, for the sequence $\{X_1, X_2, \ldots, X_n\}$, because probabilities conditional on the frequency counts depend only on $\mathbf{n}$ and are independent of the choice of the exchangeable probability P, which assigns the same probability to any two exchangeable patterns.

We have the de Finetti representation theorem for exchangeable sequences (de Finetti 1937): If an infinite sequence of K-valued random variables $X_1, X_2, \ldots$ is exchangeable, then the infinite limiting frequency

$$Z := \lim_{n \to \infty} \left(\frac{n_1}{n}, \frac{n_2}{n}, \ldots, \frac{n_K}{n} \right)$$

---

[2] These subscripts may be thought of as time indices or as giving the order in which samples are taken.

exists almost surely; and if

$$\mu(A) = \Pr(Z \in A)$$

denotes the distribution of this limiting frequency, then

$$\Pr(X_1 = c_1, X_2 = c_2, \ldots, X_n = c_n)$$
$$= \int_{\triangle_K} p_1^{n_1} p_2^{n_2} \cdots p_K^{n_K} d\mu(p_1, p_2, \ldots, p_{K-1}),$$

where $\triangle_K$ is the K-simplex of probabilities of K elements, $p_i \geq 0, \sum_i^K p_i = 1$. To apply the de Finetti theorem, we must choose a specific **prior** or mixing measure $d\mu$. A way to specify a prior has been suggested by William Ernest Johnson: postulate that all ordered K-partitions of n are equally likely. This Johnson postulate uniquely determines $d\mu$ to be

$$d\mu(p_1, p_2, \ldots p_K) = dp_1 \, dp_2 \cdots dp_{K-1},$$

a flat prior; see Zabell (1992).

Less arbitrary is the Johnson sufficientness[3] postulate (see Good 1965, p. 26):

$$\Pr(X_{N+1} = c_i | X_1, X_2, \ldots, X_N) = \Pr(X_{N+1} = c_i | \mathbf{n}) = f(n_i, N),$$

if $\Pr(X_1 = c_1, \ldots, X_N = c_N) > 0$ for all cs. This formula states that in predicting that the next outcome is c_i, n_i and N are the only relevant information. Zabell shows that Johnson's sufficientness postulate implies that

$$\Pr(X_{N+1} = c_i | \mathbf{n}) = \frac{n_i + \alpha}{n + K\alpha}.$$

Note that the Pólya urn model (Feller 1968, pp. 119–121) can produce the same conditional expectation. The mixing measure $d\mu$ in this case is the symmetrical Dirichlet prior with parameter α (Zabell 1992).

There is an obvious connection with the ways the entry and exit rates for agents are specified in our models. See the examples throughout this book (Chapters 4, 7, and 8 in particular) and Appendix A.3.

2.4   Partition exchangeability

We follow Zabell (1992) in describing the notion of exchangeable random partitions, which is due to Kingman (1978a, 1978b). In economic applications such as multiple-agent models of stock markets, we encounter exactly the same problem faced by statisticians in dealing with the so-called sampling-of-species problem. Sometimes this problem is referred to as the ecological

---

[3] This term is adopted to avoid confusion with the usual meaning of sufficiency in the statistics literature.

problem in the emerging literature on multiagent or agent-based modeling in economics. As Zabell clearly explains, this is not the problem of observing an event to which we assign 0 probability, that is, an event whose probability we judge to be 0. Rather, the problem is when we observe an event whose existence we did not even previously suspect. A new strategy is invented, a new type of agents is born, new goods become available, and so on. Zabell calls this the problem of unanticipated knowledge. Suppose we take a snapshot of all the agents in a market or take a sample of size n at a point in time, and observe all different trading strategies in use by agents in the snapshot or in the sample. Some or most strategies have been seen in past snapshots or samples. There may be new ones that have not so far been observed, however. To deal with this problem we need Kingman's construction of random partition exchangeability. A probability function P is partition-exchangeable if the cylinder-set probabilities $P(X_1 = c_1, X_2 = c_2, \ldots, X_n = c_n)$ are invariant with respect to permutations of the subscripts of the Xs (time index) *and* the category index.

The partition vector plays the same role relative to partition-exchangeable sequences that the frequency vector plays for exchangeable sequences. Two sequences are equivalent, in the sense that one can be obtained from the other by a permutation of the time set and a permutation of the category set, if and only if the two sequences have the same partition vector.

For example, suppose you roll a die, and you obtain a sample $\{5, 2, 1, 5, 4, 4, 6, 4, 6\}$. Here $K = 6$. Rearrange the time index, i.e., the samples, into the standard form of descending order of observed frequency of each face of the die: $\{4, 4, 4, 5, 5, 6, 6, 1, 2\}$. Then perform the category permutation $(1, 2)$ $(3, 5)$ $(4, 6)$, that is, $1 \to 2 \to 1, 3 \to 5 \to 3, 4 \to 6 \to 4$. Thus, in the partition-exchangeable setup, we have

$$P(5, 2, 1, 5, 4, 4, 6, 4, 6) = P(6, 6, 6, 3, 3, 4, 4, 2, 1).$$

Define the frequencies of the frequencies (called abundances in the population-genetics or sampling-of-species literature) by the partition vector $\mathbf{a} = (a_1, a_2, \ldots, a_n)$, where a_r is the number of n_j that are exactly equal to r. This vector is an example of state variables of second specification according to Sachkov, mentioned in Chapter 1. In the above example, the original sample has the frequencies $n_1 = 1, n_2 = 1, n_3 = 0, n_4 = 3, n_5 = 2, n_6 = 2$; hence the frequecy vector is

$$\mathbf{n} = (1, 1, 0, 3, 2, 2) = 0^1 1^2 2^2 3^1,$$

where the last expression is in the notation of Andrews (1971), originally used to indicate cyclic products of permutations with a_i cycles of size i. Here $a_1 = 2, a_2 = 2, a_3 = 1, a_4 = a_5 = \cdots = a_{10} = 0$. Note also that $a_0 = 1$.

We can thus alternatively characterize partition exchangeability by the fact that all sequences having the same partition vector have the same probability. Probabilities conditional on the partition vector are independent of P, just as probabilities conditional on the frequency vector (empirical means) are independent of P.

Definition. We formally call a random partition **exchangeable** if any two partitions π_1 and π_2 having the same partition vector have the same probability:

$$\mathbf{a}(\pi_1) = \mathbf{a}(\pi_2) \quad \Rightarrow \quad P(\pi_1) = P(\pi_2).$$

Since partition-exchangeable sequences are exchangeable, they can be represented by $d\mu$ on the K-simplex $\triangle_K$. To prepare our way for letting K becomes large, we use order statistics. We denote by $\triangle_K^*$ the simplex of the ordered probabilities

$$\triangle_K^* := \left\{ (p_1^*, p_2^*, \dots, p_K^*); p_1^* \geq p_2^* \geq \cdots \geq p_K^* \geq 0, \sum_i p_i^* = 1 \right\}.$$

In the case of the partition-exchangeable sequences, the conditional probability becomes

$$P(X_{N+1} = c_i | X_1, X_2, \dots, X_N) = f(n_i; \mathbf{a}).$$

There are $K!$ permutations of the integers $\{1, 2, \dots, K\}$. To every permutation there corresponds the set defined by

$$\triangle_{K,\sigma} := \{(p_1, p_2, \dots, p_K) \in \triangle_K; p_{\sigma(1)} \geq p_{\sigma(2)} \geq \cdots \geq p_{\sigma(K)}\}.$$

The map of the probability vector into the vector of probabilities with permuted indices defines a homeomorphism of $\triangle_{K,\sigma}$ onto $\triangle_K^*$. This map can be used to transfer $d\mu$ on $\triangle_K^*$ to the subsimplex $\triangle_{K,\sigma}$. See Hansen (1990) or Donnelly and Joyce (1989).

When K is finite, $P(X_1 = c_1) = P(X_2 = c_2) = \cdots = P(X_K = c_K) = 1/K$. When K is not finite, we cannot use this relation. Instead of focusing on the probability of sequence of outcomes or the probability of a frequency vector, we focus on the partition vector and its probability when K is infinite.

In the sampling-of-species context, such as taking a snapshot of a market at a point in time and counting the numbers of agents by the types of strategies they are using at that point in time, the relevant information received is an exchangeable random partition of $\mathbf{N} := \{1, 2, \dots, N\}$, where N is the total number of agents in the market at that time. Individual types, algorithms, or categories have no significance. We observe the first type, then possibly later the second, and so on. We therefore partition **N** as

$$\mathbf{N} = A_1 \cup A_2 \cup \cdots,$$

where $A_i \cap A_j = \emptyset$, $i \neq j$, and where

$$A_1 := \left\{ t_1^1, t_1^2, \ldots ; 1 = t_1^1 < t_1^2 < \cdots \right\}.$$

This means that the type of the first agent observed is called type 1. Agents of the same type 1 may be observed later at times t_1^2, t_1^3, and so on. An agent of a different type, called type 2, is first observed at t_2^1. We construct a set

$$A_2 := \left\{ t_2^1, t_2^2, \ldots ; t_2^1 < t_2^2 < \cdots \right\},$$

where t_2^1 is the first positive integer not in the set A_1.

Example. Given a sample 6, 3, 4, 2, 3, 1, 6, 2, 2, 3, we have

$$\{1, 2, \ldots, 10\} = \{1, 7\} \cup \{2, 5, 10\} \cup \{3\} \cup \{4, 8, 9\}.$$

These partitions may be interpreted as the cyclic product of permutations.

The partition vector is $\mathbf{a} = (2, 1, 2, 0, \ldots, 0)$. This indicates that there are 2 singletons, 1 partition with two numbers, and 2 partitions with three elements, and the others are empty. The sum $\sum_i a_i = 5$ means that five types are observed in this sample.

2.5   Transition rates

We mostly use transition rates that are standard in the birth–death or birth–death-with-immigration models in the probability textbooks, with one important modification. In our economic models, not all parameters in the transition rates are exogenously given; some are endogenously determined. In particular, some parameters in the transition rates are to be determined by the value-maximization processes of agents. We have several examples of this nature in this book. See, for example, the Diamond model in Chapter 9.

Initially, however, this aspect is not involved here. We take it up later when we discuss evaluation of alternative choices by agents in Chapter 6.

Rates at which agents enter the model in open models are specified by the entry rates. For example, if an agent of type i enters the model, the number of agents of type i increases by one. This is represented by the vector **n** becoming $\mathbf{n} + \mathbf{e}_i$, where $\mathbf{e}_i$ is the K-dimensional vector with sole nonzero element 1 at component i. This event has the transition rate $w(\mathbf{n}, \mathbf{n} + \mathbf{e}_i)$. In discrete-time models, this event has the conditional probability $\Pr(\mathbf{n} + \mathbf{e}_i | \mathbf{n})$.

In closed models, changing of decisions by agents may be modeled as entry together with exit. For example, an agent of type i, where type is associated with decision or choice, may become type j by exiting from a group or cluster of agents made up of type i and entering a cluster of agents of type j. This is expressed as having the transition rate $w\,(\mathbf{n}, \mathbf{n} + \mathbf{e}_j - \mathbf{e}_i)$.

More will be said in Chapter 4 as well as in a section of the Appendix at the end of the book.

2.6 Detailed-balance conditions and stationary distributions

Agents also cluster into several groups, or change their minds and leave one cluster to join another in the model. We introduce the notion of stationary or equilibrium distributions, reversibility, and detailed-balance conditions, all of which are used extensively in this book. We refer the reader to Kelly (1979, Chap. 1) as a convenient source of these notions. Some of the materials in Kelly go back to Kingman (1969), or to Kendall (1949).

When there are K types of agents, we have earlier described one state vector as

$$\mathbf{n} = (n_1, n_2, \ldots, n_K),$$

where n_i is a non negative integer that denotes the number of agents of type i, $i = 1, 2, \ldots, K$. The vector $\mathbf{n}$ describes the clusterings of agents over K types. The total number of agents in the model is given by

$$n = \sum_{i=1}^{K} n_i.$$

In modeling closed binary models, n_1 alone can serve as the state variable because $n_2 = N - n_1$.

The vector of fractions, $\mathbf{n}/N$, is an empirical distribution. In the above and in what follows we omit the time variable from expressions such as $n_i(t)$.

As you notice in Kelly (1979), Markov chains are described in terms of conditional probabilities,

$$p(j, k) := P(X(t + 1) = k | X(t) = j),$$

where the next time instant after t is denoted as $t + 1$ by a suitable choice of time unit, and where, without loss of generality, the state space is $\mathcal{S} = \{1, 2, \ldots, K\}$. The notion of the transition rate from state j to k is then defined as

$$w(j, k) \times \tau = P(X(t + \tau) = k | X(t) = j) + o(\tau)$$

for some small positive τ. We follow this practice of developing discrete-time and continuous-time versions in parallel when convenient or needed.

Before we discuss dynamics, which are determined once we specify transition rates between the states under conditions to rule out pathological behavior by Markov processes,[4] we describe how stationary or equilibrium distributions are determined by the transition rates.

Writing $w(\mathbf{n}, \mathbf{n}')$ to denote the transition rate from state $\mathbf{n}$ to $\mathbf{n}'$, the equilibrium distribution satisfies

$$\pi(\mathbf{n}) \sum_{\mathbf{n}'} w(\mathbf{n}, \mathbf{n}') = \sum_{\mathbf{n}'} \pi(\mathbf{n}') w(\mathbf{n}', \mathbf{n}), \tag{0.1}$$

where $\pi(\mathbf{n})$ is the equilibrium probability of state vector $\mathbf{n}$, and where the summation is over all possible next states; for example, six possible next states in the case of an open binary model, and two in the case of a closed binary model. See the formulation of Kelly (1979, (1.3)). This equation states that the probability influx and outflux balance out in stationary states. The method for constructing a Markov process with these transition rates is standard (due to Feller). See Kelly (1983) for a short description.

In deriving the stationary or equilibrium distributions, we appeal to the notion of detailed-balance conditions extensively. The conditions are that there exists a set of positive numbers $\pi(j)$, $j \in \mathcal{S}$, summing to unity, such that

$$\pi(j)p(j, k) = \pi(k)p(k, j)$$

for any state $j, k \in \mathcal{S}$. These $\pi(j)$ are the components of the equilibrium distribution. In the continuous-time version, the detailed-balance conditions are

$$\pi(j)w(j, k) = \pi(k)w(k, j)$$

for all $j, k \in \mathcal{S}$.

Kelly (1979, Sec. 1.2) shows that a stationary Markov chain is reversible if and only if the detailed-balance conditions hold. Similarly for a stationary Markov processes.

A necessary and sufficient condition for reversibility is the Kolmogorov cycle condition (Kendall 1959, Eq. (5.12)). Kingman shows that it is sufficient to consider two three-cycles (1969, Eqs. (17), (18)). See also Kelly (1979, Exercise 1.5.2).

We later show that some well-known distributions result from some specific choices for the transition rates.

---

[4] The conditions rule out the process making an infinite number of jumps in a finite time. See Kendall (1975) or Kelly (1983).

CHAPTER 3

The master equation

This chapter summarizes briefly the main tool of our dynamical analysis, that is, the basic dynamical equation for stochastic systems or models in this book. It is known as the master equation in the literature of physics, and as the backward Chapman–Kolmogorov equation in the probability literature.

After decribing the transition rates that appear in the master equation, we explain, following van Kampen (1992, p. 253), a power-series expansion method of solving the master equation, by which we extract dynamical equations for the aggregate variables and derive equations for fluctuations about the locally stable equilibria. This equation, which governs probability distributions for the fluctuations about the equilibria, is known as the Fokker–Planck equation. These methods are illustrated and discussed further in Chapters 4 and 5. See Aoki (1996a, Secs. 5.2, 5.3). See also Risken (1989, p. 11) or Gardiner (1990, Chap. 7).

3.1   Continuous-time dynamics

The probability distribution for a state variable $X(t)$ is governed by the master equation

$$\frac{\partial P(X, t)}{\partial t} = \int \{w(X', X)P(X', t) - w(X, X')P(X, t)\} \, dX',$$

where the transition rate from state X to X' is denoted by $w(X, X')$. If we want to be explicit about the size of the model, or the number of agents in the model, we introduce a parameter N, and denote the transition rates with N as subscript: $w_N(X', X)$. More generally, any extensive variable may be used to represent a size of the problem or model.

We make one key assumption: that the change in the state variable, i.e., $X' - X$, remains the same for different values of N. This assumption is certainly met in birth-and-death processes, since jumps are restricted to be ± 1 in binary choice models in Chapter 4, or $+1$ and -2 in the search models in

Chapter 9, from any state, regardless of the total number N. This assumption actually is concerned with the scaling properties or homogeneity properties of the transition rates. Loosely put, it means that each of the N microeconomic units may contribute approximately equally to the transition events. The transition rates reflect combinatorial ways certain events take place in a short interval of time. To make this explicit, we express the transition rate as a function of the starting state X' and the jump (vector) $r = X - X'$ and write

$$w_N(X', X) = w_N(X', X' + r) := w_N(X'; r),$$

and assume that

$$w_N(X'; r) = w_N\{N(X'/N); r\} = N w_N(X'/N; r) = N\Phi(x'; r)$$

for some function Φ, where $x' = X'/N$.

Using the same function, we can express the transition rate in the opposite direction as

$$w_N(X, X') = N\Phi(x; -r).$$

A scaling property that is seemingly more general is

$$w_N(X'; r) = f(N)\Phi(x'; r)$$

for some positive function $f(N)$. Actually, this factor $f(N)$ is arbitrary, since it can always be absorbed into the choice of time unit.

More generally, the transition rates may take the form of a power-series expansion in some inverse expression of N, such as N^{-1}:

$$w_N(X', X) = f(N)\{\Phi_0(x'; r) + N^{-1}\Phi_1(x'; r) + N^{-2}\Phi_2(x'; r) + \cdots\},$$

where higher-order terms in N^{-1} may represent higher-order interactions among microeconomic agents.

In terms of these transition rates, the master equation may be rewritten as

$$\frac{\partial P(X, t)}{\partial t} = f(N) \int \left\{ \Phi_0\left(\frac{X-r}{N}; r\right) + N^{-1}\Phi_1\left(\frac{X-r}{N}; r\right) + \cdots \right\} P(X - r, t)\, dr$$

$$- f(N) \int \left\{ \Phi_0\left(\frac{X}{N}; r\right) + N^{-1}\Phi_1\left(\frac{X}{N}; r\right) + \cdots \right\} P(X, t)\, dr.$$

Example.   A Markov chain with finite states. Suppose that a state variable $X(t, \omega)$ is defined on a probability space $(\Omega, \mathcal{F}, P)$ with values in a finite state space $I = \{1, 2, \ldots, N\}$. We write

$$p_{i,j}(t) := \Pr[\omega : X(t, \omega) = j \mid X(0) = i].$$

We assume that

$$\Pr(X(h) = k \,|\, X(0) = i) = \delta_{i,k} + q_{i,k}h + o(h)$$

uniformly in t as $h \downarrow 0$, where $q_{i,i} := -\sum_{k \neq i} q_{i,k}$. We drop ω for brevity. In this example we write the transition rate from state i to k, $w(i, k)$, as $q_{i,k}$.

Then the differential equation for $p_{i,j}$ is obtained by examining

$$\Pr(X(t + h) = j \,|\, X(0) = i)$$
$$= \sum_{k \in I} \Pr(X(h) = k \,|\, X(0) = i)\, \Pr(X(t + h) = j \,|\, X(h) = k),$$

where we note that $\Pr(X(t + h) = j \,|\, X(h) = i) = \Pr(X(t) = j \,|\, X(0) = i)$ by the time homogeneity, which is assumed. By substituting the transition-rate expression into the above,

$$p_{i,j}(t + h) = \sum_{k \in E}(\delta_{i,k} + q_{i,k}h + o(h))p_{k,j}(t),$$

from which we obtain

$$\dot{p}_{i,j}(t) = \sum_{k \neq j} q_{i,k}p_{k,j}(t) - q_{i,j}p_{i,j}(t).$$

We define matrices $P := (p_{i,j})$, and $Q := (q_{j,k})$. Note that each row of Q sums to zero.

This differential equation can be written as a matrix equation

$$\frac{dP}{dt} = QP,$$

which is known as Kolmogorov's backward equation in the probability literature; see Cox and Miller (1965, p. 181), for example. With E finite, the solution, $P(t) = \exp(tQ)$, with $P(0)$ the $N \times N$ identity matrix, also satisfies

$$\frac{dP}{dt} = PQ,$$

called Kolmogorov's forward equation.

Let ρ be a row vector of initial probabilities. Then $p_j(t) = (\rho P)_j$ is governed by the master equation

$$\frac{dp_j(t)}{dt} = \sum_{k \neq j} q_{k,j}p_k(t) - p_j(t) \sum_{k \neq j} q_{j,k}.$$

(To shorten notation we omit the condition on subscripts j and k that they belong to I.) The initial contitions are such that $0 \leq p_i(0) \leq 1$ and $\sum_i p_i(0) = 1$. See also Brémaud (1999, p. 342) for proof of differentiability, assumed above.

The steady-state solution of this master equation, denoted by $\bar{p}_i$, is obtained by setting the left-hand side of the master equation equal to zero:

$$\sum_j q_{i,j} \bar{p}_j = 0$$

for each $i \in I$. A nontrivial steady state exists, because $\det(Q) = 0$.

When the master equation is summed over j, we obtain

$$\sum_j \frac{dp_j(t)}{dt} = \sum_{j,k} q_{k,j} p_k(t) = 0.$$

So the sum of the probabilities remains at 1: $\sum_i \bar{p}_i = \sum_i p_i(0) = 1$.

We show next that there is a positive τ such that $p_j(t) > 0$ for all $j \in I$ and t in the interval $(0, \tau)$. This is clearly so if none of the initial conditions is zero. Under the assumption that the graph G underlying this Markov process[1] is connected, we eventually arrive at the conclusion that some mth derivative of the probability of some state, say p_{j^*} is positive at zero after some repeated differentiation. From this we conclude that $p_{j^*}(t) > 0$ in $0 < t < \tau$ for some positive τ. Arguing this way, we can show none of $p_j(t)$ vanishes for some $t > 0$.

We next show that the dynamics for deviational probabilities, $\delta p_j(t) = p_j(t) - \bar{p}_j$, are asymptotically stable by introducing a *Lyapunov function*.[2] The dynamical equations are

$$\frac{d}{dt} \delta p_j(t) = \sum_k \delta J_{j,k}$$

for all $j \in I$, where

$$J_{j,k} := q_{j,k} p_j - q_{k,j} p_k$$

is the net inflow of the probability flux from state j to k.

As a Lyapunov function, we use

$$V(p_1, p_2, \ldots, p_N) := \sum_i p_i \ln \frac{p_i}{\bar{p}_i}.$$

Note that it is positive except for zeros at $p_i = \bar{p}_i$, $i = 1, 2, \ldots, p_N$. We have $\delta V = 0$ at the steady-state solution. Writing $V(p_1, \ldots, p_N)$ as $V(p)$ for brevity, we have

$$\delta V = V(p + \delta p) - V(p) = \sum_i \delta p_i \ln \frac{p_i}{\bar{p}_i} + \frac{1}{2} \sum_i \frac{(\delta p_i)^2}{\bar{p}_i} + \cdots,$$

---

[1] This graph has vertices at states of the Markov chain, with edges connecting two states when the transition rates between the two states are nonzero.
[2] See Aoki (1996a, p. 261) for example.

that is,

$$\delta^2 V = \frac{1}{2} \sum_i \frac{(\delta p_i)^2}{\bar{p}_i} > 0.$$

Its time derivative along the trajectory is nonpositive:

$$\frac{dV}{dt} = \sum_j \dot{p}_j \ln \frac{p_j}{\bar{p}_j} = \sum_{j,k} q_{k,j} p_k \ln \frac{p_j}{\bar{p}_j} - \sum_{j,k} q_{j,k} p_j \ln \frac{p_j}{\bar{p}_j},$$

$$\sum_{j,k} q_{k,j} p_k \ln \frac{p_j \bar{p}_k}{\bar{p}_j p_k} \leq \sum_{j,k} q(k, j) p_k \left[\frac{p_j \bar{p}_k}{\bar{p}_j p_k} - 1 \right] = 0,$$

where we use Gibbs's inequality $\ln x \leq x - 1$ for $x > 0$.

This shows that the steady states of the master equation are asymptotically stable.

3.2 Power-series expansion

As above we expanded the transition rate in inverse powers of N, we may expand the master equations in N^{-1} to solve it by retaining terms only up to $O(N^{-1})$.[3] In some models, we anticipate that the probability density, the time evolution of which is governed by the master equation, will show a well-defined peak at some X of order N, with spread (standard deviation) of order $\sqrt{N}$, if the initial condition is

$$P(X, 0) = \delta(X - X_0).$$

In such cases, we change the variable by introducing two variables ϕ and ξ, both of order one, and set (recall that $x(t) = X(t)/N$)

$$x(t) = \phi(t) + N^{-1/2} \xi(t).$$

Later we show that ϕ is the mean of the distribution when this change of the variable is applicable, i.e., $\phi(t)$ keeps track of the mean of $x(t)$, and the spread about the mean is expressed by a random variable $\xi(t)$. This decomposition or representation is expected to work when the probability density has a well-defined peak, and it does, as we will soon demonstrate.

We next show that the terms generated in the power-series expansion of the master equation separate into two parts. The first part, which is the larger in magnitude, is an ordinary differential equation for ϕ. This is interpreted to

---

[3] When these terms are zero, we may want to retain terms of order N^{-2}. Then we have diffusion-equation approximations to the master equation. See Aoki (1996a, Sec. 5.14) for diffusion approximations.

be the macroeconomic or aggregate equation. The remaining part is a partial differential equation for ξ with coefficients that are functions of ϕ, the first term of which is known as the Fokker–Planck equation. We have several examples of this in Chapters 4, 5, and 7 through 9. To obtain the solution of the master equation, we may set the initial condition by $\phi(0) = X_0/N$.[4]

We rewrite the probability density for ξ as

$$\Pi\{\xi(t), t\} = P\{X(t), t\}$$

by substituting $N\phi + N^{1/2}\xi$ into X.[5] In rewriting the master equation for Π we must take the partial derivative with respect to time keeping $x(t)$ fixed, i.e., we must impose the relation

$$\frac{d\xi}{dt} = -N^{1/2}\frac{d\phi}{dt},$$

and we obtain

$$\frac{\partial P}{\partial t} = \frac{\partial \Pi}{\partial t} - \frac{\partial \Pi}{\partial \xi}\frac{d\xi}{dt} = \frac{\partial \Pi}{\partial t} - N^{1/2}\frac{d\phi}{dt}\frac{\partial \Pi}{\partial \xi}.$$

We also note that we need to rescale time by

$$\tau = N^{-1}f(N)t.$$

Otherwise, the random variable ξ will not be $O(N^0)$, contrary to our assumption, and the power-series expansion will not be valid. But we also assume $f(N) = N$ in this section. In general it is the case that $\tau \neq t$. We use τ from now on to accommodate this more general scaling function.

The master equation in the new notation is given by

$$\frac{\partial \Pi(\xi, \tau)}{\partial \tau} - N^{1/2}\frac{d\phi}{d\tau}\frac{\partial \Pi}{\partial \xi}$$

$$= -N^{1/2}\frac{\partial}{\partial \xi}\{\alpha_{1,0}(x) \cdot \Pi\} + \frac{1}{2}\frac{\partial^2}{\partial \xi^2}\{\alpha_{2,0}(x) \cdot \Pi\}$$

$$- \frac{1}{3!}N^{-1/2}\frac{\partial^3}{\partial \xi^3}\left\{\alpha_{3,0}(x) \cdot \Pi - N^{-1/2}\frac{\partial}{\partial \xi}\alpha_{1,1}(x) \cdot \Pi\right\}$$

$$+ O(N^{-1}), \tag{3.1}$$

---

[4] We need not be precise about the initial condition, since an expression of $O(N^{-1})$ or $O(N^{-1/2})$ can be shifted between the two terms without any consequence. Put differently, the location of the peak of the distribution can't be defined more precisely than the width of the distribution, which is of order $N^{1/2}$. See Section 9.6 for an illustration.

[5] Following the common convention that the parameters of the density are not carried as arguments in the density expression, we do not explicitly show ϕ when the substitution is made.

where $x = \phi(\tau) + N^{-1/2}\xi$, and where we define the moments of the transition rates by

$$\alpha_{\mu,\nu} = \int r^{\mu} \Phi_{\nu}(x; r)\, dr. \tag{3.2}$$

See van Kampen (1992, p. 253) for the terms not shown here.[6]

In this expression we note that the dominant terms $O(N^{1/2})$ on the two sides are equated to extract dynamical relations for the aggregate variables. Terms of $O(N^0)$ yield what is known as the (linear) Fokker–Planck equation. See Aoki (1996a, p. 157). In the next section, the first moment of the leading term of the transition rate $w_N(X|X')$, $\alpha_{10}(\phi)$, will be shown to determine the macroeconomic equation.

3.3   Aggregate dynamics and Fokker–Planck equation

Equating the highest-order terms in N on the two sides of (Eq. 3.1) yields the aggregate equations for ϕ,

$$\frac{d\phi}{d\tau} = \alpha_{1,0}(\phi).$$

The zeros of the function $\alpha_{1,0}(\phi) = 0$ defined by (Eq. 3.2) are the critical points of the aggregate dynamics. If its derivatives there are negative, then those critical points are locally stable. When $\alpha_{1,0}(\phi)$ are continuous functions of ϕ in the range between 0 and 1, then the zeros are alternately locally stable and unstable. The aggregate dynamics of the Diamond model in Chapter 9 turns out to have a discontinuity. There are two critical points, and both of them are locally stable.

3.4   Discrete-time dynamics

Here we record the discrete-time version of the master equation described earlier. We follow Costantini and Garibaldi (1999) in the derivation.

Given a discrete-time Markov chain with state vector $\{\mathbf{s}(t), t = 0, 1, 2, \ldots\}$, it satisfies

$$P[\mathbf{s}(t+1) = \mathbf{n}] = \sum_{\mathbf{n}'} P[\mathbf{s}(t) = \mathbf{n}'] P(\mathbf{n}|\mathbf{n}').$$

We use the exit probability

$$P(\mathbf{n} - \mathbf{e}_i|\mathbf{n}) = \frac{n_i}{n},$$

---

[6] Note that

$$\frac{\partial}{\partial \xi}\{\alpha_{10}(x)\Pi\} = \alpha_{10}(\phi)\frac{\partial \Pi}{\partial \xi} + N^{-1/2}\alpha'_{10}(\phi)\frac{\partial}{\partial \xi}(\xi\Pi) + O(N^{-1}).$$

and the entry probability

$$P(\mathbf{n}_k + \mathbf{e}_k | \mathbf{n}) = \frac{\alpha_k + n_k}{\alpha + n},$$

where $\alpha = \sum_i \alpha_i$ and where vector $\mathbf{e}_i$ has entry 1 at the ith component and zeros elsewhere. See the Appendix for further detail on specifications of entry and exit rates.

Using the relation $\sum_{\mathbf{n}'} P(\mathbf{n}' | \mathbf{n}) = 1$, we rewrite the dynamical equation in the form of the difference equation for the probabilities:

$$P[\mathbf{s}(t + 1) = \mathbf{n}] - P[\mathbf{s}(t) = \mathbf{n}]$$
$$= \sum_{\mathbf{n}' \neq \mathbf{n}} [P[\mathbf{s}(t) = \mathbf{n}'] P(\mathbf{n} | \mathbf{n}') - P[\mathbf{s}(t) = \mathbf{n}] P(\mathbf{n}' | \mathbf{n})].$$

This is the discrete-time master equation.

When the detailed-balance condition holds, it has a unique stationary solution, $\pi(\mathbf{n})$, which is the solution of

$$\pi(\mathbf{n}) P(\mathbf{n}' | \mathbf{n}) = \pi(\mathbf{n}') P(\mathbf{n} | \mathbf{n}').$$

In particular, we use $\mathbf{n}' = \mathbf{n} - \mathbf{e}_i + \mathbf{e}_j$, recalling that

$$P(\mathbf{n} - \mathbf{e}_i + \mathbf{e}_j | \mathbf{n}) = P(\mathbf{n} - \mathbf{e}_i | \mathbf{n}) P(\mathbf{n} - \mathbf{e}_i + \mathbf{e}_j | \mathbf{n} - \mathbf{e}_i),$$

with $P(\mathbf{n} - \mathbf{e}_i | \mathbf{n}) = n_i / n$, $P(\mathbf{n} - \mathbf{e}_i + \mathbf{e}_j | \mathbf{n} - \mathbf{e}_i) = (\alpha_j + n_j - 1)/(n - 1 + \alpha)$, and its inverse transition probability

$$P(\mathbf{n} | \mathbf{n} - \mathbf{e}_i + \mathbf{e}_j) = \frac{(n_j + 1)(\alpha_i + n_i - 1)}{n(\alpha + n - 1)},$$

with $\alpha = \sum_i \alpha_i$.

The difference equation for the stationary probability distribution is

$$\pi(\mathbf{n}) = \frac{n_j + 1}{n_i} \frac{\alpha_i + n_i - 1}{\alpha_j + n_j} \times \pi(\mathbf{n} - \mathbf{e}_i + \mathbf{e}_j).$$

The solution is a generalized Pólya distribution

$$P(\mathbf{n}, \alpha) = \frac{n!}{\alpha^{[n]}} \prod_{r=1}^{K} \frac{\alpha_r^{[n_r]}}{n_r!},$$

where $\alpha = \sum_i \alpha_i$.

CHAPTER 4

Introductory simple and simplified models

This chapter collects some solved examples of simple or simplified models, which are developed more fully later in this book. The first example describes a simplified two-sector version of a K-sector model with underutilized factors of production. As a starter we just describe its equilibrium distributions. Later, in Chapter 8, we discuss dynamics of equilibria and a general K-sector version. The rest of the examples illustrate how to solve master equations. In these examples, agents choose one of a discrete set of choices or decisions. We classify agents by their decisions or the algorithms they are using into distinct classes, or **types**. When the total number of agents is fixed, we speak of **closed** models, that is, closed to entry or exit by agents. When there are random entries and exits, we have **open** models, in which the number of agents is a random variable. When agents have two alternative decisions (algorithms or choices), we speak of binary choice or binary decision models. Such models are perhaps the simplest for a large group of microeconomic agents, and are suitable to illustrate a number of points that we wish to make.

4.1   A two-sector model of fluctuations

This model is a simplified two-sector version of a more general model of an economy composed of K-sectors (agents), which is similar to the one described more fully in Section 8.6. Here, for simplicity, we assume that the two sectors produce identical or close-substitute goods. The two sectors (agents), each has an underutilized factor of production.

A more completely analyzed model in Section 8.6 has patterns of output fluctuations and growth that are similar to those of models of more complex economic structures. This full version of the model has three novel features. First, it uses a stochastic adaptive scheme that is different from those in many adaptive models in general and in agent-based computational economic models in particular. Second, the notion of holding, or sojourn, times of continuous-time Markov chains is used to select the next sector (agent) who acts. Thirdly, it

27

introduces new types or sectors in a way similar to that of changing the number of types in the Ewens sampling formula in the population-genetics literature. See Ewens (1990) or Section A.7 of the Appendix on the Ewens distribution. New sectors or type are created and sectors disappear randomly and in a way correlated with excess demands. Sectors with positive excess demands create new ones randomly as new branches. This feature is in line with the findings by Schmookler (1966). He found evidence in the U.S. patent data that invention and technical progress are strongly influenced by demand conditions. This last feature is absent in this simplified version.

In this simplified two-sector version, we examine the stationary (equilibrium) distribution of the sizes of the two sectors. Resources are stochastically allocated to the two sectors in response to excess demands or supplies of the sectors. The output of the model randomly fluctuates. More importantly, this model demonstrates what we believe to be a generic property that the level of aggregate activities is influenced stochastically by the patterns of demands.

Sector i has productivity coefficient c_i, which is exogenously given and fixed. In our simplified version, $c_1 = c_2$ is assumed. Sector i employs N_i units of a factor of production. It is a nonnegative integer-valued random variable. We call its value the **size** of the sector. When $N_i(t) = n_i, i = 1, 2, \ldots, K$, the output of sector i is $c_i n_i$, and the total output (GDP) of this economy is

$$Y(t) := \sum_{i=1}^{K} c_i n_i(t) = cn(t), \tag{4.1}$$

where $n(t) = n_1(t) + n_2(t)$ for $K = 2$.

Demand for the output of sector i is denoted by $s_i Y(t)$, where $s_i > 0$ is the share of sector i, and $\sum_i s_i = 1$. The shares are also assumed to be exogenously given and fixed. We denote the excess demand for goods of sector i by

$$f_i(t) := s_i Y(t) - c_i n_i(t),$$

$i = 1, 2$.

In a closed model n is fixed and Y remains constant, even though n_1 and $n_2 = n - n_1$ will fluctuate. In an open model n_1 and n are random numbers. We do not discuss the dynamics of the model here. However, it is convenient to introduce the notion of holding-time here, which is important in developing the full version of the model in Section 8.6. We assume that the time it takes for sector i to adjust its size by one unit, up or down, T_i, is exponentially distributed,

$$\Pr(T_i > t) = \exp(-b_i t).$$

This time is called the sojourn time or **holding time** in the probability literature. See Lawler (1995) or Section A.4.1. We assume that the random variables T_i

of the sectors with nonzero excess demand are independent. The sector that adjusts first is then the sector with the shortest holding time. Let T^* be the minimum of all the holding times of the sectors with nonzero excess demands.

Let $T_* := \min(T_1, T_2)$. Then, noting that $\Pr(T_* > t) = \Pr(T_1 > t)\Pr(T_2 > t)$ $= e^{-(b_1 + b_2)t}$, the probability that sector 1 adjusts its size first is given by

$$\Pr(T_1 = T_*) = \int_0^\infty \Pr(T_2 > t)\, d\Pr(T_1 = t) = \int_0^\infty e^{-b_2 t} b_1 e^{-b_1 t}\, dt = \frac{b_1}{b_1 + b_2}.$$

Similarly, we can calculate the probability that sector 2 adjusts its size first to be $b_2/(b_1 + b_2)$. These bs will be specified in Section 8.6.

After a change in the size of a sector, the total output of the economy changes to

$$Y(t + h) = Y(t) + \mathrm{sgn}\{f_a(t)\}\, c_a,$$

where a is the sector that jumped first by the time $t + h$.[1]

These two equations show the effects of an increase of size in one sector. An increase by c_a of output increases GDP by the same amount. However, sector a experiences an increase of its demand by only a fraction s_a of it, while the other sectors experience increase of their demands by $s_i c_a$, $i \neq a$.

In this simplified version the sum of the excess demands after a size change is the same as before:

$$f_1'(t) + f_2'(t) = f_1(t) + f_2(t),$$

where

$$f_1'(t) := s_1 c_2 n_2(t) - s_2 c_1 [n_1(t) + 1] = f_1(t) - c_1(1 - s_1),$$

and

$$f_2'(t) := f_2(t + h) = s_2 c_1 [n_1(t) + 1] + s_2 c_2 n_2(t) - c_2 n_2(t) = f_2(t) + s_2 c_1.$$

Analogous equations hold when sector 2 changes its size by one:

$$f_1''(t) := f_1(t) + s_1 c_2\, \mathrm{sgn}[f_2(t)],$$

and

$$f_2''(t) := f_2(t) - c_2 s_1\, \mathrm{sgn}[f_2(t)].$$

Note also that $f_1''(t) + f_2''(t) = f_1(t) + f_2(t)$.

---

[1] For the sake of simplicity, we may think of the skeleton Markov chain in which the directions of jump are chosen appropriately but the holding times themselves are replaced by a fixed unit time interval. The limiting behavior of the original and the skeletal version are known to be the same under certain technical conditions, which hold for this example. See Çinlar (1975).

When excess demands of all sectors are zero, no section changes its output. We solve two equations $f_i = 0$, $i = 1, 2$, for zero excess demands and denote the equilibrium sizes with superscript e. With $c := c_1 = c_2$, the solution is particularly simple:

$$Y^e = cn^e,$$

where $n^e = n_1^e + n_2^e$, with

$$n_i^e = s_i n^e,$$

$i = 1, 2$, so that we have

$$n_2^e = \beta n_1^e,$$

with $\beta = s_2/s_1$.

In this preliminary stage of our analysis of the model, we just examine the equilibrium situation, and drop superscript e from now on. There are $C_{n,n_1} = n!/n_1!(n - n_1)!$ many microeconomic configurations of n_1 and $n_2 = n - n_1$ for this given macroeconomic situation, where $C_{n,k}$ denotes the binomial coefficient for choosing k objects out of n. This happens with probability

$$C_{n,n_1} s_1^{n_1} s_2^{n-n_1}.$$

With large n and n_1, we use the Stirling formula for factorials to approximate the binomial coefficients by

$$C_{n,n_1} \approx \exp\left[nH\left(\frac{n_1}{n}\right)\right],$$

where $H(x) = -x\ln x - (1 - x)\ln(1 - x)$ is the Shannon entropy, and see that the probability is given by

$$\pi(n_1; n) \approx \exp[nD(P_{n_1}, Q)],$$

where $D(\cdot, \cdot)$ is the Kullback–Leibler distance (divergence) between the two distributions $P_{n_1} = (n_1/n, (n - n_1)/n)$ and $Q = (s_1, 1 - s_1)$.

The most probable configuration is that of $n_1 = s_1 n$ condidtional on n being given. If s_1 is adjustable by some means, then assuming that the goods of the two sectors are close substitutes, the expected total output is maximized at $s_1 = 1/2$. In this simple model, the expected output is maximized when demands fall equally on the two sectors.

4.2 Closed binary choice models

For examples with agents with discrete choice sets, we begin with binary choice models to introduce our notation, basic formulation for the dynamics, and stationary or equilibrium distributions in the context of jump Markov processes. Consider a model for a large collection of agents, each of whom chooses from two alternative decisions. For this reason, we call it a binary choice model or simply a binary model.

Each of n agents chooses from a set of two alternatives, which we call choice one and choice zero, denoted by $x_i = 1$ or $x_i = 0$, $1 \leq i \leq n$. We later generalize this model in several ways by incorporating richer choice sets, or by examining consequences of various alternative specifications for transition rates. In binary choice models, the vector $\mathbf{x} = (x_1, x_2, \ldots x_n)$ can take on 2^n possible patterns, or configurations. The fraction n_1/N, or more generally the set of empirical distributions or frequencies, is the information we have on configurations.

The average choice, X/n, where $X = \sum_{i=1}^{n} x_i$, is perhaps the simplest example of macroeconomic signals of the model. We can also deal with the average of some function of choices, $f(x_i)$, for example. This model is simple enough to allow complete description of the probability distribution of the possible configurations. Later, we introduce a method for approximatng the probability expressions (which can naturally be expressed in terms of entropy functions), because the method applies equally well to more complex models than the one we discuss here.

There is a famous urn model, the Ehrenfest urn model, in elementary physics and probability textbooks. This model may be reinterpreted as a closed binary choice model by specifying the two transition rates by $w(k, k + 1) = \lambda(n - k)$ for $k = 0, 1, \ldots, n - 1$ and $w(k, k - 1) = \mu k$ for $k = 1, 2, \ldots, n$.

These transition rates reflect the fact that agents make their choices independently. For example, when there are $n - k$ type 2 agents, each switches to type 1 in the small time interval dt with probability $\lambda \, dt + o(dt)$, so that the aggregate or total probability is approximately $\lambda(n - k) \, dt$. Externalities among agents' decisions are introduced in the next section.

These transition rates produce the stationary probability distribution, obtained by setting the left-hand side of the master equation equal to zero, with these transition rates substituted into the right-hand side. The solution is $\pi_k = (1 + \lambda/\mu)^{-n} C_{n,k} (\lambda/\mu)^k$, because of the relation $1 = \sum_{k=0}^{n} C_{n,k} (\lambda/\mu)^k \pi_0 = (1 + \lambda/\mu)^n \pi_0$, which determines the constant π_0.

4.2.1 A Pólya distribution model

Next, we describe a closed binary choice model with a Pólya distribution as the equilibrium distribution. This distribution arises from the entry and exit transition rates specified by

$$w(k, k - 1) = dk$$

for $k > 1$, and

$$w(k, k + 1) = c(k + f)$$

for $k \geq 0$, for some positive constants f, c, and d.[2] A model of these transition rates is called a birth–death-with-immigration model, where the constant term represents a constant flow of immigrants. In the economic interpretation, the constant term may represent some economic inducement for entry, such as excess profit, shortage of production capacity, or the like. In some cases, the constant term may depend on previous history of decisions made by agents. See the business-cycle model in Section 8.6 for an example of such an interpretation.[3]

The detailed-balance condition, given by

$$\pi(k)w(k, k - 1) = \pi(k - 1)w(k - 1, k)$$

is a first-order difference equation for the equilibrium probability $\pi(j)$, and gives

$$\pi(k) = (1 - g)^f g^k \Gamma(f + k)/\Gamma(f)$$

for $k \geq 0$, where $g = c/d$. The ratio of gamma functions is often written as

$$f^{[k]} := f(f + 1)(f + 2)\cdots(f + k - 1).$$

This model may be used to analyze market shares of two brands of consumer goods, for example. We may model growth of a sector of an economy by associating choices with investment or no-investment decisions of firms, as we later describe. Further, we may model growth in a macroeconomic context by associating agents' choices with relocation decisions in a two-sector economy. For example, models of intersectoral capital reallocation under uncertainty such as that of Dixit (1989) may be redone using the framework of our binary choice model.

4.3   Open binary models

There are six admissible state transitions in an open binary choice model: entry of each of two types of agents, departure of each of two types, a change of

---

[2] When f is negative, we obtain another distribution. See Costantini and Garibaldi (1999).

[3] Although we do not explicitly discuss microeconomic factors involved in decisions by agents to enter, exit, or change strategies, such as cumulative profit or loss figures or explicit evaluations of merits of alternative choices, they are implicit in the specifications of transition rates we employ. See Aoki (1996a, Secs. 3.3, 5.5, 6.3) for further elaborations. In the face of uncertain consequences of any choice, these specifications may be thought of as first-order approximations, since transition rates are likely to be complicated nonlinear functions of state-vector components. Linearly specified transitions rates may be thought of as the first-order approximations to nonlinear transition rates ϕ and/or ψ. See Aoki (1996a, p. 121) for higher-order terms of transition rates.

strategy by a type one agent into a type two, and the reverse transition of an agent from type two to type one. These transitions are conveniently expressed by defining two vectors

$$\mathbf{e}_1 = (1, 0),$$

and

$$\mathbf{e}_2 = (0, 1).$$

Entry and exit by a type i agent are the events denoted by state transition

$$\mathbf{n} \rightarrow \mathbf{n} + \mathbf{e}_i, \quad \text{and} \quad \mathbf{n} \rightarrow \mathbf{n} - \mathbf{e}_i$$

for $i = 1, 2$. The number of agents in the market changes by one in these two transitions. Change of strategy by an agent from strategy i to j is denoted by

$$\mathbf{n} \rightarrow \mathbf{n} - \mathbf{e}_i + \mathbf{e}_j,$$

where $i, j = 1, 2$, and $i \neq j$, since n_i is decreased by one and n_j is increased by one. For example $\mathbf{n} - \mathbf{e}_2 + \mathbf{e}_1 = (n_1 + 1, n_2 - 1)$ means that one of type two participants changes into a type one agent. Note that unlike entries or exits, the total number of agents in the market remains the same in the type changes.

Now we posit, as in Kingman (1969),[4]

$$w(\mathbf{n}, \mathbf{n} - \mathbf{e}_i) = \phi_i(n_i), \tag{4.2}$$

where $\phi(0) = 0$,

$$w(\mathbf{n}, \mathbf{n} + \mathbf{e}_j) = \psi_j(n_j), \tag{4.3}$$

and

$$w(\mathbf{n}, \mathbf{n} - \mathbf{e}_i + \mathbf{e}_j) = \lambda_{i,j} \phi_i(n_i) \psi_j(n_j), \tag{4.4}$$

where the λ's are positive, $i \neq j$, and $i, j = 1, 2$. These transition rates are special cases, called simple by Kingman. He calls them **simple** if it is possible to write in (4.2) $\sim$ (4.4)

$$\phi_i(\mathbf{n}) = \phi_i(n_i), \qquad \psi_j(\mathbf{n}) = \psi_j(n_j).$$

In addition, we assume that $\gamma_{i,j}$ in the transition from state i to j is proportional to the product of the exit rate from state i and the entry rate to state j. See Costantini and Garibaldi (1999) for more on this point.

---

[4] To avoid a trivial situation in which every agent chooses the same decision, we assume that agents who are seemingly identical (or, more technically, assumed to be exchangeable) may choose differently because outcomes of a choice may be random or only incompletely or partially known.

Equations (4.2) through (4.4) specify that an agent of either type may enter or change his or her type at rates that are influenced by the number of agents of the same type in the market.

In general, stationary probability distributions cannot be obtained analytically. When the equality holds term by term, that is, when we assume that the detailed-balance conditions hold, we can sometimes solve for the equilibrium distributions. This is the case with $K = 2$. Although there are six separate equations when we impose the detailed-balance condition, the solution of any one of the six equations turns out to satisfy the remainder of the equations with suitable conditions imposed on the model transition parameters. For example, we start with (4.2):

$$\pi(\mathbf{n})w(\mathbf{n}, \mathbf{n} + \mathbf{e}_i) = \pi(\mathbf{n} + \mathbf{e}_i)w(\mathbf{n} + \mathbf{e}_i, \mathbf{n})$$

for $i = 1, 2$, or with (4.2) or (4.3). It does not matter how we begin.

We first verify for the case with $K = 2$ that the stationary probabilities in product form satisfy the detailed-balance condition. That is, we posit

$$\pi(n_1, n_2) = \pi_1(n_1)\pi_2(n_2).$$

This is the same as what Kingman calls simple transition rates. The detailed-balance condition using (4.2) yields the first-order difference equations

$$\pi_i(n_i + 1) = \frac{w(\mathbf{n}, \mathbf{n} + \mathbf{e}_i)}{w(\mathbf{n} + \mathbf{e}_i, \mathbf{n})}\pi_i(n_i) = \frac{\psi(n_i)}{\phi(n_i + 1)}\pi_i(n_i),$$

$i = 1, 2$. Note that $w(\mathbf{n} + \mathbf{e}_i, \mathbf{n})$ is the departure rate when the number of type i agents is $n_i + 1$. This is a first-order difference equation for the probabilities. Iterating this relation, we obtain

$$\pi_i(n_i) = b_i \prod_{r=1}^{n_i} \frac{\psi_i(r - 1)}{\phi_i(r)},$$

where b_i is the normalizing constant.

As a special linear case, we may use $\phi(n_i) = d_i n_i$, $d_i \neq 0$, and $\psi_i(n_i) = a_i + c_i n_i$. This specification is used in Kelly (1979, p. 139). The specified process is sometimes called a birth–death-with-immigration process, since there is a term a_i that is independent of n_i in the entry transition rate.

In economic applications, the constant term in the entry rate is important. It may represent exogenous (policy) effects either to encourage or facilitate entry in the case of positive a_i, or to discourage or retard entry in the case of negative a_i. Sutton (1997) speaks of niche effects, such as increases in demand that affect only a subset of the sectors of economy – that are not **economy-wide**. Positive as produce (generalized) Pólya distributions, and negative ones produce hypergeometric distributions. We return to these distributions later, and discuss one example.

4.3.1 Examples

Here are three examples with $n = \infty$. When a model has transition rates specified by $w(k, k - 1) = \alpha$ and $w(k, k + 1) = \beta$, the equilibrium distribution is

$$\pi_k = (1 - \theta)\theta^k,$$

with $\theta = \beta/\alpha$. This is a geometric distribution.

With $w(k, k - 1) = \mu k$ and $w(k, k + 1) = \nu$, the equilibrium distribution is a Poisson distribution

$$\pi_k = e^{-\theta}\frac{\theta^k}{k!},$$

where $\theta = \nu/\mu$.

A third example is the case where $w(k, k - 1) = \mu k$ and $w(k, k + 1) = \nu + \lambda k$. In this case the equilibrium distribution is

$$\pi_k = (1 - \theta)^{\nu/\lambda}\theta^k C_{\nu/\lambda+k-1,k},$$

which is called a negative binomial distribution with $\theta = \lambda/\mu$.

4.4 Two logistic process models

In at least two places in this book, we discuss models that exhibit logistic growth patterns. As preparation, we describe two models that generate logistic curves as the expected values of the random number n – the number of agents of type 1 or choice 1, say. See the Section 7.4 for related models.

4.4.1 Model 1: The aggregate dynamics and associated fluctuations

This model is described in Karlin and Taylor (1981, p. 144). We discuss a particular case of it with $N_1 = 1$ in their notation. See also Kendall (1949). Define the transition rates for the right move,

$$r_k = \lambda\frac{k}{n}\frac{n - k}{n},$$

and the left move,

$$l_k = \mu\frac{k}{n}\frac{k - 1}{n},$$

where n is the upper bound on k. (N_2 in Karlin and Taylor and in Kendall.) We may interpret the parameter λ as the constant of proportionality between the birth rate per individual and the deviation from the upper bound, $n - k$, and the parameter μ as that between the death rate per individual and the deviation from the floor, $k - 1$, when k is the number of individuals.

So far, this is a deterministic model. It may be converted into a stochastic model governed by the master equation

$$\frac{d P_k(t)}{dt} = r_{k-1} P_{k-1}(t) + l_{k+1} P_{k+1}(t) - (r_k + l_k) P_k(t).$$

This master equation has the equilibrium distribution determined by

$$\lambda(k - 1)(n - k + 1)\pi_{k-1} = \mu k(k - 1)\pi_k,$$

with $1 \leq k \leq n$. The solution is

$$\pi_k = \frac{1}{k} \binom{n - 1}{k - 1} \left(\frac{\lambda}{\mu}\right)^{k-1}.$$

To obtain approximate solutions to the master equation as n goes to infinity, we change variables to

$$k = n\phi + \sqrt{n}\xi.$$

We have already seen several instances in which this type of change of variables was carried out. In this example we need to change the time scale as well, by

$$n\tau = t.$$

Define

$$\Pi(\xi, t) := P(k, t),$$

and note that

$$\frac{\partial P}{\partial t} = \frac{\partial \Pi}{\partial t} + \frac{\partial \Pi}{\partial \xi} \frac{d\xi}{dt},$$

where

$$\frac{d\xi}{dt} = -\sqrt{n}\frac{d\phi}{dt}.$$

We rearrange the terms depending on μ as $(r_{k-1} - r_k) P_k(t) + r_{k-1}[P_{k-1}(t) - P_k(t)]$, that is, as n^{-2} times

$$(k - 1)(n - k + 1)P(k - 1, t) - k(n - k)P(k, t)$$
$$= (k - 1)(n - k + 1)[P(k - 1, t) - P(k, t)] - (n - 2k + 1)P(k, t),$$

and group them as $(l_{k+1} - l_k) P_k(t) + l_{k+1}[P_{k+1}(t) - P_k(t)]$, that is, as n^{-2} times

$$k(k + 1)P(k + 1, t) - k(k - 1)P(k, t)$$
$$= k(k + 1)[P(k + 1, t) - P(k, t)] + 2k P(k, t).$$

Now we use the Taylor series expansion

$$P(k-1,t) - P(k,t) = -\frac{1}{\sqrt{n}}\frac{\partial \Pi}{\partial \xi} + \frac{1}{2n}\frac{\partial^2 \Pi}{\partial \xi^2} + \cdots.$$

We expand $P(k+1,t) - P(k,t)$ analogously.

To match the largest terms in n, we change t into τ defined above. The largest orders yield the aggregate dynamic equation

$$\frac{d\phi}{d\tau} = \lambda\phi(1-\phi) - \mu\phi^2.$$

Its solution is

$$\phi = \frac{\lambda}{\lambda + \mu - ce^{-\beta\tau}},$$

where c is a constant of integration, $c = 1 - \lambda/[\phi(0)(\lambda+\mu)]$, and $\beta = (\mu+\lambda)^2/\lambda$. This is called a **logistic curve**.

The next largest order of terms gives

$$\frac{\partial \Pi}{\partial \tau} = [-\lambda(1-2\phi) + 2\mu\phi]\frac{\partial(\xi\Pi)}{\partial \xi} + \frac{\lambda\phi(1-\phi)+\mu\phi^2}{2}\frac{\partial^2 \Pi}{\partial \xi^2}.$$

Its stationary solution is obtained by setting the time derivative on the right to zero. We can integrate the result and obtain

$$X(\xi) = \text{const } \exp[-\xi^2/2\sigma(\phi)],$$

where we use $X(\xi)$ to denote the stationary distribution of Π as time goes to infinity, and where $\sigma(\phi) = [\lambda\phi(1-\phi)+\mu\phi^2]/[2\mu\phi - \lambda(1-2\phi)]$. Since $\lambda/(\lambda+\mu)$ is the positive equilibrium value for ϕ, the variance is well defined, because it is positive.

The equation for ϕ can be thought of as the growth equation for the expected value, and the equation for ξ as giving the fluctuations about the mean, which is normally distributed with zero mean and variance $\sigma(\phi)$ in this case.

4.4.2 Model 2: Nonlinear exit rate

Suppose the transition rates of the previous model are changed slightly to

$$r_k = \lambda\frac{k}{n},$$

and

$$l_k = \mu\left(\frac{k}{n}\right)^2.$$

(Other variations are possible in specifying the transition rates.)

In solving the master equation we again use the change of variables introduced in connection with Model 1. We omit the detail of calculations, since they are quite similar to those for Model 1. We obtain the aggregate dynamics as

$$\frac{d\phi}{d\tau} = \lambda\phi - \mu\phi^2,$$

and the Fokker–Planck equation for ξ for a stationary distribution is

$$0 = (2\mu\phi - \lambda)\frac{\partial(\xi\Pi)}{\partial\xi} + \frac{\lambda\phi + \mu\phi^2}{2}\frac{\partial^2\Pi}{\partial\xi^2}.$$

The solution is the normal distribution with mean zero and variance

$$\sigma(\phi) = \frac{\lambda\phi + \mu\phi^2}{2(2\lambda\phi - \lambda)},$$

provided that the expression in the denominator is positive. The aggregate equation has a positive equilibrium at λ/μ, and the denominator of the variance expression is positive near it.

4.4.3   A nonstationary Pólya model

We have described in Section 4.1 a closed binary choice model that has a Pólya distribution as its equilibrium distribution. We use the number of agents of type 1, say k, as the state variable for a closed model with the total number of agents fixed at n.

The transition rates are specified by

$$w(k, k - 1) = \lambda_{1,2}c_2d_1k(n - k + f_2),$$

and

$$w(k, k + 1) = \lambda_{2,1}c_1d_2(n - k)(k + f_1).$$

The detailed-balance conditions are satisfied with $\lambda_{1,2} = \lambda_{2,1}$, and the parameters are all positive.

The stationary probability density is given in the product form

$$\pi(k) = \pi_1(k)\pi_2(n - k) = BC_{-f_1,k}C_{-f_2,n-k}(-g_1)^k(-g_2)^{n-k},$$

where B is the normalization constant, and $g_i = c_i/d_i, i = 1, 2$. By calculating the constant B, we see that $\pi(k)$ is a Pólya distribution

$$\pi(k) = C^{-1}_{-f_1-f_2,n}C_{-f_1,k}C_{-f_2,n-k}.$$

To examine the dynamic aggregate behavior, we have two choices.

One is to change the state variable from n to

$$\frac{k}{n} = \phi + \frac{\xi}{\sqrt{n}},$$

where ϕ denotes the mean of the fraction of type 1 agents, and ξ denotes the fluctuation about the mean. We know from Aoki (1996a, p. 136) that the aggregate or average dynamics for ϕ is given by

$$\frac{d\phi}{d\tau} = \alpha_0(\phi),$$

where $\tau = nt$, with $\alpha_0(\phi) := -\rho_0(\phi) + \gamma_0(\phi)$, and where

$$\rho_0(\phi) = n\lambda c_2 d_1 \phi(1 - \phi + f_2/n),$$

and

$$\gamma_0(\phi) = n\lambda c_1 d_2(1 - \phi)(\phi + f_1/n).$$

Exercise. Suppose that $c_1/d_1 = c_2/d_2 = g$. Show that there is a unique locally stable equilibrium at $\phi_e = f_1/(f_1 + f_2)$.

Around this equilibrium point, ξ has a stationary normal distribution, since up to $O(N^{-1})$, the distribution for ξ is governed by the Fokker–Planck equation, and its stationary solution is given by solving

$$\alpha_0'(\phi_e)\xi\,\Pi_e(\xi) = \frac{\beta_0(\phi_e)}{2}\frac{d}{d\xi}\Pi_e,$$

with

$$\beta := \rho_0 + \gamma_0,$$

where ϕ_e denotes the locally stable critical point of the aggregate dynamics, and Π_e is the stable distribution for ξ, which is a mean-zero normal distribution. See Aoki (1996a, pp. 137, 158). Integrating this equation, the variance is seen to be $\sigma_e^2 := -\beta_0/2\alpha_0'/2$, evaluated at ϕ_e. Note that $-\alpha_0'$ is nonnegative at ϕ_e.

The critical point of the aggregate dynamics yields information about ϕ_e. The Fokker–Planck equation tells us about fluctuation of the state variable n/N, that is, about the fraction of type 1 agents about the equilibrium point.

Alternatively, if we are interested in obtaining information about the mean and the variance but not necessarily about the distribution, we can use the cumulant generating function. This method produces ordinary differential equations for these two moments. Their stationary solutions coincide with the information obtained above.

Exercise.   Derive the ordinary differential equation for the mean and variance from the cumulant generating function. (First, obtain the partial differential equation for the probability generating function, $G(z)$ say, from the master equation. Then, let $K(\theta, t) = \ln G(z, t)$ with $z = e^{-\theta}$.)

4.5   An example: A deterministic analysis of nonlinear effects may mislead!

Kendall (1949) describes an effect discovered by Feller in 1939, which showed that deterministic equations give erroneous results in population models.

Given transition rates $r_k := w(k, k + 1) = \alpha(n_2 - k)k$ and $l_k := w(k, k - 1) = \beta(k - n_1)k$, where $n_1 \leq k(t) \leq n_2$, the deterministic equation

$$dk/dt = \alpha(n_2 - k)k - \beta(k - n_1)k$$

has the stationary solution

$$\bar{k} = \frac{\alpha n_2 + \beta n_1}{\alpha + \beta}.$$

For convenience, set $n_1 = 1$. In the limiting case of $n_2 \to \infty$, $\alpha \to 0$ while $\alpha n_2 \to \lambda_0$, the equilibrium value is

$$\bar{k} = 1 + x,$$

with $x = \lambda_0/\beta$.

The equilibrum distribution is obtained from the detailed-balance condition

$$\pi_{k-1} w(k - 1, k) = \pi_k w(k, k - 1),$$

which yields

$$\pi_{n_1+k} = \frac{B}{n_1 + k} \binom{n_2 - n_1}{k} \left(\frac{\alpha}{\beta}\right)^k,$$

where B is the normalizing constant to ensure that the sum of π_k from $k = n_1$ to n_2 equals one. Now let n_2 and α approach their respective limits as above, and $n_2\alpha$ approach λ_0. Then

$$\pi_{k+1} = (e^{\lambda_0/\beta} - 1)^{-1} \frac{(\lambda_0/\beta)^k}{k!},$$

$k = 1, 2, \ldots$, because $\{(n_2 - 1)!/(n_2 - 1 - k)!\}\alpha^k$ approaches λ_0^k.

With this distribution the expected value of k is less than $\bar{k}$ of the deterministic model:

$$\langle k \rangle = \frac{x}{1 - e^{-x}} < 1 + x.$$

This is the result of Feller (1939).

CHAPTER 5

Aggregate dynamics and fluctuations of simple models

Here, we illustrate the notion of aggregate dynamics and fluctuations about locally stable equilibria using simple models, and in so doing introduce some important tools. We begin this chapter with a closed binary model with slightly more complex transition rates than the ones in Chapter 4. For this model we derive the dynamics of aggregate variables and fluctuations about the aggregate mean, both are derivable from the master equation.

Agents in this section still face binary choices, but no longer choose their decisions independently. Their choices are subject to externality. A simple way to incorporate interactions among the decision processes by agents in the model is to use nonlinear transition rates l_n and r_n. More specifically, we now assume that they depend on the fraction of agents with the same choice. This is a type of feedback effect of aggregate effects of the decisions by all the agents in the model.

The proposed reformulation illustrates a simple way of analyzing stochastic interaction patterns of a large number of microeconomic agents who are subject to aggregate effects, or field effects. These effects are distinguished from pairwise or neighborhood interactions among agents, patterned after the Ising model, or anonymous interaction patterns, often used in the literature on search. The kind of externalities discussed in this section is called social influence in Becker (1974, 1990) and is discussed in Akerlof (1980), and Akerlof and Milbourne (1980). They are called mean field or simply field effects in Aoki (1995, 1996a) and Aoki and Miyahara (1993).

5.1 Dynamics of binary choice models

As the first look at the dynamics or derivation of nonstationary probability distribution for the state vector, let us suppose that in a small time interval Δt the probability that the number of agents with choice 1 increases by one from k to $k + 1$ is given by $r_k \Delta t + o(\Delta t)$, and the probability that the number decreases by one from k to $k - 1$ is given by $l_k \Delta t + o(\Delta t)$. The probability that the number of agents does not change is then given by $1 - (r_k + l_k)\,\Delta t + o(\Delta t)$.[1] Probabilities of changes by more than one are of higher order of smallness, by assumption here.[2]

We do not stop here to discuss how r_k and l_k may depend on k and possibly on other parameters in the model. We have seen some examples earlier. For the simple binary choice model under consideration, each of k agents may change his or her mind independently of the others at the rate μ, and each of $n - k$ agents may do so at the rate ν over a small interval of time. For this illustrative example, we postulate

$$l_k = \mu k \quad \text{and} \quad r_k = \lambda(N - k).$$

For the purpose of this simple model analysis, assume that μ and λ are constant. In more realistic or complex models, they may be functions of states (the so-called state-dependent models).

We derive the differential equation for the probability distribution that there are k agents with choice 1 at time t. Denote this by $P(k, t)$.

Keeping track of inflows and outflows of probability flux, we obtain

$$P(k, t + \Delta t) = l_{k+1}\,\Delta t\,P(k + 1, t) + r_{k-1}\,\Delta t\,P(k - 1, t)$$
$$+ [1 - (l_k + r_k)\,\Delta t]P(k, t) + o(\Delta t),$$

from which the master equation in the limit of letting Δt go to zero is

$$\frac{dP(k, t)}{dt} = l_{k+1}P(k + 1, t) + r_{k-1}P(k - 1, t) - (l_k + r_k)P(k, t)$$

for positive k. We need the boundary condition for $k = 0$,

$$\frac{dP(0, t)}{dt} = l_1 P(1, t) - r_0 P(0, t).$$

There are many references to this kind of derivation of the equation. On the backward Chapman–Kolmogorov equation, see Taylor and Karlin (1994, p. 325) for example.

When the total number of agents is fixed at n, then we need another boundary condition

$$\frac{dP(n, t)}{dt} = r_{n-1}P(n - 1, t) - l_n P(n, t).$$

---

[1] In closed binary models, the state space is the set $\{0, 1, \dots, n\}$.
[2] This can be deduced in some cases. See Çinlar (1975), for example.

5.2 Dynamics for the aggregate variable

We mention here only the dynamics for the conditional mean of the fraction of agents with choice 1 in situations where $P(n, t)$ is expected to have a well-defined peak of order N, and fluctuations or variation of order $\sqrt{N}$. The differential equations for the fluctuations are introduced later in connection with the search model. To capture this feature, we change variables from $n(t)$ to

$$n(t) = N\phi(t) + \sqrt{N}\xi(t),$$

where $\phi(t)$ is the mean of the fraction, and ξ is a random variable to represent fluctuation about the mean. The idea of this scaling is to make ϕ and ξ about $O(1)$. Let

$$\Pi(\xi, t) := P(n, t),$$

with n defined above. We have

$$\frac{dP}{dt} = \frac{\partial \Pi}{\partial t} + \frac{\partial \Pi}{\partial \xi} \frac{d\xi}{dt},$$

where the partial derivative with respect to time is taken keeping n fixed, i.e., we have

$$\frac{d\xi}{dt} = -\sqrt{N} \frac{d\phi}{dt}.$$

To simplify our derivation of approximate dynamics, regroup the right-hand side of the master equation by the **lead** and **lag** operators

$$z[l_n P_n(t)] = l_{n+1} P_{n+1}(t),$$

and

$$z^{-1}[r_n P_n(t)] = r_{n-1} P_{n-1}(t)$$

as

$$\frac{\partial P_n(t)}{\partial t} = (z - 1)[l_n P_n(t)] + (z^{-1} - 1)[r_n P_n(t)].$$

Then, note that the change from n to $n + 1$ entails change of ξ by a factor $N^{-1/2}$. Thus, for any smoothly differentiable function $a(n)$,

$$(z - 1)a(n) = a(n + 1) - a(n) = \frac{\partial a}{\partial n} + \cdots = \frac{\partial a}{\partial \xi} N^{-1/2} + \frac{1}{2} \frac{\partial^2 a}{\partial \xi^2} N^{-1} + \cdots.$$

We write this in shorthand as

$$z - 1 = N^{-1/2} \frac{\partial}{\partial \xi} + \frac{1}{2} N^{-1} \frac{\partial^2}{\partial \xi^2} + \cdots.$$

Analogously, we write

$$z^{-1} - 1 = -N^{-1/2}\frac{\partial}{\partial \xi} + \frac{1}{2}N^{-1}\frac{\partial^2}{\partial \xi^2} + \cdots.$$

The expressions for the transition rates are also expanded into Taylor series. To balance the orders in N, we change the time scale by

$$\tau = t/N.$$

Then, we equate the highest-order term in N, which is $N^{-1/2}$, with the terms on the right of the same order to obtain the differential equation for ϕ, which was introduced at the beginning of this section in changing the variable from n to ξ:

$$\frac{d\phi}{dt} = G(\phi).$$

This is the dynamic equation for the aggregated variable, the fraction.[3]

This aggregate equation is thus obtained by equating the highest-order terms from each side of the master equation. It is more comprehensive and more informative than a set of equations for the moments, which can be easily derived. See Aoki (1995) and Aoki (1996a, p. 136) for more detail. If the right-hand side is identically zero, we see that $\phi(\tau) = \phi(0)$ for positive τ, that is, any small deviation in $\phi(0)$ does not decay to zero. In this case we need to use a different time scaling than the one used above in expanding the master equation. This leads to what is known as the **diffusion approximation**. See Aoki (1996a, Sec. 5.4).

As an example, consider transition rates given by

$$r_n = h(N)\lambda \left(1 - \frac{n}{N}\right) \eta_1 \left(\frac{n}{N}\right),$$

and

$$l_n = h(N)\mu \frac{n}{N} \eta_2 \left(\frac{n}{N}\right),$$

where n is now the number of agents making choice 1, N is the total number of agents in the model, and where η's are some function of n/N. At the boundaries, we set $r_N = 0$ and $l_0 = 0$ because the model is closed with no entry and no exit. Then, we derive as the right-hand side of the aggregate dynamics

$$G(\phi) := -\mu\phi\eta_2(\phi) + \lambda(1 - \phi)\eta_1(\phi).$$

There are two differences between the transition rates in the previous closed model and those of this section, one minor and the other major. The function $h(n)$ is introduced to represent some scale effects. This is a minor point, and

---

[3] Equating the terms of order N^{-1}, we derive what is known as the Fokker–Planck equation. We discuss it later.

we set it to 1 without loss of generality, since it can be absorbed into the units of time. The η's are a major difference. They represent externalities and the perceived advantages of alternative choices as functions of the fraction k/n, i.e., the state variable of the model.

In the next section, we show that the zeros of this function $G(\phi)$ satisfy the same equation as the critical points of the potential of the stationary distribution

$$\frac{\eta_1(\phi)}{\eta_2(\phi)} := e^{2\beta g(\phi)} = \frac{\phi}{1-\phi},$$

that is, the critical points of the potential and the zeros of G are the same. See Aoki (1996a, pp. 118, 140) for further points on potentials. To pick out the critical points that correspond to local minima, we sign the derivative of G. Calculating its derivative

$$G'(\phi) = -(\eta_1/\phi)[1 - 2\phi(1 - \phi)\beta g'(\phi)],$$

we obtain the condition for the local asymptotic stability of the critical points as

$$2\phi(1 - \phi)\beta g'(\phi) < 1.$$

5.3   Potentials

With these transition rates, the expression for the equilibrium distribution becomes

$$\pi_k = \pi_0 \left(\frac{\lambda}{\mu}\right)^k C_{N,k} \prod_{r=1}^{k} \frac{\eta_1(\frac{r-1}{N})}{\eta_2(\frac{r}{N})}, \tag{5.1}$$

where $C_{N,k}$ is the binomial coefficient $N!/k!(N-k)!$. We see that the binomial coefficient we encountered in the earlier model is now modified by the product of the ratios of η's.

We express π_k as an exponential function

$$\pi_k = \frac{1}{Z} \exp\left[-\beta N U\left(\frac{k}{N}\right)\right],$$

where Z is a normalizing constant

$$Z = \sum_k \exp\left[-\beta N U\left(\frac{k}{N}\right)\right]$$

and is assumed to be finite, and where β is a nonnegative parameter we have introduced. It plays a key role in our analysis from now on. Informally, it represents the effect of uncertainty or incompleteness of information in making the choices. We return to this in the next subsection. The function U introduced above is called potential, and is related to the η's by

$$-\beta N U\left(\frac{k}{N}\right) - \ln Z = \ln \pi_0 + k \ln q + (N - k)\ln(1 - q)$$

$$+ \ln C_{N,k} + \sum_r \ln\left\{\frac{\eta_1(\frac{r-1}{N})}{\eta_2(\frac{r}{N})}\right\},$$

with $q = \lambda/(\lambda + \mu)$.

This function U in the exponent of π_k is called a potential, since it is independent of the path from state 0 to state k (or k/N, to be more precise), and depends only on the initial and the current state. This is known as the Kolmogorov criterion; see Kelly (1979, p. 23).

To proceed further we need to specify the η's more explicitly. Suppose that they are given by

$$\eta_1(f) = X^{-1}\exp[\beta g(f)],$$

and

$$\eta_2(f) = 1 - \eta_1(f) = X^{-1}\exp[-\beta g(f)],$$

with

$$X = e^{\beta g(f)} + e^{-\beta g(f)},$$

for $0 \le f \le 1$. A nonnegative function $g(f)$ expresses the relative merits of alternative choices in a sense that we will explain shortly.

The parameter β incorporates into the transition rates the (intrinsic or extrinsic) uncertainty or incompleteness of information that surrounds agents' decision-making processes. As specified above, larger values of β with positive values of $g(f)$ cause $\eta_1(f)$ to be larger than $\eta_2(f)$, and make transitions associated with r_n more likely to occur than those associated with l_n. One the other hand, near-zero values of β make η_1 and η_2 nearly equal to a half. This makes the choice between the alternatives nearly a fair coin toss by independent agents.

Next, we show heuristically that $g(f)$ may be interpreted as the difference of the perceived benefits of the two choices, conditional on the value of the fraction f, when we approximate the uncertain consequences of choices as normally distributed. Alternative interpretations are also possible, and they are discussed later.

Returning to the definition of the potential, we approximate the binomial coefficient by the entropy expression to derive

$$U(f) = -\frac{2}{N}\sum_{r=1}^{k} g\left(\frac{r}{N}\right) - \frac{1}{\beta}H(f) + o\left(\frac{\ln N}{N}\right),$$

where $f = k/N$, and where $H(f) = -f \ln f - (1-f)\ln(1-f)$. We approximate $g(\frac{r-1}{N}) + g(\frac{r}{N})$ by $2g(r/N)$. Treating f as continuous for N sufficiently large, $df \approx \Delta f = \frac{k+1}{N} - \frac{k}{N}$, and we write $df = 1/N + o(1/N)$. Hence

$$U(f) \approx -2 \int^f g(y)\, dy - \frac{1}{\beta} H(f).$$

Next, we locate the value of f at which the stationary probability is maximal, i.e., at which the potential U is minimal. Differentiating $U(f)$ with respect to f and setting the derivative equal to zero, we derive

$$\exp[2\beta g(f)] = \frac{f}{1-f} \frac{1-q}{q},$$

or

$$f = \frac{q e^{\beta g(f)}}{q e^{\beta g(f)} + (1-q)e^{-\beta g(f)}}, \tag{5.2}$$

with $\lambda = \mu$, $q = 1/2$, and $f = \eta_1(f)$, where $f = e^{\beta g(f)}/(e^{\beta g(f)} + e^{-\beta g(f)})$, which is the Gibbs distribution (Aoki 1996a, pp. 50–51).

This is one of the main results of this section. It is the equation for the fraction value at which the potential is minimized, i.e., at which the stationary probability is maximized. The resulting value is then the maximum-likelihood estimate of the fraction f. As we discuss next, the role of β, i.e., the role of the degree of incompleteness or uncertainty surrounding alternative choices, becomes very apparent when searching for the critical values of the potential or the roots of this equation. Depending on the value of β, there may be one or three equilibria, for example.[4]

5.4   Critical points and hazard function

Here, we relate the critical points for the potential to the notion of hazard function. In the current model, we have seen that the stationary probability distribution for the fraction of agents with choice 1 is of the form $\exp\{-\beta N U(x)\}$, where $U(x)$ is a potential of the form

$$U(x) \approx -2 \int^x g(y)\, dy - \frac{1}{\beta} H(x).$$

---

[4] In a pioneering paper of Kirman (1993), the transition rates he used are $\eta_1(x) = \epsilon + (1-\delta)x$ and $\eta_2(x) = \epsilon + (1-\delta)(1-x)$, in the notation of this section. He used α/N for ϵ and $2\alpha/N$ for δ. In other words, in Kirman, $\beta g(x) = \ln\{x + (\alpha/N)(1-2x)\}$ is the key equation. Note that in his model β plays no role and there is only one critical point. His model does not exhibit interplay of uncertainty with the number of equilibria.

With a large value for β, the critical points are nearly the same as the zeros of $g(x)$, $0 = dU(x^*)/dx \approx -2g(x^*)$. This equation shows that x^* is the value of the fraction of agents with choice 1 such that the mean of the difference of the alternative present values is zero, conditional on x^*:

$$0 \approx g(x^*) = E(V_1 - V_0|x^*),$$

where V_0 is the present discounted value associated with choice 0, and V_1 with choice 1. (See the next chapter on value functions.) In other words, at x^* agents are indifferent between the alternative choices.

As the value of β descreases, the second term in the expression for the potential causes the critical point to deviate from the zeros of the function g:

$$0 = \frac{dU(x^*)}{dx} = -2g(x^*) - \frac{1}{\beta} \ln\left(\frac{1 - x^*}{x^*}\right).$$

Putting this differently, at a zero point of g, the potential is still increasing if the zero is between 0.5 and 1, and the potential is decreasing if the zero is between 0 and 0.5.

To interpret the condition for minimal potential with smaller values of β where the zero of the function g is not the minimizing point, we adapt the notion of hazard function (rate) in the reliability literature.[5] Cox and Miller (1965, p. 253) define the hazard function for a random variable Y as

$$\lambda(y) = \lim_{v \downarrow 0} \frac{\Pr(y < Y < y + v|y < Y)}{v}.$$

In terms of the distribution function F for Y, we can put it as

$$\lambda(y) = -\frac{d}{dy} \ln\{1 - F(y)\}.$$

Suppose we set

$$F(y) = \Pr(Y \le y) = \frac{1}{1 + e^{-2\beta y}}.$$

This expression should remind the reader of the expression for the first-passage time of a standard Brownian motion (Grimmett and Stirzaker 1992, p. 500), or to the error-function approximation by Ingber (1982) in Aoki (1996a, pp. 132, 179). Then,

$$\lambda(y) = \frac{2\beta}{1 + e^{-2\beta y}}.$$

---

[5] In this literature, the notion of hazard rate is applied to the life of durable goods such as light bulbs. The hazard rate gives the conditional probability that a light bulb fails in the next hour, given that it has lasted 1000 hours, say. In our application here, we look for the conditional probability that an agent switches his or her choice in response to a (perceived) small increase in the return difference, conditional on the current choice at a current fraction x.

Now, let $g(x^*)$ be our Y, and use the probabilities conditional on x^*. We start with

$$\Pr(\epsilon \le V_1 - V_0 | x^*) = \frac{1}{1 + e^{-2\beta g(x^*)}}$$

as our conditional distribution. Then, the conditional hazard function is given by

$$\lambda(V_1 - V_0 | x^*) = \frac{2\beta \eta_1(x)}{1 + e^{-2\beta g(x)}}.$$

Alternatively, the conditional hazard function is approximately given by

$$\frac{\Pr(V_1 - V_0 < \epsilon < V_1 - V_0 + v | x^*)}{\Pr(V_1 - V_0 < \epsilon | x^*)}.$$

In words, given that $\hat{V}_0 < \hat{V}_1$, where $\hat{V}_i := V_i + \epsilon_i, i = 0, 1$, where ϵ_i stands for some errors in perception or observation noise, a slight increase in the difference by $v > 0$ will switch the preferred choice from choice 0 to 1: $\hat{V}_1 + v > \hat{V}_0$. This switching of the choices, or crossing of the boundary between the choices, occurs when $x = x^*$.

In our context, the potential minimization condition can be put as

$$\eta_1(x^*) = x^*,$$

from which we conclude that

$$\lambda(V_1 - V_0 | x^*) = 2\beta \eta_1(x^*) = 2\beta x^*.$$

This equation shows that for small values of β the conditional hazard function is approximately equal to β, that is, β may be considered as the conditional hazard rate in the range where β is small. We may state that the potential is minimized at a fraction x at which the conditional hazard function is approximately equal to β.

5.5 Multiplicity—An aspect of random combinatorial features

Here, we return to the factor η_1 / η_2 introduced in (5.1) that multiplies the binomial coefficients and interpret it. Suppose we are interested in the fraction of agents with choice 1. This fraction is given by

$$f = \frac{1}{N} \sum_i x_i,$$

with $x_i = 1$ or 0. How many different ways can a given value of f be realized? To put this differently, how many microeconomic patterns of choices are compatible with the average value f? We suppose agents are symmetrical average value in their choices, i.e., agents are exchangeable in the technical sense to be described later. What this assumption implies is that any agent may choose choice 1 or 0 with the same probabilities, and hence $\mu = \lambda = 1/2$,

$$r_n = \frac{N - n}{2N},$$

and

$$l_n = \frac{n}{2N}.$$

Substituting these into (5.1), we derive the stationary distribution as

$$\pi_n = \frac{N!}{n!(N - n)!} 2^{-N}.$$

We recognize here the binomial coefficient for choosing n out of N, denoted by $C_{N,n}$, i.e.,

$$\pi_n = C_{N,n} p^n q^{N-n},$$

with $p = q = 1/2$. More generally, if an agent chooses 1 with probability p and 0 with probability $1 - p := q$, then the above formula holds without p and q being equal to $1/2$.

Given the fraction f, then, there are $C_{N,Nf}$ ways of getting that fraction. Put differently, there are this many ways of realizing the fraction f. Thus, we are led naturally to assess the magnitude of the binary coefficient for large N. We use Stirling's formula

$$N! \approx (2\pi N)^{1/2}(N/e)^N = (N/e)^N + O(\ln N/N),$$

where the second expression on the right ignores the factor $\sqrt{2\pi N}$ when we write $N!$ as $\exp\{N(\ln N!/N)\}$.

Applying this approximation to the binomial coefficient, we derive

$$C_{N,n} 2^{-N} \approx \frac{N^N}{n^n(N - n)^{N-n}} 2^{-N} \approx \left(\frac{n}{N}\right)^{-n} \left(1 - \frac{n}{N}\right)^{-(N-n)} 2^{-N},$$

which becomes

$$C_{N,n} 2^{-N} \approx \exp\{-ND\{(n/N, 1 - n/N); (1/2, 1/2)\},$$

where

$$D(P; Q) := p \ln \frac{p}{q} + (1 - p) \ln \frac{1 - p}{1 - q},$$

with P standing for the discrete distribution $(p, 1 - p)$, and Q for $(q, 1 - q)$, both for $x = 1$ and $x = 0$. This expression is a special case of the relative entropy $D(P; Q)$ of one distribution P with respect to another Q. We can show that the relative entropy, also called the Kullback–Leibler divergence or information measure, is nonnegative and equals zero if and only if the two distributions are equal. See, for example, Dupuis and Ellis (1997, p. 32) or Kullback and Leibler (1951).

With $p = 1/2$, the most likely distributions of N agents are $N/2$ with choice 1 and $N/2$ with 0, when N is even. With $n = Nf$, the probability is approximately given by $\exp\{D((f, 1 - f); (1/2, 1/2))\}$. We have

$$\frac{1}{N} \ln \Pr(n/N = f) \approx -D((f, 1 - f); (1/2, 1/2)).$$

Exercise. Suppose that $\mu \neq \lambda$, and introduce them into the transition rates: $r_n = \lambda(1 - n/N)\eta_1(n/N)$ and $l_n = \mu(n/N)\eta_2(n/N)$. Show that the expression for the potential is now given by replacing the entropy term $H(f)$ by

$$D(P; Q) := f \ln\left(\frac{f}{q}\right) + (1 - f) \ln\left(\frac{1 - f}{1 - q}\right),$$

where $q = \lambda/\mu$, and P and Q are the distributions $(f, 1 - f)$ and $(q, 1 - q)$, respectively.

CHAPTER 6

Evaluating alternatives

How do economic agents assess the relative merits of alternative choices? There are many questions to be resolved in choosing alternatives, such as the length of planning horizons, the degrees of precisions with which the factors or variables are known or estimated, and the degree to which agents are able to allow for externalities caused by other agents' decisions. In this chapter, for simplicity, we examine this question by assuming that agents all face the same choice set, although that is not necessary.

To partially answer this important question, we assume that economic agents calculate or estimate *present values* of the consequences of their alternative choices, and choose the ones with the largest present value. Agents do this by calculating the discounted present values of alternative streams of profits, utilities, or whatever other "things" contribute to their benefits. Agents' decision-making problems are complex, partly because alternative streams of revenues, utilities, and the likes are only incompletely and imperfectly known or estimated. Their future choice sets may also be altered by past positions or by choices they or others have made. They may also be unaware of aggregate effects of choices made by others. Agents usually are not able to allow for the externalities completely. The utility or cost of individual decisions is often affected by these aggregate effects.

Actually, such calculations of present values are by no means straightforward, being affected at least by the same set of difficulties. In our approach, these externalities are reflected in the specifications of the transition rates that govern the behavior of a group of agents. In economic applications of jump Markov processes, transition rates may be endogenously determined, as we illustrate later. Here, we describe the way value functions are calculated by individual agents. Search-theoretic examples in later chapters show how the differences in the calculated present values enter the transition rates in dynamic search models.

6.1   Representation of relative merits of alternatives

We offer three interpretations for our specifications of the functions η in the transition rates of the last chapter. The first is based on some approximate calculations of the perceived difference of the expected utilities, or advantages of one choice over the other. A second interpretation is based on discrete choice theory as in Anderson et al. (1993) or McFadden (1972, 1974). These are related to the extreme-value distributions of type I, which are discussed in the Section 6.3 and Section A.6. See also Aoki (1996a, Chap. 3). The third is via constrained maximization of entropy or minimization of the Kullback–Leibler divergence, subject to some constraints such as the size of the model and other macroeconomic signals. All three explain heuristically how distributions called Gibbs distributions arise, and how they are related to error functions.

Let us start with the first interpretation. Denote by $u_1(x)$ the expected return from choice 1, given that fraction x has selected choice 1. For definiteness, think of the discounted present value of the benefit stream based on the assumption that fraction x remain the same over some planning horizon. Define $u_2(x)$ analogously. Let

$$\eta_1(x) = \Pr\{u_1(x) \geq u_2(x)\}.$$

Next, assume that the difference $\Delta u(x) = u_1(x) - u_2(x)$ is approximately distributed as a normal random variable with mean $g(x)$ and variance ϕ^2. We calculate the probability that it is nonnegative,

$$\Pr\{\Delta u(x) \geq 0\} = \frac{1}{2}[1 + \mathrm{erf}(u)],$$

where the error function is defined by

$$\mathrm{erf}(u) := \frac{2}{\sqrt{\pi}} \int_0^u e^{-y^2} dy,$$

with $u = g(x)/(\sqrt{2}\phi)$. See Abramovitz and Stegun (1968) for example. We follow Ingber (1982) in approximating the error function by

$$\mathrm{erf}(u) \approx \tanh(\kappa u),$$

with $\kappa = 2/\sqrt{\pi}$. This approximation is remarkably good and useful. For example, for small $|x|$, we note that

$$\mathrm{erf}(x) = \kappa \left(x - \frac{x^3}{3} + \frac{x^5}{5} + \cdots \right),$$

and

$$\tanh(\kappa x) = \kappa \left(x - \frac{x^3}{2.36} + \frac{x^5}{4.63} + \cdots \right).$$

By letting β be $\sqrt{2/\pi}\phi^{-1}$, we deduce the desired expression for the probability

$$\Pr\{\Delta u(x) \geq 0\} \approx X^{-1} \exp[\beta g(x)],$$

with the same X introduced in Chapter 5. This offers one interpretation of β that appears in the transition rates: large variances mean large uncertainty in the expected difference of the alternative choices.

Alternatively put, we may interpret $g(x)$ as the conditional mean of a measure that choice 1 is better than choice 2, conditional on the fraction x having decided on choice 1.

See Aoki (1996a, Chaps. 3, 8) on the partition functions and how β arises as a Lagrange multiplier to incorporate macrosignals as constraints. The parameter β is related to the elasticity of the number of microeconomic configurations with respect to macrosignals. Small values of β mean that the number of microeconomic configurations responds little when macroeconomic signals change. See Aoki (1996a, p. 216).

6.2   Value functions

Here, we outline the use of value functions in making the best choice out of K possible ones. Value functions correspond to potentials associated to discrete-time or continuous-time Markov chains. We briefly describe the connection after some introductory comments. We observe that the appeal to value functions is useful for a small number of alternatives such as $K = 2$ or 3, with no uncertainty about future interest rates, perfect knowledge of externalities, and so on. With a large number of alternatives, practical implementation of the ideas behind the value functions may become problematical due to imperfect information for making decisions, let alone the computational complexities, among other things.

Suppose that K alternative choices are associated with K alternative streams of profits or utilities. These alternative streams may depend, in addition, on the state of the "world," which may represent the summaries of aggregate choices of all agents involved. The values of these alternatives are calculated as the present values of the discounted sums of the streams of profits, utilities and the like, which render the values dependent on the state of the world. Using the risk-neutral interest rate r, the value V must satisfy, in a continuous-time formulation,

$$rV = \rho + E(dV/dt),$$

where the first term on the right is the flow of rewards or revenues and the second is the expected capital gain term. In the finance literature, V refers to the value of some financial asset. The sum of flow return and the capital-gain term must equal the yield or return to the asset on the left-hand side in order for the asset to be willingly held. In the finance literature, the underlying stochastic processes are usually taken to be some diffusion processes. Here in evaluating alternative choices using value functions, the underlying stochastic processes are (jump) Markov processes.

Strictly speaking, we don't know time profiles of r, nor of ρ. For now, we proceed with our examination assuming that r and ρ are known. The flow ρ must be replaced by its expected value or some kind of estimate if it is not a known deterministic quantity. We incorporate impreciseness and incompleteness of information later into the probability distribution functions we specify.

To each state i of the state space S having at most countably many states, the value function with infinite horizon with the initial state i is defined by

$$V_i = E_i \int_0^\infty e^{-rt} \rho(X_t) \, dt,$$

where E_i denotes the expectation with the initial condition $X_0 = i$ of a jump Markov process $\{X_t\}$, $t \geq 0$. It is known that $V = (V_i : i \in S)$ is the unique bounded solution to

$$(r - W)V = \rho,$$

where W is the generator matrix of the jump process with transition rate $w(i, j)$,

$$\Pr(X_{t+h} = j | X_t = i) = \delta_{i,j} + w(i, j)h + o(h),$$

that is, the matrix of transition rates, $P(t) = (p_{i,j}(t))$, satisfies the backward equation

$$\frac{dP(t)}{dt} = W P(t),$$

with $P(0) = I$. See Norris (1997, Sec. 4) for a readable introduction. See also Kelly (1979) and Doyle and Snell (1984) for relations of value functions to potentials and their representation as electrical networks.

Here is a simple illustration of the approach with two states, $s = 1$ and $s = 2$, say, without recourse to Ito calculus. Assume simply that state changes are two-state jump Markov processes, described by the transition rates $w(1, 2)$ and $w(2, 1)$. The first is the transition rate from state 1 to 2, and the second from 2 to 1. In a small time interval of duration Δt, then, the probability of state 1 changes to 2 with probability $w(1, 2) \Delta t + o(\Delta t)$, for example. The value function over an infinite horizon is given by

$$r V_1 = \rho_1 + w(1, 2)(V_2 - V_1),$$

and

$$rV_2 = \rho_2 + w(2, 1)(V_1 - V_2),$$

where the subscript refers to the state. For example, ρ_1 is the flow revenue in state 1. Recall that $w(1, 1) = -w(1, 2)$.

Solving them for the values, we see that they are the weighted averages of the two present values of the flow revenues

$$V_1 = p_1 \frac{\rho_1}{r} + (1 - p_1)\frac{\rho_2}{r},$$

and

$$V_2 = (1 - p_2)\frac{\rho_1}{r} + p_2 \frac{\rho_2}{r},$$

where

$$p_1 = \frac{r + w(2, 1)}{r + w(1, 2) + w(2, 1)},$$

and

$$p_2 = \frac{r + w(1, 2)}{r + w(1, 2) + w(2, 1)}.$$

The expression ρ_1/r is the present value of the streams ρ_1, and similarly for ρ_2/r. Given that the state changes, the expression $1 - p_1$ gives the probability that state 1 changes to state 2 and analogously for the expression $1 - p_2$.

In choosing alternatives, it is the difference of the two present values that matters, not their magnitudes. With this setup, the difference in values of the preceding example is given by

$$V_1 - V_2 = \left(\frac{\rho_1 - \rho_2}{r}\right)\frac{r}{r + w(1, 2) + w(2, 1)}. \qquad (6.1)$$

With the deterministic flows, the first fraction is the difference of the present values. The second factor shows how much that is reduced by the fluctuations of states.

If there are two choices that affect the revenue flows, then we may represent these effects by making the ρ's and V's functions of the choice variables as well as some (vector-valued) parameter θ to represent other (macroeconomic) variables to represent economic environments. Fractions of agents of the same choice may be among its components. For example, $V_1(c, ; \theta)$ may stand for the present value of state 1, given the choice c and (environmental) parameter θ. Similary for $V_0(c, ; \theta)$. If the numbers of states are different for different choices, we just focus on the states we are interested in, and compare their values.

Suppose we are interested in $V_1(c, ; \theta)$ for two alternative choices of $c : c = c_1$ and $c = c_2$. Suppose further that we know

$$V_1(c_1; \theta) \geq V_1(c_2; \theta)$$

for $\theta \in \Theta$, and the inequality is reversed when θ is not in Θ. We may use the likelihood ratio

$$\ln[P(+)/P(-)] = a(+) - a(-),$$

where $P(+) = \Pr[V_1(c_1) \geq V_1(c_2)]$ and $P(-) = 1 - P(+)$, to express the status of agents' information about these possibilities. We then express the probability of one choice being superior to the alternative as

$$P(+) = \frac{e^{a(+)}}{e^{a(+)} + e^{a(-)}}.$$

Here, we have introduced a Gibbs distribution for the discrete choice. This type of distribution is also found in the literature on discrete choice models. See for example Anderson et al. (1993) or Amemiya (1985).

The approach outlined above goes back at least to McFadden (1972), and we turn to his approach next.

6.3   Extreme distributions and Gibbs distributions

In the last part of the previous section, we calculated the probability that one choice has higher present value than the alternative. In this section, we pursue this further.

Suppose that we calculate the probability that the discounted present value V_1 is higher than the value V_2, associated with alternative choices 1 and 2 respectively. Suppose further that we represent some of the incompleteness and impreciseness of information or uncertainty of consequences surrounding the value calculation by adding random terms to the present values:

$$\hat{V}_1 = V_1 + \epsilon_1,$$

and

$$\hat{V}_2 = V_2 + \epsilon_2.$$

One interpretation is that these ϵs are noises to represent inevitable fluctuations in the present values. A second interpretation is to think of them as (additional) evidence to support a particular choice. Other interpretations are certainly possible. For example, McFadden (1973) speaks of common or community preference and individual deviations from the common norm in the context of utility maximization.

One quick assumption to obtain a Gibbs distribution expression in the case of two alternative choices is to assume that $\epsilon = \epsilon_2 - \epsilon_1$ is distributed according to

$$\Pr(\epsilon \le x) = \frac{1}{1 + e^{-\beta x}}$$

for some positive β. With this distribution, a larger value of ϵ supports more strongly the possibility that $V_1 > V_2$. The parameter β controls to what extent changes in x translate into changes in probabilities. With a smaller value of β, a larger increase in x — that is, in evidence – is needed to increase the probability that favors choice 1, for example. The larger β is, the smaller is the increase in x needed to change the probability by a given amount.

With this distribution, then, immediately we obtain

$$P_1 = \Pr(\hat{V}_1 \ge \hat{V}_2) = \frac{e^{\beta V_1}}{e^{\beta V_1} + e^{\beta V_2}} = \frac{e^{\beta g}}{e^{\beta g} + e^{-\beta g}},$$

with $g = (V_1 - V_2)/2$. We obtain also $P_2 = 1 - P_1$, of course.

To reiterate an important point, we see that a smaller value of β implies a smaller difference of $|P_1 - P_2|$. Namely, with a large value of β, one of the alternatives tends to dominate.

In the next subsection, this type of approach, which involves explicit calculations of probabilities of relative sizes of present values, is developed further.

For the third way, we call attention to the conditional limit theorem; see Aoki (1996a, Secs. 3.7, 3.8).

6.3.1   Type I: Extreme distribution

McFadden models agents' discrete choice as the maximization of utilities, i.e., by deriving the distribution for the maximum of U_j, $j = 1, 2, \ldots, K$, where U_j is associated with choice j, and K is the total number of available choices. Assume that the observed utility is corrupted by noise,

$$U_j = V_j + \epsilon_j,$$

and we are really interested in picking the maximum of V's, not U's.

Define

$$P_i = \Pr\left(\max_j U_j = U_i\right).$$

It is known that P_i has the form of a Gibbs distribution, i.e., the exponential form, when the noise is distributed according to

$$\Pr(\epsilon_i \le x) = \exp(-e^{-x}).$$

This distribution may look very exotic. However, it is not so. In the literature on extreme distributions, this distribution is known as the type I extreme distribution. This distribution has nonzero domain of attraction, and conditions under which distributions converge weakly to this distribution are known. See Galambos (1987, Chaps. 2, 3) or Leadbetter et al. (1993) for example.

This distribution arises as follows: Suppose the ϵs are i.i.d. with distribution function F. Then we know that the maximum of a large number n of samples is distributed as

$$\Pr\left(\max_{1 \le j \le n} \epsilon_j \le x\right) = [F(x)]^n.$$

Taking the logarithm and writing $F(x) = 1 - [1 - F(x)]$, we see that if

$$\lim_n n[1 - F(a_n + b_n y)] = u(y)$$

for some constant positive a_n and b_n, then

$$\lim_K \Pr\left(\max_j U_j \le a_K + b_K y\right) = \exp[-u(y)].$$

See Galambos (1987, p. 11).

Choose $F(x) = 1 - e^{-x}$, $a_n = \ln n$, and $b_n = 1$. Then $1 - F(a_n + x) = (1/n)e^{-x}$, and $\exp(-e^{-x})$ follows. By interpreting ϵs as evidence for Vs, we may think of the type I distribution as the result of using the strongest or best possible evidence for each alternative V.

To illustrate, suppose K is three. The probability for the second choice to be maximal is given by

$$P_2 = \int_{-\infty}^{\infty} f(x) \Pr(\epsilon \le V_2 - V_1 + x, \epsilon_3 \le V_2 - V_3 + x) \, dx,$$

with

$$f(x) = \frac{d}{dx} \exp(-e^{-x}) = e^{-x} \exp(-e^{-x}).$$

By the independence assumption, the probability in the integrand becomes a product $\Pr(\epsilon_1 \le V_2 - V_1 + x)\Pr(\epsilon_3 \le V_2 - V_3 + x) = \exp[-(e^{-x+V_1-V_2} + e^{-x+V_3-V_2})]$. When the integration is carried out, the result is the Gibbs distribution

$$P_2 = \frac{e^{V_2}}{\sum_j e^{V_j}}.$$

6.4   Approximate evaluations of value functions with a large number of alternatives

Although the use of value functions is theoretically appealing, it is not easily implemented in practice in situations with a large number of alternatives. An example of this is in Aoki and Shirai (2000), in which there are as many value functions as there are employed agents in the model. In this case, they could just use the value function for the mean. See also Chapter 9, where this kind of approximation is used.

With many alternatives, the expressions for the value functions involve sums of many terms on the right-hand side. We discuss two aspects of value-function evaluations in such context. First, we discuss how the value functions discussed in the preceding section may be obtained under some circumstances. Then, we point out an interesting connection with the extreme values in evaluations of value functions consisting of many alternative returns. This connection is helpful in value-function evaluations.

6.5   Case of small entry and exit probabilities: An example

This example arises in connection with the well-known search model of Diamond (1982), discussed in Chapter 9. This model uses an infinite number of agents with fractions of employed as deterministic state variables. Aoki and Shirai (2000) reworked the same model with a finite number N of agents. In the model, the reservation cost for undertaking production opportunities, which arrive at a rate a to a pool of unemployed, is determined by value maximization. There are values $V_e(n/N)$ and $V_u(1 - n/N)$ for $n = 0, 1, \ldots, N$, where the subscripts e and u mean employed and unemployed, respectively. Therefore, there are about $2N$ value functions to determine. (There are also some boundary-condition equations.)

To simplify, we look for the average relation between the values of being employed and unemployed, using the change of variables

$$\frac{n}{N} = \phi + \frac{1}{\sqrt{N}}\xi,$$

where ϕ is the average fraction of employed, and ξ is a random variable to account for random fluctuation about the mean value of the fraction. We refer the reader to the cited paper for detail, and give here just a brief exposition to convey the essential points.

The approximate value functions become

$$r V_u(\phi) = a(G^* c^* - \bar{c}) \approx -a\bar{c},$$

and

$$r V_e(\phi) = b(\phi)(v - c^*),$$

where r is the interest rate, and where the reservation cost is given by

$$c^* = V_e(\phi) - V_u(\phi) \text{ and } \bar{c} = \int^{c^*} z \, dG(z).$$

Here $G^* = G(c^*)$ is the cumulative cost up to c^*, and aG^* is the transition rate from the pool of unemployed to that of employed, when the fraction of employed is ϕ. We have ignored the effects of externalities as being small. They vanish exactly at equilibrium points $\phi = \phi_e$ of the aggregate dynamics where

$$\frac{d\phi}{dt} = \Phi(\phi),$$

that is, ϕ_e is a zero point of the dynamics Φ.

Solving this set of approximate value-function equations on the assumption that aG^* and bG^* are smaller than r, we arrive at familiar-looking expressions

$$V_e = \frac{b(\phi)v}{r},$$

and

$$V_u = -a\frac{\bar{c}}{r}.$$

The reservation cost is approximately given by

$$c^* \approx \frac{bv + a\bar{c}}{r}.$$

These expressions give the value functions as discounted present values of the benefit and average cost streams, adjusted for the quantities a and b, which are related to the transition rates.

6.6 Approximate evaluation of sums of a large number of terms

We often need to evaluate approximately expressions involving sums of infinitely many terms. Such sums may arise for example in evaluating partition functions, or as total probabilities of certain events. We discuss approximate evaluation procedures for deterministic sums and for stochastic sums. Some of the methods come under the heading of the method of Laplace. These are discussed separately. Here, we present another approximate method for the deterministic sums in the next section. Some known methods for sums composed of random terms are also collected, to justify a procedure for approximating sums by the maximum terms in the sums.

Historically, Darling (1952) was the first to derive a result on this topic. He showed that for i.i.d. Xs. $E(Z_n)$ approaches 1, where $Z_n = S_n/X_n^*$, with $X_n^* = \max(X_1, \ldots, X_n)$, and $S_n = \sum X_i$. Let the distribution function F of X have density ϕ.

The characteristic function of Z_n is

$$E(e^{itZ_n}) = \int_0^\infty \phi(\beta) \, d\beta \int_0^\beta \cdots \int_0^\beta e^{it(\beta+\beta_2+\cdots+\beta_n)/\beta} n\phi(\beta_2) \cdots \phi(\beta_n) \, d\beta_2 \cdots d\beta_n,$$

because there is no loss of generality in assuming that $X_n^* = X_1$. Changing variables to $\alpha_2 = \beta_2/\beta$, etc., we have

$$E(e^{itZ_n}) = ne^{it} \int_0^\infty \beta^{n-1}\phi(\beta) \left\{\int_0^1 e^{it\alpha}\phi(\beta\alpha) \, d\alpha\right\}^{n-1} d\beta.$$

Differentiating the characteristic function with respect to it and setting t equal to 0, we obtain the mean of Z_n as

$$E(Z_n) = 1 - n(n-1) \int_0^\infty F(\beta)^{n-2}[1 - F(\beta)] \int_0^1 \left[\frac{1 - F(\beta\alpha)}{1 - F(\beta)} - 1\right] dF(\beta).$$

In deriving this expression, we note that the derivative of $F(\beta)^n$ with respect to β is $n\phi(\beta)F(\beta)^{n-1}$, and the integral of $\alpha\beta\phi(\beta\alpha)$ with respect to α over the interval from 0 to 1 is $F(\beta\alpha) - F(\beta)$.

Darling then shows that the expression in the square bracket goes to zero as β goes to infinity if the tail of the distribution is slowly varying. This is more or less the definition of the notion of slow variation. See Bingham et al. (1987) on slowly varying functions.

6.7   Approximations of error functions

There is another approximate way of introducing a Gibbs distribution, which links up with the distribution $(1 + e^{-\beta x})^{-1}$ at the end of the previous section.

Assume that $\epsilon_1 - \epsilon_2$ is normally distributed with mean zero and variance b. Then, a simple calculation reveals that

$$\Pr(\epsilon_1 - \epsilon_2 \geq x) = \frac{1}{2}\left[1 - \operatorname{erf}\left(\frac{x}{\sqrt{2b}}\right)\right].$$

Next we follow Ingber (1982) and approximate the right-hand side by

$$\frac{1}{2}\left[1 - \operatorname{erf}\left(\frac{x}{\sqrt{2b}}\right)\right] \approx \frac{1}{1 + e^{2\beta x}}.$$

Now let $x = V_1 - V_2$. Then

$$\Pr(\hat{V}_1 \geq \hat{V}_2) = \frac{e^{\beta V_1}}{e^{\beta V_1} + e^{\beta V_2}},$$

which can be put in the form $e^{\beta g}/[e^{\beta g} + e^{-\beta g}]$ by setting $g = (V_1 - V_2)/2$.

Consider the case where transition rates are given by

$$w(1, 2) = \mu(N - n)\eta(x),$$

and

$$w(2, 1) = \mu n[1 - \eta(x)],$$

where $x = n/N$ is the fraction of agents with choice (state) 1, and where N is the total number of agents in the group, assumed constant, as in the binary choice model in Section 5.3, where η is specified by

$$\eta(x) = \Pr(\hat{V}_1 \geq \hat{V}_2 | x) = \frac{e^{\beta g(x)}}{e^{\beta g(x)} + e^{-\beta g(x)}}.$$

Then, the second factor of the difference of the two present values in (6.1) becomes

$$\frac{r}{r + \mu[(N - n)\eta + n(1 - \eta)]}.$$

The expression in the square bracket is $N[x + (1 - 2x)\eta]$. In our discussion of a binary choice model, we have seen that $\eta(x^*) = x^*$, where x^* denotes a critical point of the aggregate dynamics for the mean of the fraction x. We showed there that it is the same as the local minimum point of the potential that defines the stationary probability distribution of n, i.e., the fraction x.

We note that

$$x + (1 - 2x)\eta = 2x^*(1 - x^*).$$

Thus, the second factor in (6.1) becomes

$$\frac{r}{r + 2\mu N x^*(1 - x^*)}.$$

We know from experience that the expression $x(1 - x)$ is related to the variance term in diffusion equations.

The logistic function belongs to the domain of attraction of this type I extreme distribution, as we can easily verify. Given

$$F(x) = \frac{e^{\kappa x} - 1}{e^{\kappa x} + 1},$$

choose $a_n = (\ln 2n)/\kappa$ and $b_n = 1$. Then

$$\lim n[1 - F(a_n + y)] = e^{-\kappa y},$$

and hence

$$\lim \Pr\left(\max_j U_j \le y + a_n\right) = \exp(-e^{-y}).$$

6.7.1   Generalization

Let $G(y_1, \ldots, y_K)$ be nonnegative and homogeneous of degree one in the region of nonnegative ys, such that G approaches zero when any one of the arguments goes to minus infinity, and G goes to infinity when all of the arguments go to infinity. The derivative $\partial^j G/\partial y_{i_1} \cdots \partial y_{i_j}$ is nonpositive for odd j and nonnegative for even j. Then

$$F(y_1, y_2, \ldots, y_K) = \exp[-G(e^{-y_1}, \ldots, e^{-y_K})]$$

is a K-dimensional distribution, and $f(y_{i_1}, \ldots, y_{i_j})$ defined by the jth partial derivatives of F with respect to the appropriate arguments is the density, because of our assumption on the signs of the partial derivatives of F.

Now divide the region of nonnegative ys into K disjoint regions by taking region i to be such that $\max_j(V_j + \epsilon_j)$ is achieved by $j = i$, and the ϵs have the joint distribution F. To simplify the derivation we calculate the probability of region 1, P_1. It is given by

$$P_1 = \int G(e^{-x}, e^{-x-V_1+V_2}, \ldots, e^{-x-V_1+V_K}) f(x)\, dx,$$

where the density for ϵ_1 is given by

$$f(x) = e^{-x} G_1(e^{-x}, e^{-x-V_1+V_2}, \ldots, e^{-x-V_1+V_K}).$$

Change the variable of integration from x to $w = x + V_1$, then use the assumed linear homogeneity to rewrite P_1 as

$$P_1 = \int \exp[-e^{-w} G(e^{V_1}, \ldots, e^{V_K})] G_1(e^{V_1}, \ldots, e^{V_K}) e^{V_1-w}\, dw.$$

By further changing the variable of integration to $u = e^{-w}$, we can express this as

$$P_1 = e^{V_1} G_1(e^{V_1}, \ldots, e^{V_K}) \int_0^{e^{-V_1}} \exp[-u G(e^{V_1}, \ldots, e^{V_K})]\, du = \frac{e^{V_1} G_1}{G}.$$

6.7.2   Example

The next example is due to Tiago de Oliveira (1973). Let $G(x, y) = [x^\beta + y^\beta]^{1/\beta}$. Then it is linear homogeneous and we have $G_i \geq 0$, $i = 1, 2$, and $G_{1,2} \leq 0$. We obtain

$$P_x = \frac{e^{\beta V_1}}{e^{\beta V_1} + e^{\beta V_2}}.$$

McFadden calls these generalized extreme value (GEV) functions.

CHAPTER 7

Solving nonstationary master equations

Often, we need to analyze nonstationary probability distributions to investigate, for example, how the distributions behave as time progresses. For instance, we may be interested in knowing how the distributions of market shares of firms behave in some sector as the sector or industry matures.

If we can't solve master equations directly in the time domain, we may try to solve them by the method of probability generating functions. In cases where that approach does not work, we may try solving ordinary differential equations for the first few moments of the distributions by the method of cumulant generating functions; see Cox and Miller (1965, p. 159). Alternatively, we may be content with deriving probabilities such as $P_0(t)$, this being the probability for extinction of certain types (of their sizes being reduced to zero).

This section describes the probability- and cumulant-generating-function methods for solving the master equations. In those cases where the transition rates are more general nonlinear functions of state variables than polynomials, we can try Taylor series expansions of transition rates to solve the master equations approximately.

In this chapter, we illustrate some procedures to obtain nonstationary probability distributions on some elementary models. (See also the method of Langevin equations, which is discussed in Section 8.7.) This leads to (approximate) solutions of Fokker–Planck equations.

7.1 Example: Open models with two types of agents

The next example is an open market or sector model with two types of agents. By reinterpreting the number of agents as measured in some basic units, we may translate the results in terms of the number into results in terms of sizes of agents such as firms. We solve this problem both for stationary and for nonstationary distributions. For stationary solutions we use the detailed-balance conditions. For nonstationary solutions, we use the generating-function methods. We first dispose of the stationary case, since it is straightforward.

7.1.1 Equilibrium distribution

Assume that all transition rates are time-homogeneous. Suppose that the entry probability intensity is given by

$$w(\mathbf{n}, \mathbf{n} + \mathbf{e}_i) = v_i$$

for $n_i \geq 0$, and the exit transition rate is specified by

$$w(\mathbf{n}, \mathbf{n} - \mathbf{e}_i) = \mu_i n_i$$

for $n_i \geq 1$, $i = 1, 2$. In addition, agents change from type 1 to type 2 with probability intensity

$$w(\mathbf{n}, \mathbf{n} - \mathbf{e}_1 + \mathbf{e}_2) = \lambda_{12} n_1,$$

and likewise from type 2 to type 1 with the coefficient λ_{21}.

The detailed-balance conditions hold, and it is easy to see that the equilibrium probability distribution is given by

$$\pi(\mathbf{n}) = \pi_1(n_1)\pi_2(n_2),$$

with

$$\pi_i(n_i) = c_i \frac{\alpha_i^{n_i}}{n_i!},$$

$i = 1, 2$, where c_i is the normalizing constant and the constants are $\alpha_i = v_i/\mu_i$, and provided $\lambda_{12}\alpha_1 = \lambda_{21}\alpha_2$.

Exercise 1. Verify that with the expression for the equilibrium distributions, the detailed-balance conditions are satisfied.

Exercise 2. Change the entry transition rate specification to $w(\mathbf{n}, \mathbf{n} + \mathbf{e}_i) = v_i n_i$, and the type switching transition rates to $\lambda_{12} n_1 n_2$ and $\lambda_{21} n_2 n_1$, respectively. Assume that α's are less than one in magnitude. Show that π_i changes to $c_i \alpha_i^{n_i}/n_i$.

7.1.2 Probability-generating-function method

The master equation is given by

$$
\begin{aligned}
\frac{dP(n_1, n_2)}{dt} &= \mu_1(n_1 + 1)P(n_1 + 1, n_2) + \mu_2(n_2 + 1)P(n_1, n_2 + 1) \\
&+ v_1 P(n_1 - 1, n_2) + v_2 P(n_1, n_2 - 1) \\
&+ \lambda_{12}(n_1 + 1)P(n_1 + 1, n_2 - 1) \\
&+ \lambda_{21}(n_2 + 1)P(n_1 - 1, n_2 + 1) \\
&- \{\mu_1 n_1 + \mu_2 n_2 + v_1 + v_2 + \lambda_{12} n_1 + \lambda_{21} n_2\}P(n_1, n_2),
\end{aligned}
$$

where we supress the time argument of n_1 and n_2, and where z_1 and z_2 below are dummy or auxiliary variables of the generating function to extract appropriate probabilities from the function. See Feller (1968) for example.

Define the probability generating function by

$$G(z_1, z_2; t) = \sum_{n_1} \sum_{n_2} z_1^{n_1} z_2^{n_2} P(n_1, n_2).$$

Multiply the master equation by $z_1^{n_1} z_2^{n_2}$, and sum over n_1 and n_2. Using relations such as $\sum_{n_1} \sum_{n_2} n_1 z_1^{n_1} z_2^{n_2} P(n_1, n_2) = z_1 \frac{\partial G}{\partial z_1}$, we deduce the partial differential equation for the probability generating function G:

$$\begin{aligned}
\frac{\partial G}{\partial t} &= [\nu_1(-1 + z_1) + \nu_2(-1 + z_2)]G \\
&\quad + [\mu_1(1 - z_1) + \lambda_1(z_2 - z_1)]\frac{\partial G}{\partial z_1} \\
&\quad + [\mu_2(1 - z_2) + \lambda_2(z_1 - z_2)]\frac{\partial G}{\partial z_2},
\end{aligned}$$

where we abbreviate λ_{12} as λ_1, and likewise for λ_2.

7.1.3   Cumulant generating functions

Often, we are interested in the time response patterns of the first few moments such as the mean, variance, and skewness. Now, by using the device in Cox and Miller (1965, p. 159), we derive the ordinary differential equations for the mean and variance.

Given a random variable $X(t)$, its probability generating function is changed into the moment generating function by setting $z = e^{-\theta}$ and defining

$$H(\theta, t) = E\left(e^{-\theta X(t)}\right) = G(e^{-\theta}, t).$$

Next introduce the cumulant generating function by

$$K(\theta, t) = \ln H(\theta, t).$$

Denoting the rth cumulant by κ_r, we extract it from $K(\theta, t)$ as the coefficient of $(-\theta)^r/r!$.

Now, instead of solving the partial differential equation for G, we derive equations to determine the mean and the second moments. Letting $z_i = e^{-\theta_i}$, $i = 1, 2$, and $K(\theta_1, \theta_2, t) = \ln G(z_1, z_2, t)$, we obtain, by noting that $\partial/\partial z_i = -e^{\theta_i}\,\partial/\partial\theta_i$, $i = 1, 2$,

$$\frac{dK}{dt}(\theta_1, \theta_2; t) = \nu_1(e^{-\theta_1} - 1) + \nu_2(e^{-\theta_2} - 1)$$

$$+ [\mu_1(1 - e^{-\theta_1}) + \lambda_1(1 - e^{\theta_1-\theta_2})]\frac{\partial K}{\partial\theta_1}$$

$$+ [\mu_2(1 - e^{\theta_2}) + \lambda_2(1 - e^{\theta_2-\theta_1})]\frac{\partial K}{\partial\theta_2}.$$

Expand the function K in a power series of θ_i as

$$K = -\kappa_{10}\theta_1 - \kappa_{01}\theta_2 + \frac{1}{2}\left(\kappa_{20}\theta_1^2 + 2\kappa_{11}\theta_1\theta_2 + \kappa_{02}\theta_2^2\right) + \cdots.$$

By collecting expressions for the coefficients of θ_i, θ_i^2, $i = 1, 2$, and that of $\theta_1\theta_2$, we derive

$$\frac{d\kappa_{10}}{dt} = \nu_1 - (-\mu_1 + \lambda_1)\kappa_{10} + \lambda_2\kappa_{01},$$

$$\frac{\kappa_{01}}{dt} = \nu_2 - (-\mu_2 + \lambda_2)\kappa_{01} + \lambda_1\kappa_{10},$$

$$\frac{d\kappa_{11}}{dt} = -(-\mu_1 + \mu_2 + \lambda_1 + \lambda_2)\kappa_{11} - \lambda_1(\kappa_{10} - \kappa_{20}) - \lambda_2(\kappa_{01} - \kappa_{02}),$$

$$\frac{d\kappa_{20}}{dt} = \nu_1 + (\lambda_1 + \mu_1)\kappa_{10} - 2(\lambda_1 - \mu_1)\kappa_{20} + 2\lambda_2\kappa_{11},$$

and at last the equation for κ_{02}, which is obtained from that for κ_{20} by substituting 2 for 1 in the subscripts, κ_{10} by κ_{01}, and κ_{20} by κ_{02}.

7.2   Example: A birth–death-with-immigration process

We may reinterpret this model as a representation of a process that governs the growth of a firm by interpreting a birth as the addition of a basic unit to the firm size, death as a reduction in size, again in some basic unit, and immigration as an innovation that increases the size of a firm by a unit. This last term may also represent the feedback effects of the average (field) effect. We let μ denote the rate of size reduction and λ the rate of size increase by one unit, and α the innovation rate. Accordingly, the transition rates are specified by

$$l_k = \mu k$$

for size reduction by a unit, and

$$r_k = \alpha + \lambda k$$

for size increase by a unit, which comes either as random innovation or as random proportional growth. We assume that $0 < \lambda \le \mu$.

The master equation is

$$dP_k/dt = (k+1)\mu P_{k+1} + [\alpha + \lambda(k-1)]P_{k-1} - [\alpha + (\lambda+\mu)k]P_k,$$

with the initial condition that $k(0) = k_0$. A model with $\alpha = 0$ is discussed in Cox and Miller (1965, p. 165). We discuss only the case of λ strictly less than μ. See Kendall (1948a) for other cases.

7.2.1   Stationary probability distribution

Setting the left-hand side of the master equation equal to zero, and applying the detailed-balance conditions, which hold for this model because of the tree graph structure, we derive the stationary probability for k, π_k, as a negative binomial distribution

$$\pi_k = (1-\gamma)^\theta \binom{\theta+k-1}{k} \gamma^k,$$

where $\gamma = \lambda/\mu$ and $\theta = \alpha/\lambda$.

The maximum of the probability occurs at k^*, which satisfies

$$1 \le \frac{\alpha-\mu}{\mu-\lambda} \le k^* \le \frac{\alpha-\lambda}{\mu-\lambda},$$

provided that $\alpha > \mu$ and $\mu < (\alpha+\lambda)/2$.

Next, we verify that the time-dependent solution of the master equation indeed approaches this steady-state solution.

7.2.2   Generating function

Let the probability generating function be defined by

$$G(z,t) = \sum_{k \ge 0} z^k P_k(t).$$

Note that $\sum_{k \ge 0} z^k P_{k-1}(t) = z\,G(z,t)$, $\sum_{k \ge 1}(k+1)z^k P_{k+1}(t) = \partial G/\partial z$, $\sum_{k \ge 1} kz^k P_k(t) = z\,\partial G/\partial z$, and $\sum_{k \ge 1}(k-1)z^k P_{k-1}(t) = z^2\,\partial G/\partial z$.

Using these relations, the master equation is transformed into a partial differential equation for the generating function:

$$\frac{\partial G}{\partial t} = (\lambda z - \mu)(z-1)\frac{\partial G}{\partial z} + \alpha(z-1)G.$$

This equation is solved by the method of characteristics. See Hildebrand (1976, Chap. 8) for example. A brief outline of the method is in the Section A.1.

The characteristic curves are defined by[1]

$$\frac{dt}{1} = \frac{dz}{-(\lambda z - \mu)(z-1)} = \frac{dG}{\alpha(z-1)G}.$$

From the first pair we derive

$$\frac{z-1}{\lambda z - \mu} = C(z,t)e^{\beta t},$$

with $\beta = \mu - \lambda$, and from the second pair we derive

$$G(z,t) = D(z,t)(\lambda z - \mu)^{-\alpha/\lambda},$$

where C and D are the constants of integration. From the initial condition, we note that

$$G(z,0) = z^{n_0} = D(z,0)(\lambda z - \mu)^{\alpha/\lambda},$$

and we replace z by

$$z = \frac{C(z,0)\mu - 1}{C(z,0)\lambda - 1}$$

to obtain the relation between $C(z,0)$ and $D(z,0)$, which is

$$D(z,0) = z^{n_0}(\lambda z - \mu)^{\alpha/\lambda},$$

in which z is substituted out by the expression above.

Now to obtain the expression for $G(z,t)$, we substitute into $G(z,t) = (\lambda z - \mu)^{-\alpha/\lambda} D(z,t)$ the relation between $D(z,t)$ and $C(z,t)$ by replacing 0 with t. The result is

$$G(z,t) = (\lambda z - \mu)^{-\alpha/\lambda} \left\{ \frac{\mu C(z,t) - 1}{\lambda C(z,t) - 1} \right\}^{n_0} \left\{ \frac{\mu - \lambda}{\lambda C(z,t) - 1} \right\}^{\alpha/\lambda},$$

which, after substituting $C(z,t)$ out, becomes

$$G(z,t) = \left\{ \frac{\mu - \lambda}{\lambda(z-1)e^{-\beta t} - (\lambda z - \mu)} \right\}^{\alpha/\lambda} \left\{ \frac{\mu(z-1)e^{-\beta t} - (\lambda z - \mu)}{\lambda(z-1)e^{-\beta t} - (\lambda z - \mu)} \right\}^{n_0}.$$

The effect of the initial condition disappears as t becomes large, because the second factor above approaches one. The mean, which is calculated as $\partial G/\partial z|_{z=1}$, can be shown to approach a constant α/β at the rate $e^{-\beta t}$. With

---

[1] In general, when a term dependent on G is absent, the equation becomes $dt/1 = dz/h(z) = dG/0$. This equation has $G = a$, with some constant a, as one of the two independent solutions. The other solution is obtained from the first equality, $\phi(z,t) = b$, say. See Cox and Miller (1965, p. 158) for the necessary relation between the two constants.

$\alpha = 0$ and the initial condition $n_0 = 1$, the mean is one: $\bar{n}_t = 1$. The probability $P_0(t)$ approaches $(1 - \lambda/\mu)^{\alpha/\lambda}$, which is less than 1, as time goes to infinity. With $\alpha = 0$ it approaches as time goes to infinity.

Exercise 3.

(a) A process with $r_n = vn$, and $l_n = 0$ is governed by

$$\frac{\partial P_n(t)}{\partial t} = -vn P_n(t) + v(n-1)P_{n-1}(t).$$

Suppose that the initial condition is $P_n(0) = \delta_{n-n_0}$ for some positive integer n_0. Show that its moment generating function is given by

$$G(z, t) = e^{-vn_0 t} z^{n_0}[1 - (1 - e^{-vt})z]^{-n_0}.$$

By extracting the coefficient of z^n obtain the expression

$$P_n(t) = C_{n-1, n-n_0} e^{-vn_0 t}(1 - e^{-vt})^{n-n_0}$$

for $n \geq n_0$. Use the identity that $C_{-n,k} = C_{n+k-1}(-1)^k$. Suppose that the parameter v above is replaced with v/n, i.e., the birth rate is monotonically descreasing in n. Then, $P_n(t)$ has the Poisson distribution.

(b) Derive the moment generating function for the stationary and nonstationary probability distributions with the initial condition $P_n(0) = \delta(n - n_0)$, and the transition rates $l_n = n\mu$ and $r_n = (N - n)v$ where $v > \mu$. It is given by

$$G(z, t) = \left(\frac{v}{v + \mu}\right)^N \left\{\frac{z + (\mu/v) + (\mu/v)(z - 1)e^{\theta t}}{z + (\mu/v) - (\mu/v)(z - 1)e^{-\theta t}}\right\}^{n_0} H^N,$$

where

$$H = \left\{\frac{z + (\mu/v) - (z - 1)e^{-\theta t}}{z + (\mu/v) - (\mu/v)(z - 1)e^{-\theta t}}\right\}^N, \quad \text{with} \quad \theta = v + \mu.$$

(c) Suppose that each agent is characterized by a set of K attributes, each of which takes on the value of 1 or -1. The resulting K-dimensional vector is his state vector. The distance between the states of two agents is measured by the Hamming distance, which is the number of attributes on which the two agents are different. Let $P_k(t)$ be the probability at time t that the Hamming distance is k between two specified agents. Assume that attributes change with time in such a way that μ is the rate of change, that is, in a short time span dt, the Hamming distance changes by one with probability $\mu\, dt + o(dt)$. The probability is governed by the master equation

$$dP_k(t)/dt = \mu\{(k + 1)P_{k+1}(t) + (K - k + 1)P_{k-1}(t) - kP_k(t)\}.$$

Show that the solution of this equation is

$$P_k(t) = \frac{K!}{2^K k!(K-k)!}(1 - e^{-2\mu t})^k(1 + e^{-2\mu t})^{K-k}.$$

Verify that the average Hamming distance is $(K/2)(1 - e^{-2\mu t})$.

7.2.3 Time-inhomogeneous transition rates

We follow Kendall (1948a) in discussing solutions of master equations with time-varying transition rates. Consider

$$\frac{\partial G}{\partial t} = f(z)\frac{\partial G}{\partial z},$$

where $f(z) = (\lambda z - \mu)(z - 1)$. The associated differential equation $dz/dt = f(z)$ is a known Riccati type. The general solution is of the form (Watson 1952, Sec. 8.4)

$$z = \frac{f_1 + Cf_2}{f_3 + Cf_4},$$

where the fs are functions of time. Solving for the constant we have

$$C = \frac{zf_3 - f_1}{f_2 - zf_4}.$$

The generating function with the initial condition $P_0(0) = 1$, $P_n(0) = 0$, $n \neq 1$, is

$$G(z,t) = \frac{g_1 + zg_2}{g_3 + zg_4}$$

for some gs. Expanding G in power series in z, we obtain

$$P_0(t) = g_1(t)/g_3(t) := \xi(t),$$

and

$$P_n(t) = \eta P_{n-1}(t),$$

with $\eta(t) = -g_4(t)/g_3(t)$. Normalizing the probabilities to sum to one, we have

$$P_n(t) = (1 - P_0(t))(1 - \eta(t))\eta(t)^{n-1},$$

$n \geq 1$.

To determine the functions ξ and η, substitute the generating function thus determined, $G(z,t) = \{\xi + (1 - \xi - \eta)z\}/(1 - \eta z)$, into the partial differential equation. From it we derive

$$\xi'\eta - \xi\eta' + \eta' = \lambda(1 - \xi)(1 - \eta),$$

and

$$\xi' = \mu(1 - \xi)(1 - \eta),$$

where the prime denotes differentiation with respect to time. Next, change variables to $U = 1 - \xi$ and $V = 1 - \eta$. The differential equation for V becomes

$$V' = (\mu - \lambda)V - \mu V^2.$$

On further changing the variable to $W = 1/V$, this becomes

$$W' = -(\mu - \lambda)W + \mu,$$

which is integrated to give

$$W = e^{-\rho}\left[1 + \int_0^t e^{\rho(u)}\mu(u)\,du\right]$$

with $\rho(t) = \int_0^t [\mu(u) - \lambda(u)]\,du$.

The differential equation for U becomes

$$U'/U = -\mu/W = -W'/W - (\mu - \lambda).$$

From these we derive

$$\xi(t) = 1 - e^{-\rho(t)}/W,$$

and

$$\eta(t) = 1 - 1/W.$$

These can be used to show that $P_0(t)$ goes to one with time going to infinity if and only if $I = \int_0^\infty e^{\rho(u)}\mu(u)\,du$ is infinite.

7.2.4 The cumulant-generating-function

Now, instead of solving the partial differential equation for G as we have done above, we derive ordinary differential equations to determine the means, the covariance, and the variances. For this purpose we use the cumulant generating function. We set $z = e^{-\theta}$ in the probability generating function to convert it to the moment generating function, and take the logarithm of it to obtain the cumulant generating function

$$K(\theta; t) = \ln G(e^{-\theta}; t).$$

Noting that

$$\frac{\partial}{\partial z} = -e^\theta \frac{\partial K}{\partial \theta},$$

we rewrite the partial differential equation for G of Section 7.2.2 as

$$\frac{\partial K}{\partial t} = -(\lambda e^{-\theta} - \mu)(1 - e^{\theta})\frac{\partial K}{\partial \theta} + \alpha(e^{-\theta} - 1).$$

Let $K(\theta, t) = -\kappa_1(t)\theta + \kappa_2\theta^2/2 + \cdots$, where κ_1 is the mean and κ_2 is the variance of the state variable k. We derive the ordinary differential equations

$$d\kappa_1/dt = -\beta\kappa_1 + \alpha,$$

and

$$d\kappa_2/dt = -2\beta\kappa_2 + (\lambda + \mu)\kappa_1 + \alpha.$$

Solving these, we derive the mean and variance. We see that the variance approaches its steady-state value at least as fast as $e^{-2\beta t}$.

We use next the cumulant generating function to discuss market shares of firms.

7.3 Models for market shares by imitation or innovation

We compare deterministic and master-equation treatments of imitation and innovation processes by two types of firms. We expect the deterministic solutions to be identical or analogous to those of the mean dynamic equations provided the variances about the mean asymptotically vanish, although we should be aware of the possibility of disappointment, as Feller's example in Chapter 5 shows. The expectation is indeed satisfied for the examples in this section except for the last one.

We provide additional illustration of these generating-function techniques in the context of market shares with two types of firms, one technically advanced and the other technically less advanced. The exact natures of the two classes of firms are not important so long as firms of one class can become firms of the second class.

To be concrete, we consider a collection of n firms. This assumption allows us to use one state variable rather than two, by taking the number of firms of the advanced type to be the state variable, $k = 0, 1, 2, \ldots, n$, where n is fixed. The disadvantage of this approach is that we must provide separate boundary conditions for $k = 0$ and $k = n$, which look different from the master equations valid for $0 < k < n$. Since we are merely illustrating the use of generating functions, we do not bother with these boundary conditions here. In Chapter 5 we show how to deal with models with two state variables without assuming that the total number of firms is exogenously fixed. Elsewhere, we have dealt with a model with two types of agents. There, the transition rates $w(k, k+1) = \lambda n(1 - k/n)\eta_1(k/n)$ and $w(k, k-1) = \mu n(k/n)\eta_2(k/n)$ have been used. In other words, the birth and death rates are not constant but state-dependent. Then, the functional form of η_1 is specified as $e^{\beta h(k/n)}/\{e^{\beta h(k/n)} + e^{-\beta h(k/n)}\}$, where β is a parameter to incorporate uncertainty or imprecise information about alternative choices, and $h(\cdot)$ is a function equal to the difference of means of the alternative discounted present values associated with the alternative choices. When this function h is expanded in Taylor series, we see that we obtain both the terms $x(1 - x)$ and $x^2(1 - x)$, which are singled out in the imitation process of this chapter, and effects of congestion. For the latter, see Hirsch and Smale (1974, Chap. 12) for example.

7.3.1   Deterministic innovation process

Suppose we divide the firms into two groups: group A of k firms with superior technologies to the firms in group B, consisting of the remainder, i.e., $n - k$ firms. The identities of the firms belonging to the groups are not important. What matters is the number – or the value of the fraction, $x = k/n$ – of firms belonging to group A.

Suppose, for the sake of simplicity, that an innovation, when it occurs to firms of group B, turns them into members of group A. The fraction is then often modeled by

$$\frac{dx}{dt} = \lambda(1 - x). \tag{7.1}$$

The solution is

$$x(t) = 1 - [1 - x(0)]e^{-\lambda t}.$$

This shows that eventually all firms belong to group A, that is, the fraction converges to 1. The reason, of course, is that no firm leaves the market; hence eventually all firms belong to group A. Our purpose is not to implement more realistic assumptions, but rather to justify the ordinary differential equation above, which is often used without much justification.

We now reformulate this process as the birth process with transition rate $w(k, k + 1) = \lambda(n - k)$. This specifies that firms of the less advanced class can have individual probability rates λ of advancing to the superior class. The master equation is

$$dP_k(t)/dt = P_{k-1}(t)w(k - 1, k) - P_k(t)w(k, k + 1),$$

except for the boundary conditions for $P_0(t)$ and $P_n(t)$, with which we do not bother here.

Next, convert this equation into the partial differential equation for the probability generating function,

$$\frac{\partial G(z, t)}{\partial t} = \lambda n(z - 1)G - \lambda z(z - 1)\frac{\partial G}{\partial z}.$$

We can solve this equation by the characteristic-curve method as shown in Section 7.2. When we do this, $G(z, t)$ approaches z^n as t goes to infinity for all initial numbers of firms in group B. This shows that all firms become technically advanced as time progresses.

Our purpose is to point out that the posited ordinary differential equation can be derived from the cumulant generating function, to show the relations between it and the partial differential equations, and to show that it can be used by itself, since no coupling exists between the mean and variance dynamics for this simple process.

Let $K(\theta, t) = \ln G(e^{-\theta}, t)$. The partial differential equation now becomes

$$\frac{\partial K}{\partial t} = \lambda n(e^{-\theta} - 1) + \lambda(e^{-\theta} - 1)\frac{\partial K}{\partial \theta}.$$

Expand $K(\theta, t) = -\kappa_1\theta + \kappa_2\theta^2/2 + \cdots$, from which we derive

$$d\kappa_1/dt = -\lambda\kappa_1 + \lambda n,$$

with $\kappa_1(0) = k_0$, and

$$\frac{d\kappa_2}{dt} = -2\lambda\kappa_2 + \lambda(n - \kappa_1),$$

with $\kappa_2(0) = 0$. Note that κ_3 does not appear in this set of equations.

In this example there is no dynamic coupling from the variance to the mean. The solutions are

$$\kappa_1(t) = n - (n - k_0)e^{-\lambda t};$$

hence κ_1/n may be interpreted as the deterministic counterpart of the fraction x defined by $x = \kappa_1/n$, and

$$\kappa_2(t) = (n - k_0)(e^{-\lambda t} - e^{-2\lambda t}).$$

This shows that the variance asymptotically vanishes. Hence, the above interpretation is justified.

7.3.2 Deterministic imitation process

We next introduce interactions between firms of different classes. We follow Iwai (1984a,b, 1996) and assume that firms in group B individually imitate firms in group A and succeed in becoming members of group A at the rate μ. Using the deterministic approach, this is expressed by[2]

$$\frac{dx}{dt} = \mu x(1 - x).$$

---

[2] If only firms with backward technology die, we add $-d(1 - x)$ to the next equation. This does not introduce anything new. Change the variable from x to $y = x - d$. Then, for $y \geq 0$ y approaches $1 - d$ as time goes to infinity.

Writing this as $dx/x(1-x) = \mu\, dt$ and integrating it, we obtain its solution as

$$x(t) = \frac{x(0)}{x(0) + [1 - x(0)]e^{-\mu t}}.$$

Again, we see that all firms succeed in becoming members of the advanced class.

In terms of the master equation, we respecify the transition rate to be $w(k, k+1) = \mu k(n-k)$, in

$$dP_k(t)/dt = P_{k-1}(t)w(k-1,k) - P_k(t)w(k, k+1).$$

Now, the partial differential equation for the probability generating function is slightly more complicated:

$$\frac{\partial G}{\partial t} = \mu n z(z-1)\frac{\partial G}{\partial z} - \mu z(z-1)\left[\frac{\partial G}{\partial z} + z\frac{\partial^2 G}{\partial z^2}\right].$$

Going directly to the partial differential equation for the new cumulant generating function, we note that $[z\partial^2 G/\partial z^2 + \partial G/\partial z]$ equals $Ge^{2\theta}[(\partial K/\partial\theta)^2 + \partial^2 K/\partial\theta^2]$. We derive

$$\frac{\partial K}{\partial t} = \mu(1 - e^{-\theta})\left[n\frac{\partial K}{\partial\theta} + \left(\frac{\partial K}{\partial\theta}\right)^2 + \frac{\partial^2 K}{\partial\theta^2}\right].$$

The ordinary differential equations for the mean and variance are now coupled:

$$d\kappa_1/dt = \mu(n - \kappa_1)\kappa_1 - \mu\kappa_2,$$

and

$$d\kappa_2/dt = \mu(2n - 1)\kappa_2 + \mu(n - \kappa_1)\kappa_1 - 4\mu\kappa_1\kappa_2 - 2\mu\kappa_3.$$

However, as κ_1 approaches n, the effect of the variance on the mean vanishes. Thus dropping the κ_2 term in the differential equation for κ_1 leads to the correct limiting value.

The reader may have noticed the absence of the phenomenon of firms going out of business – the death process in the birth-and-death process models. When bankruptcy is modeled, we must drop the assumption that n is fixed exogenously. See Chapter 10 for discussions of processes with both birth and death effects on firm market shares.

7.3.3   A joint deterministic process

We now combine these two effects into a single equation:

$$\frac{dx}{dt} = \mu x(1 - x) + \lambda(1 - x). \tag{7.2}$$

We can solve this directly by noting that

$$\frac{1}{\mu x(1-x)+\lambda(1-x)} = \frac{1}{\mu+\lambda}\left[\frac{\mu}{\mu x+\lambda}+\frac{1}{1-x}\right].$$

The solution is

$$x(t) = \frac{C-\lambda e^{-\gamma t}}{C+\mu e^{-\gamma t}},$$

where $\gamma = \lambda+\mu$, and where $C = (\lambda+\mu x_0)/(1-x_0)$. Unsurprisingly, $x(t)$ goes to one as time progresses.

The reason for this limiting behavior is clear. No firms leave the market, and eventually all firms belong to group A. To remedy this, we must allow some firms to leave the market or go bankrupt. We need to abandon the assumption of a fixed number of firms unless we artificially allow entry to keep the number fixed. See Chapter 10 for this alternative model.

7.3.4 A stochastic dynamic model

Next, we set up the master equation for the joint processes to model market shares of group A. We assume that n is fixed. We take the transition rate of the number of firms in group A from k to $k+1$ to be

$$r_k = \mu\frac{k}{n}\left(1-\frac{k}{n}\right)+\lambda\left(1-\frac{k}{n}\right).$$

Denote the probability $P_k(t) = \Pr(k_A(t) = k)$, where k_A is the number of firms of group A. It is governed by

$$\frac{dP_k(t)}{dt} = r_{k-1}P_{k-1}(t) - r_k P_k(t)$$

for $k = 1, \ldots, n$. There is an obvious boudary equation for $k = 1$.

It is convenient to regroup the right-hand side as $[r_{k-1} - r_k]P_k(t) + r_{k-1}[P_{k-1} - P_k(t)]$, change the variable by

$$\frac{k}{n} = \phi + \frac{\xi}{\sqrt{n}},$$

and denote

$$\Pi(\xi, t) := P_k(t).$$

Then, the left-hand side of the master equation becomes

$$\frac{\partial\Pi}{\partial t} - \sqrt{n}\frac{\partial\Pi}{\partial\xi}\frac{d\phi}{dt}.$$

This change of variable was introduced earlier in Section 5.2. See also Aoki (1996a, p. 123) or Aoki (1995). As it turns out, to match orders of magnitude of terms on both sides, we need to change the time scale as well by

$$t = n\tau.$$

We rewrite the time derivative as $d\phi/dt = n^{-1} d\phi/d\tau$, and do likewise to rewrite $\partial \Pi/\partial t$.

We note that on the right-hand side

$$r_{k-1} - r_k = -\frac{\mu}{n}\left(1 - 2\phi - 2\frac{\xi}{\sqrt{n}}\right) + \frac{\lambda}{n} + o(n^{-1}),$$

and

$$P_{k-1} - P_k = -\frac{1}{\sqrt{n}}\frac{\partial \Pi}{\partial \xi} + \frac{1}{2n}\frac{\partial^2 \Pi}{\partial \xi^2}.$$

Now equate terms of the same order. The highest-order ones are of the order n. We obtain

$$\frac{d\phi}{d\tau} = \mu\phi(1 - \phi) + \lambda(1 - \phi).$$

The next highest-order terms in n produce what is known as the (linear) Fokker–Planck equation. We look for the stationary solution and set $\partial \Pi/\partial \tau$ equal to zero:

$$0 = [\lambda - \mu(1 - 2\phi)]\frac{\partial(\xi \Pi)}{\partial \xi} + \frac{\mu\phi(1 - \phi) + \lambda(1 - \phi)}{2}\frac{\partial^2 \Pi}{\partial \xi^2}.$$

The deterministic equation has the logistic curve as its solution. The Fokker–Planck equation has the Gaussian distribution with mean zero and variance $[\mu\phi(1 - \phi) + \lambda(1 - \phi)]/[\lambda - \mu(1 - 2\phi)]$ when the denominator is positive. By setting μ to zero, we recover the aggregate dynamics (7.1) and the associated Fokker–Planck equation.

7.4   A stochastic model with innovators and imitators

We examine an open model with two types of firms, called innovators and imitators, to discover the market shares of the two types. We incorporate asymmetric interactions between the two types of firms.

Let $\mathbf{n} = (n_1, n_2)$ be the state vector. We assume that the transition rates are such that

$$w(\mathbf{n}, \mathbf{n} + \mathbf{e}_1) = c_1(n_1 + h_1) = c_1 n_1 + f_1,$$

where type 1 firms grow at the innovation rate f_1 plus a proportional growth rate of $c_1 n_1$. On the other hand type 2 firms, which are less technically advanced that those of type 1, grow at the rate

$$w(\mathbf{n}, \mathbf{n} + \mathbf{e}_2) = f_2,$$

where $f_2 < f_1$.

The two types go out of business at the rates

$$w(\mathbf{n}, \mathbf{n} - \mathbf{e}_j) = d_j n_j,$$

$j = 1, 2$. We assume that type 2 firms fail more often than type 1 firms: $d_2 \geq d_1$. By imitating type 1 firms, a type 2 firm may become type 1 at the rate

$$w(\mathbf{n}, \mathbf{n} + \mathbf{e}_1 - \mathbf{e}_2) = \lambda_{21} d_2 c_1 n_2 (n_1 + h_1),$$

while a type 1 firm may slip back to type 2 at the rate

$$w(\mathbf{n}, \mathbf{n} + \mathbf{e}_2 - \mathbf{e}_1) = \lambda_{12} f_2 d_1 n_1.$$

With these transition rates, it is easily verified that the steady-state probability distribution exists by imposing the detailed-balance conditions, provided $\lambda_{12} = \lambda_{21}$. Let $g_1 = c_1/d_1$, and $g_2 = f_2/d_2$. We define $\mu := \lambda d_1 d_2$. Then we can write the transition rates more succinctly by noting that $\lambda_{21} d_2 c_1 = \mu g_1$ and $\lambda_{12} f_2 d_1 = \mu g_2$:

$$w(\mathbf{n}, \mathbf{n} + \mathbf{e}_1 - \mathbf{e}_2) = \mu g_1 n_2 (n_1 + h_1),$$

while a type 1 firm may slip back to type 2 at the rate

$$w(\mathbf{n}, \mathbf{n} + \mathbf{e}_2 - \mathbf{e}_1) = \mu g_2 n_1.$$

The number of type 1 firms is governed by a negative binomial distribution, while the number of type 2 firms has a Poisson distribution,

$$\pi(n_1, n_2) = \pi_1(n_1) \pi_2(n_2),$$

with

$$\pi_1 = (1 - g)^{h_1} \binom{n_1 + h_1 - 1}{n_1} g_1^{n_1},$$

and

$$\pi(n_2) = e^{-g_2} \frac{g_2^{n_2}}{n_2!}.$$

We next examine the nonstationary solution of the master equation

$$\partial P(\mathbf{n})/\partial t = I(\mathbf{n}, t) - O(\mathbf{n}, t),$$

where the probability influx denoted by the first term is

$$I(\mathbf{n}, t) = P_{n_1+1,n_2}(t)d_1(n_1 + 1) + P_{n_1,n_2+1}(t)d_2(n_2 + 1)$$
$$+ P_{n_1-1,n_2}(t)c_1(n_1 + h_1 - 1) + P_{n_1,n_2-1}(t)f_2$$
$$+ P_{n_1+1,n_2-1}(t)\mu g_2(n_1 + 1)$$
$$+ P_{n_1-1,n_2+1}(t)\mu g_1(n_1 + h_1 - 1)(n_2 + 1),$$

and the outflux is given by

$$O(\mathbf{n}, t) = P_{n_1,n_2}(t)[c_1(n_1 + h_1 - 1) + f_2 + d_1 n_1 + d_2 n_2$$
$$+ \mu g_1 n_2(n_1 + h_1) + \mu g_2 n_1].$$

We rewrite it in terms of the probability generating function

$$G(z_1, z_2, t) = \sum_{n_1,n_2} z_1^{n_1} z_2^{n_2} P(n_1, n_2).$$

The partial differential equation for the generating function is

$$\frac{\partial G}{\partial t} = [d_1(1 - z_1) + c_1 z_1(z_1 - 1) + \mu g_2(1 - z_1)] \frac{\partial G}{\partial z_1} + [d_2(1 - z_2)$$
$$+ \mu g_1 h_1(z_1 - z_2)] \frac{\partial G}{\partial z_2} + \mu g_1 z_2(z_1 - z_2) \frac{\partial^2 G}{\partial z_1 \partial z_2}$$
$$+ [h_1(z_1 - 1) + f_2(z_2 - 1) + c_1)] G.$$

Since this equation is rather complicated, we change it to one for the cumulant generating function defined by

$$K(\theta_1, \theta_2, t) = \ln G(e^{-\theta_1}, e^{-\theta_2}, t).$$

In doing so, we note that $\partial G/\partial t = G \, \partial K/\partial t$, $\partial G/\partial z_i = -G e^{\theta_i} \partial K/\partial \theta_i$, $i = 1, 2$, and $\partial^2 G/\partial z_1 \partial z_2 = G e^{\theta_1+\theta_2}[(\partial K/\partial \theta_1)(\partial K/\partial \theta_2) + \partial^2 K/\partial \theta_1 \partial \theta_2]$. We derive

$$\frac{\partial K}{\partial t} = -\phi_1 \frac{\partial K}{\partial \theta_1} - \phi_2 \frac{\partial K}{\partial \theta_2} + \phi_3 \left[\frac{\partial K}{\partial \theta_1} \frac{\partial K}{\partial \theta_2} + \frac{\partial^2 K}{\partial \theta_1 \partial \theta_2} \right] + \phi_4,$$

where

$$\phi_1 = d_1 \left(\theta_1 + \frac{\theta_1^2}{2} \right) + c_1 \left(-\theta_1 + \frac{\theta_1^2}{2} \right) + \mu g_2 \left(\theta_1 - \theta_2 + \frac{(\theta_1 - \theta_2)^2}{2} \right),$$

$$\phi_2 = d_2 \left(\theta_2 + \frac{\theta_2^2}{2} \right) + \mu g_1 h_1 \left(\theta_2 - \theta_1 + \frac{(\theta_2 - \theta_1)^2}{2} \right),$$

$$\phi_3 = \mu g_1 \left(\theta_2 - \theta_1 + \frac{(\theta_1 - \theta_2)^2}{2} \right),$$

and

$$\phi_4 = f_1\left(-\theta_1 + \theta_1^2/2\right) + f_2\left(-\theta_2 + \theta_2^2/2\right).$$

Then, expanding K as $K = -\kappa_1\theta_1 - \kappa_2\theta_2 + (1/2)(\kappa_{11}\theta_1^2 + 2\kappa_{12}\theta_1\theta_2 + \kappa_{22}\theta_2^2) + \cdots$, we derive coupled ordinary differential equations for the first and second moments. Unfortunately, the ordinary equations are not solvable in closed form.

We mention some special cases by imposing some conditions on the parameters in the transiton rates.

7.4.1   Case of a finite total number of firms

First, assume that $g_2 = 0$, that $d_2 = d_1 - c_1$, and that h_1 is much smaller than these parameters. The first assumption means that no type 1 firms become type 2 firms. Once technically advanced, firms remain technically advanced. The second assumption means that the net dropout rate of type 1 firm is the same as that of type 2 firms. The third assumption means that c_1 is much larger than f_1, that is, the rate of growth of type 1 firms comes primarily from existing firms generating new firms of the same type and not from new entries. Then,

$$\frac{d(\kappa_1 + \kappa_2)}{dt} = -d_2(\kappa_1 + \kappa_2) + f_1 + f_2;$$

hence the sum of the numbers of firms of both types asymptotically approaches $(f_1 + f_2)/d_2$.

Another consequence of these parameter values is that κ_{12} is constant. Suppose that it is zero at time 0. Then, it remains zero for all times. With $g_2 = 0$ and $h_1 = 0$, we can drop the assumption that $d_2 = d_1 - c_1$ and solve for κ_1 and κ_2 separately, because

$$d\kappa_1/dt = -(d_1 - c_1)\kappa_1 + f_1 + \mu g_1(\kappa_1\kappa_2),$$

and

$$d\kappa_2/dt = -d_2\kappa_2 + f_2 - \mu g_1(\kappa_1\kappa_2).$$

We can solve algebraically for the limiting values of κ_1 and κ_2 from these. Compared with the case of $\mu g_1 = 0$, interactions between firms of the two groups cause $\kappa_1(\infty)$ to be larger with $\mu g_1 \neq 0$, and $\kappa_2(\infty)$ less, as expected.

Next, suppose that type 2 firms never become type 1. Once technically behind, they remain behind. This is expressed by assuming that $g_1 = 0$. In this case, the dynamics for κ_1 is solved first, then substituted into the dynamics for κ_2. We find that $\kappa_1(\infty) = f_1/(d_1 - c_1)$ and $\kappa_2 = f_2/d_2 + \mu g_2 f_1/d_2(d_1 - c_1)$. There are more type 2 firms, while the number of type 1 firms remains the same.

In examining the joint dynamics for κ_1 and κ_2, we see that the covariance κ_{12} acts on the time derivatives of κ_1 and κ_2 with opposite signs and the same magnitude.

7.5   Symmetric interactions

7.5.1   Stationary state distribution

Suppose we now specify entry transition rates for the two groups in the same form, that is, we replace f_2 in the previous section by

$$w(\mathbf{n}, \mathbf{n} + \mathbf{e}_2) = c_2(n_2 + h_2) = c_2 n_1 + f_2,$$

and respecify the transition rate from type 1 to type 2 as

$$w(\mathbf{n}, \mathbf{n} - \mathbf{e}_1 + \mathbf{e}_2) = \mu g_2 n_1 (n_2 + h_2).$$

Then both types have negative binomial distributions as their equilibrium distributions:

$$\pi_i(n_i) = B_i g_i^{n_i} \binom{n_i + h_i - 1}{n_i},$$

$i = 1, 2$.

7.5.2   Nonstationary distributions

We derive the differential equation for the cumulant generating function as in the previous section. The detailed expressions for ϕ_1 through ϕ_4 are slightly different, but the general procedure of analysis remains the same. We do not bother with the detailed results.

Rather, we later examine in Chapter 11, after discussing some growth and business-cycle models in between in Chapters 8 and 10, what happens when the number of groups becomes large, as well as the total number of firms. We find a perhaps surprising connection with the Ewens distribution.

CHAPTER 8

Growth and fluctuations

This chapter is loosely grouped into four parts. Part one is composed of Sections 8.1 through 8.5. Part two consists of a single long Section 8.6. Part three is made up of Sections 8.7 and 8.8, and part four is Section 8.9. The first part of this chapter collects a number of bare-bones models and topics that are loosely tied to the notion of growth, market shares, and fluctuations.

The bare-bones models in this part may be used, singly or in some combinations, to construct more fully specified models of growth or fluctuation. For example, Aoki and Yoshikawa (2001) describe a model that uses some of the bare-bones models as components to show how demand saturation limits growth. A second example is described in Section 8.6. The third example is discussed in Chapter 9.

We begin this chapter by discussing two mini-models, called Poisson and urn models, for explaining how economies grow by inventing new goods or creating new industries. These models provide different explanations of growth from those in the literature on endogenous growth models.

The two models in Section 8.1 provide two explanations of economic growth that are different from standard ones based on technical progress, that is, total factor productivity models or endogenous growth models. The flavor of the difference may be captured by saying that in the endogenous growth models an economy grows by improving the quality of existing goods, whereas in our models it grows by introducing new goods.

In the first model, firms or sectors independently invent new goods or improve on the existing ones. The numbers of new goods are then functions of the number of the firms, or the size of the economy. The growth rate of this model eventually converges to the rate at which new goods are being introduced to the economy. In the second model, the numbers of goods that are introduced are independent of the numbers of the existing goods, and the rate of introduction of new goods decreases as the number of goods grows. The growth rate eventually reduces to zero. This is not a totally absurd idea. Actually, to quote Kuznets (1953), "The industries that have matured technologically account for a progressively increasing ratio of the total production of the economy. Their maturity does imply that economic effects of further improvements will necessarily be more limited than in the past."

These two linear models are followed by another set of two related models. In the first one the exit rate of goods is nonlinear, to quantify the idea that older goods disappear from the markets more quickly than newer goods. In the second, demand saturates as time goes on.

We then turn to discuss a simple stochastic business-cycle model, after taking a quick look at a deterministic version suggested by Iwai (1984a, b, 1996). His model considers an economy composed of two sectors of firms with a fixed total number of firms. The rates of change of shares of the market change in response to gaps between demands and supplies of the two sectors. The share converges monotonically to one. This generates no business-cycle-like fluctuations of the total output.

A stochastic version of this model, which keeps the central idea that shares change in response to the gaps, is next discussed for comparison. A simplified two-sector version of this model has been described in Section 4.1. The model generalizes this to a K-sector model in which sectors respond to gaps between supplies and demands of individual sectors. It is an open business-cycle model. Unlike the deterministic ones, it generates fluctuations. The expected output of the economy responds to changing patterns of demand shares. It increases as more demands are shifted to more productive sectors of the economy.

We accomplish two things by this model. First, we illustrate a possibility that fluctuations of the aggregate economy arise as an outcome of interactions of many agents/sectors in a simple model. Second, we demonstrate that the *level* of the *aggregate* economic activity depends on the structure of demand. In the standard neoclassical equilibrium, where the marginal products of production factors such as labor are equal in all activities and sectors, demand determines only the composition of goods and services to be produced, not the level of the aggregate economic activity.

There are two ways for demand to affect the aggregate level of economic activities. One is externality associated with demand, which might produce multiple equilibria as in Diamond (1982). We return to his model in Chapter 9. The other is differences in productivity across sectors/activities. Recent works by Murphy et al. (1989) and Matsuyama (1995), for example, emphasize the importance of increasing returns in order to demonstrate the role of demand in determining the level of the aggregate production. They, in effect, allow differences in productivity across sectors to draw their conclusions. In this chapter, we keep Iwai's idea and assume that productivities differ across sectors in the economy. Here, we just show how the output of the economy is maximized for a suitable choice of the demand shares by assuming that the productivity coefficients of the two sectors are not equal.

8.1 Two simple models for the emergence of new goods

Two models are introduced to explain how new goods appear. In the first model, called the *Poisson model*, firms or sectors independently invent new goods or improve on the existing ones. The numbers of new goods are then functions of the number of firms, or the size of the economy. The growth rate of this model eventually converges to that of the rate at which new goods are being introduced into the economy. In the second, called the *urn model*, the number of goods that are introduced is independent of the numbers of the existing goods, and the rate of introduction of new goods decreases as the number of goods increases.

8.1.1 Poisson growth model

Let $Q_k(t)$ be the probability that there are k goods or sectors in the economy at time t. Each firm (sector) independently has probability $\lambda \, \Delta t$ in a small time interval Δt of introducing one new good (sector). Thus the total numbers of the final goods (sectors) go from k to $k + 1$ in time interval of Δt with probability

$$\Pr(N(t + \Delta t) = k + 1 | N(t) = k) = \lambda k Q_k(t) \, \Delta t + o(\Delta t),$$

where $N(t)$ is the number of goods being produced at time t, and λk is the overall rate of new goods being introduced, on the assumption that sectors act independently. The probability $Q_k(t)$ is governed by the differential equation

$$\frac{dQ_k(t)}{dt} = -\lambda k Q_k(t) + \lambda(k - 1)Q_{k-1}(t),$$

with the initial condition $Q_k(0) = \delta(k - k_0)$. We assume goods once introduced are not withdrawn from the market. A different model is later discussed, which has different effects on goods to be introduced to the markets in the future. For simplicity take k_0 to be one.

Solving this differential equation, the probability is given by

$$Q_k(t) = e^{-\lambda t}(1 - e^{-\lambda t})^{k-1}.$$

Suppose that output at time t of a good that was introduced at time s, $s \leq t$, is given by

$$y(t; s) = \frac{\mu}{\nu + (\mu - \nu)e^{-\mu(t-s)}}.$$

For definiteness assume that $\mu > \nu$. This expression implies that the output changes monotonically from 1 at the time of introduction of the good, and incorporates the assumption that the output eventually levels off at μ/ν as time goes to infinity.

The total output of this economy is then given by

$$Y_t = \sum_{k \geq 1} \lambda k \int_0^t Q_k(s) y(t, ; s) \, ds + y(t; 0).$$

The second term is the output of the original firm that exists in the economy at time zero. Using the generating function to express the sum, it is straightforward to show that the rate of growth of the total output converges to λ, that is, the rate of entry of new goods (sectors) as time goes to infinity:

$$g_t := \frac{d \ln Y_t}{dt} = \lambda + \frac{y(t, 0)}{Y_t} \frac{d \ln y(t, 0)}{dt} \to \lambda,$$

since $d \ln y(t, 0)/dt \to 0$.

In this subsection, we have used a constant λ. More realistically, λ may be a decreasing function of N. For example, by interpreting N as proxy for the stock of R&D, diminishing returns to R&D due to congestion in research, increasing difficulties, and such may cause the growth rate to approach zero, as in Jones (1995), Jones and Williams (1998), Segerstrom (1998), and Young (1998) among others. In the next model, we present a different take on this aspect.

8.1.2   An urn model for growth

The model of this subsection incorporates the idea that goods/sectors that will emerge are not directly linked to R&D, so that their rate of emergence is not tied to the birth rate of the Poisson process, but is strongly conditioned on some opportunities for innovations, which are independent of stock or flows of R&D, such as advances in basic scientific knowledge. We assume that a new good or sector is introduced at time t with probability

$$P(t) = \frac{\omega}{\omega + t},$$

for some positive ω, and $t = 1, 2, \ldots$. We use a discrete-time description for brevity.

Here, the rate of innovation is simply a descreasing function of time. This probability may be regarded as a probability of drawing a black ball from an urn that initially contains ω black balls. After each drawing, the drawn ball is returned, and one white ball is added to the urn. At time t, then, the urn contains ω black balls and t white balls. Urns to which one or more balls of different colors are added belong to a class of urn models called *Pólya urns*. Such models are extensively used in population genetics models. See Hoppe (1984, 1987), or Appendix A.2.

Pólya urns are used also in the standard R&D-based total factor productivity models such as Jones (1995), Jones and Williams (1998), Segerstrom (1998), and Young (1998). Their rate of innovation is a decreasing function of the R&D capital stock. Here, the rate of innovation is simply a decreasing function of time.

The probability of k goods being available in the market at time t is denoted as before by $Q_k(t)$, but is now governed by the difference equation

$$Q_k(t+1) = [1 - P(t)]Q_k(t) + P(t)Q_{k-1}(t),$$

with the boundary conditions

$$Q(1, t) = \frac{1}{\omega + 1} \frac{2}{\omega + 2} \cdots \frac{t - 1}{\omega + t - 1}$$

and

$$Q(t, t) = \frac{\omega^t}{(\omega + 1)(\omega + 2) \cdots (\omega + t)}.$$

The first is the probability that no new goods are introduced up to time t, and the second is the probability that new goods are introduced at each and every period up to time t.

We introduce a notation for the ascending factorial

$$\omega^{[t]} := \omega(\omega + 1) \cdots (\omega + t - 1).$$

The difference equation has the solution

$$Q_k(t) = \frac{c(k, t)\omega^k}{\omega^{[t]}}.$$

Here, we have introduced also an important number, the (unsigned) Stirling number of the first kind. It satisfies the recursion relation

$$c(k, t + 1) = tc(k, t) + c(k - 1, t).$$

This number is also defined by

$$x^{[m]} = \sum_{j=0}^{m} c(m, j)x^j,$$

for some positive integer m, i.e., the coefficient of x^j in the expansion of the ascending factorial $x^{[m]}$. See Appendix A.5 on Stirling numbers, as well as Abramovitz and Stegun (1968, p. 825). Aoki (1997, p. 279) has some nongenetic applications.

The total output is now given by

$$Y_t = \sum_{l=1}^{y} \sum_{j=1}^{l} \frac{c(l - 1, j - 1)\omega^{j-1}}{\omega^{[l-1]}} \frac{\omega}{\omega + l} y(t - l),$$

where $y(t - l)$ is the production at time t of the final good that emerged at time l, $l < t$.

For simplicity take ω to be a positive integer. Then

$$\sum_{l=1}^{t} \frac{\omega}{\omega + l} = \omega \left(\sum_{k=1}^{\omega+l} \frac{1}{k} - \sum_{k=1}^{\omega} \frac{1}{k} \right) \approx \ln \frac{\omega + t}{\omega}.$$

Thus, approximately,

$$Y_t = \ln(\omega + t).$$

The growth rate goes asymptotically to zero.

Alternatively, suppose that $P(t)$ depends on the number of existing goods. We define the probability that the kth good is invented during period t by

$$P_k(t) = \frac{\omega(k - 1)}{\omega + k}.$$

In this case, the rate of growth is given by

$$\frac{d \ln Y_t}{dt} = \frac{1}{t} + \frac{1}{t \ln t}.$$

When opportunities for innovation declines, sustained growth is not possible. Solow (1994) makes a similar point about endogenous innovations. He points out that if R&D does not produce a proportional increase in the (Hicks-neutral) technical progress factor A in the production function $AF(K, L)$, but only an absolute increase in A, then greater allocation of resources to R&D buys a one-time jump in productivity, but no faster productivity growth. The model in the first Subsection 8.1.1 corresponds to proportionate growth in A, and the second to an absolute increase in A.

8.2　Disappearance of goods from markets

In the standard economic literature, diminishing returns to capital stocks essentially restrain economic growth. The model of this section is constructed to have its growth impeded by demand saturation, and is led by new goods, which randomly appear on the markets.[1] We examine a process of invention of goods and disappearance of goods as a nonlinear birth–death process.

Put simply, we assume that the stochastic process for demand changes is a birth-and-death process with birth rate λ and death rate μn_t. The only non-standard feature is a nonlinear death rate in order to embody an idea that older

---

[1] This section is based in part on Aoki and Yoshikawa (2000).

products have higher probability of dying out. This aspect is somewhat reminiscent of the old-age effect of Arley referred to in Kendall (1948b). Arley use μt with constant μ to indicate that older particles die faster, probabilistically, than newly formed particles in his study of cosmic showers. We can handle an alternative senario of constant death rate and diminishing birth rate by replacing λ by λ/n_t. Basically the same qualitative conclusion follows from this alternative. We do not pursue this alternative further.

8.2.1 Model

Write the probability that output is n (in a suitable unit) as $P_n(t)$. The master equation for this growth process is

$$\frac{\partial P_n(t)}{\partial t} = \lambda(n-1)P_{n-1}(t) + \mu(n+1)^2 P_{n+1}(t) - (\lambda + \mu n)n P_n(t),$$

$n > 1$. The boundary condition is $\partial P_0(t)/\partial t = \mu P_1(t)$. We assume that $\lambda > \mu$. In this model the birth rate is a constant λ, but the death rate is taken to be μ times the number n. This effect may be congestion effects or old-age effect.

We can solve the master equation for a steady-state (stationary) distribution by setting the left-hand side equal to zero and replacing $P_n(t)$ by π_n. Try the detailed-balance condition

$$\lambda(n-1)\pi_{n-1} = \mu n^2 \pi_n,$$

$n > 1$. This has the solution

$$\pi_n = \frac{1}{Z}\frac{(\lambda/\mu)^n}{nn!},$$

where $n \geq 1$, and where $Z = \sum_n (\lambda/\mu)^n/nn! < \infty$.

All stationary moments are finite. For example, $\bar{n} = \sum_n n\pi_n = e^{\lambda/\mu}/Z$, $\overline{n^2} = (\lambda/\mu)\bar{n}$, $\overline{n^3} = (\lambda/\mu)(\lambda/\mu + 1)/Z$, and so on.

To obtain some information on nonstationary behavior of the growth process, we next derive the probability generating function $G(z, t) = \sum_n z^n P_n(t)$. Since this does not seem to have a closed-form solution, we convert it to the cumulant generating function and derive the ordinary differential equations for the first two cumulants.

The probability generating function is

$$\frac{\partial G}{\partial t} = \lambda z(z-1)\frac{\partial G}{\partial z} + \mu(1-z)\left\{\left(\frac{z\partial^2 G}{\partial z^2} + \frac{\partial G}{\partial z}\right)\right\},$$

and the cumulant generating function is

$$\frac{\partial K}{\partial t} = -\lambda(e^{-\theta} - 1)\frac{\partial K}{\partial \theta} + \mu(e^{\theta} - 1)\left[\left(\frac{\partial K}{\partial \theta}\right)^2 + \frac{\partial^2 K}{\partial \theta^2}\right],$$

where $K(\theta, t) = G(e^{-\theta}, t)$.

We expand K as $-\kappa_1\theta + \kappa_2\theta^2/2 - \kappa_3\theta^3/3! + \cdots$. Then, equating the expressions of the same powers in θ on both sides, we obtain the differential equations for the first two cumulants, κ_1 and κ_2:

$$d\kappa_1/dt = \lambda\kappa_1 - \mu(\kappa_1^2 + \kappa_2),$$

and

$$d\kappa_2/dt = (2\lambda + \mu)\kappa_2 + \lambda\kappa_1 + \mu\kappa_1^2 - 4\mu\kappa_1\kappa_2 - 2\mu\kappa_3.$$

Unfortunately, the equations for the cumulants do not terminate at any finite moments. By assuming that the steady state of κ_3 is a small bounded number, we can solve for the steady-state values of the first two moments by ignoring this term. We then examine if the linearized differential equations are asymptotically stable. If the answer is yes, then the stationary values are such that the third cumulants are zero. For certain ranges of the ratio λ/μ, there are two steady-state variance values for a positive stationary value of the mean.

8.2.2   Stability analysis

We drop the time argument for simplicity. Assume that $\mu < \lambda \le 2\mu$. With this assumption, the linearized equations for x and v about x_∞ and v_∞ are asymptotically stable, as we show later, and the stationary values are obtained by setting the left-hand side of the differential equation equal to zero, and assuming that the third central moment remains bounded for all time and has a stationary value as well. The stationary values are given by

$$\lambda x_\infty = \mu(x_\infty^2 + v_\infty),$$

and

$$(2\lambda + \mu)v_\infty + \lambda x_\infty + \mu x_\infty^2 - 4\mu x_\infty v_\infty = 2\mu\kappa_3(\infty).$$

In terms of x_∞, the stationary values are related by

$$v_\infty = \left(\frac{\lambda}{\mu} - x_\infty\right)x_\infty,$$

and

$$\kappa_\infty = x_\infty\frac{\lambda}{\mu} + \left(\frac{\lambda}{\mu} - 2x_\infty\right)\left(\frac{\lambda}{\mu} - 2x_\infty\right)x_\infty.$$

When the third central moment does not have zero steady-state value, we need to bound the effects of this nonzero value by the Gronwall inequality. We drop these inessential complications here.

The steady-state variance needs to be smaller than $(\mu/2\lambda)^2$ to have positive x_∞; we assume that, and focus on the mean of n, or equivalently on the mean of the demand, which becomes

$$\bar{A}(t) = \frac{\lambda A_0}{\mu A_0 + (\lambda - \mu A_0)e^{-\lambda t}}.$$

The expected demand follows the logistic curve. Suppose that the initial value A_0 is smaller than λ/μ. Then, the mean demand initially grows almost exponentially, but eventually the growth diminishes to zero and the mean demand approaches its ceiling value λ/μ.

Subtract the steady-state values obtained by setting the derivatives equal to zero, and let $\xi = x - x_\infty$ and $\zeta = v - v_\infty$. Retaining only linear terms in the differential equations for these newly introduced variables, we have

$$\frac{d\xi}{dt} = \lambda\xi - \mu\zeta - 2\mu x_\infty\xi,$$

and

$$\frac{d\zeta}{dt} = (\lambda - 4\mu v_\infty + 2\mu x_\infty)\xi + (2\lambda + \mu - 4\mu x_\infty)\zeta - 2\mu(\kappa - \kappa_\infty).$$

The eigenvalues of this set of two equations have negative real part if the trace is negative and the determinant is positive of the matrix of the two equations above. At $x_\infty = \lambda/\mu$, for example, v_∞ is zero, and the two eigenvalues of this linearized equation both have negative real part, under the condition $\mu \leq \lambda \leq 2\mu$.

8.3 Shares of dated final goods among households

This section applies the techniques and elementary building blocks for models, discussed in Chapter 7, to analyze a model in which new final goods become available randomly over time, and they are being adopted or purchased gradually by some fraction of n households. To simplify presentation we work with expected values of stochastic variables. These new goods sustain growth of the economy.[2]

The mechanism of growth of the model is basically that of the Ramsey model. Unlike the latter, which relies on the shift of preference of a representative household for the engine of growth, growth in our model is due to diffusion or spread of consumption of the newly available goods for purchase by the households. Spread of consumption of new goods among households creates demand, which

---

[2] This section is based in part on Aoki and Yoshikawa (2000).

in turn induces capital investment and growth. Higher growth rate creates higher income among households, which induces more households to consume.

Because the amount of final goods purchased by households is bounded, growth of production of goods necessarily decelerates. Creation of new goods is the ultimate engine to sustain growth in the model.

8.3.1   Model

For simplicity, assume that there are n households, where n is exogenously fixed. Household i either buys or does not buy good j at time t. See Aoki and Yoshikawa (2000) for full specification of the model.

The purchase pattern is denoted by $q_{i,j}(t, \tau)$, which is 1 if household i purchases good j at time or period t and zero otherwise. Actually this depends also on the epoch τ at which good j has appeared on the market. To shorten notation, we sometimes drop this argument. We should and can treat $q_{i,j}$ as stochastic, but for simplicity we stay with the deterministic version.

The total number of households that buy good i is given by

$$\sum_{i=1}^{n} q_{i,j}(t, \tau) := d_j(t, \tau),$$

where $d_j(t, \tau)$ is the number of households that buy good j, which has existed since time τ.

We model the spread of purchase shares among the households by the birth–death process discussed in Chapter 7. As discussed there, we incorporate a nonlinear death rate in the model to reflect the assumption that demands for older goods decline with time.

The (expected) value of the mean of the demand for good j, then, has the S-shaped time profile

$$m_j(t, \tau) = \frac{\mu}{\nu + (\mu - \lambda)e^{-\mu(t-\tau)}}.$$

This expression is obtained by solving a nonlinear master equation, having μ as the birth rate and $j\nu$ as the nonlinear exit or disappearance rate. Recall our discussion of a model with a nonlinear exit rate in Chapter 4.

Next, assume that each household has the saving rate s, which is assumed to be the same for all households. Households purchase $1 - s$ units of any final goods that they consume.

The budget constraints for household i is

$$I_i(t) = \sum_{j=2}^{\infty} \int_0^t \lambda n e^{-\lambda \tau}(1 - e^{-\lambda \tau})^{n-1}(1 - s)q_{i,j}(t, \tau)d\tau + (1 - s)m_{i,1} + sI_i(t),$$

where $I_i(t)$ is the income of household i, and $m_{i,1}$ is the purchase share of good 1, which is the initially available good at time 0. Here we assume that the number of goods initially available is 1. This budget constraint simplifies to

$$I_i(t) = \sum_{j=2}^{\infty} \int_0^t \lambda n e^{-\lambda \tau} (1 - e^{-\lambda \tau})^{n-1} q_{i,j}(t, \tau) \, d\tau + m_{i,1}.$$

Recall our discussion of the solution of the master equation

$$\frac{dQ(n, t)}{dt} = -\lambda n Q(n, t) + \lambda(n - 1)Q(n - 1, t),$$

where $Q(n, t)$ is the probability that the number of final goods available to the households is n at time t. We have seen that

$$Q(n, t) = e^{-\lambda t}(1 - e^{-\lambda t})^{n-1}.$$

Summing the incomes of all the households, we arrive at

$$\sum_i I_i(t) = \sum_j \int_0^t \lambda n e^{-\lambda \tau}(1 - e^{-\lambda \tau})^{n-1} \frac{\mu}{\lambda + (\mu - \lambda)e^{-\mu(t-\tau)}} \, d\tau$$
$$+ \frac{\mu}{\lambda + (\mu - \lambda)e^{-\mu t}}$$
$$= Y(t),$$

where $Y(t)$ is the GDP of this economy.

The equilibrium condition of the goods market is $s(\rho(t), \psi(t)) = \phi(g)$, where g is the growth rate of the economy, $\phi(\cdot)K$ is the investment in the economy with capital stock K, and ψ is a shift parameter of the saving rate. In the stationary state

$$s(\rho^*, \psi^*) = \phi(\lambda),$$

where $*$ indicate logarithmic derivative ($\phi^* := d\phi/dt$, for example), and ρ is the instantaneous rate of discount.

8.4 Deterministic share dynamics

We next switch to sectoral models. Denote the market shares of the n firms by s_i, with $s_i > 0$, for all i and $\sum_1^n s_i = 1$. These firms belong to two subgroups or clusters, denoted by A and B. We define

$$S_A := \sum_{j \in A} s_j.$$

For shorter notation we denote the sum as $\sum_A$. Similarly for $S_B = 1 - S_A$.

The rate of changes of the share of group A is

$$\frac{dS_A/dt}{S_A} = \sum_A \frac{ds_j/dt}{s_j} \frac{s_j}{S_A}.$$

We assume that individual firms' rates of change of shares are proportional to their deviations from the share-weighted average over all firms of some variable denoted as x_j, $j = 1, 2, \ldots, n$, such as the price charged by firm j or unit cost of firm j:

$$\frac{ds_j/dt}{s_j} = \gamma(\bar{x} - x_j),$$

where

$$\bar{x} = \sum_A s_j x_j + \sum_B s_j x_j.$$

The difference of the share-weighted averages between the two subgroups is

$$\delta = \frac{\sum_B s_j x_j}{S_B} - \frac{\sum_A s_j x_j}{S_A}.$$

The growth of the share of group A can be written as

$$\frac{dS_A}{dt} = \gamma \delta S_A (1 - S_A),$$

by expressing the sum over group B in terms of that over A and δ, and substituting it back into the original expression for the rate of change.

This last equation shows that the difference between the subgroups, δ, drives the dynamics for the group share, S_A. $S_A(t)$ converges to 1 if δ remains positive, and to 0 if δ remains negative. It is only with $\delta = 0$ that the shares of groups stabilize.

8.5   Stochastic business-cycle model

In this section, we consider a stochastic model in which the gap between demands and supplies of firms in subgroups drives the dynamics.

Let N denote the total number of firms, assumed to be fixed. The number of firms of group A is denoted by n. There are $N - n$ firms in group B, which is assumed to be less productive than those of firms in group A. Thus the total output of the economy is

$$y = c_1 n + c_2 (N - n) = c_2 N + (c_1 - c_2) n,$$

where $c_1 \geq c_2 > 0$, and time arguments are suppressed from y and n. We express this in terms of the fraction

$$x = \frac{n}{N}.$$

Denote the share of demand for group As goods by s. That for group B is then $1 - s$. Both efficiency of production and shares could be functions of x in our analysis.

The gap between demand and supply for group A is

$$g = sy - c_1 n = N[sc_2 - \{c_2 s + c_1(1 - s)\}x].$$

In a special case in which $c_1 = c_2 := c$, we have

$$g = cN(s - x).$$

In a deterministic model, one might postulate some adjustment mechanism that increases x if this gap is positive, and decreases x if it is negative, with $x = sc_2/[c_2 s + c_1(1 - s)]$ being the equilibrium share of group A. Instead, we use the framework of birth–death processes, similar to the one in Aoki (1996a, Chap. 5), and postulate the transition rate for the number of firms in group A as

$$r_n := w(n, n + 1) = N(1 - x)\eta_1(x),$$

and

$$l_n := w(n, n - 1) = Nx\eta_2(x),$$

with

$$\eta_1(x) = \frac{e^{\beta h(g)}}{e^{\beta h(g)} + e^{-\beta h(g)}},$$

where $h(g)$ is an increasing function of the gap g. It may include some adjustment or moving-cost component as well. The parameter β plays a crucial role. As in our earlier applications, β incorporates the effects of uncertainty, incomplete information, ignorance, and so on. In the simple case of $c_1 = c_2 = c$, g is positive when $s > x$ and η_1 is bigger than $1/2$, and is less than $1/2$ when $s < x$.

If we treat s, c_1, and c_2 as fixed parameters, then g is linear in x. If we assume that h is linear in g, then h is linear in x. With h nonlinear in g, or g made nonlinear by assuming that share the s, or efficiency of production, is a function of x, we could have situations in which h is cubic in x. In this case we know from models discussed in Aoki (1996a, Sec. 5.10) that there may be three critical points to the aggregate dynamics, two of which may be locally stable. All depends on the value of β introduced in the transition rates to embody uncertainty or lack of information on the future streams of profits that firms face. We show next how to use the master equation, the aggregate dynamics, and the Fokker–Planck equation to gain information on the fluctuations.

The master equation is

$$\partial P(n, t)/\partial t = (z - 1)P(n, t)w(n, n - 1) + (z^{-1} - 1)P(n, t)w(n, n + 1),$$

where we use the operator notation

$$z P(n, t)w(n, n - 1) := P(n + 1, t)w(n + 1, n),$$

and

$$z^{-1} P(n, t)w(n, n + 1) = P(n - 1, t)w(n - 1, n).$$

This is analogous to lead and lag operators in econometrics, and z-transforms in system theory. In physics this notation is used by van Kampen for example. Next, we change variables by

$$\frac{n}{N} = x = \phi + N^{-1/2}\xi,$$

and set

$$P(n, t) = \Pi(\xi, t).$$

With this change of the variable, we note that

$$z - 1 = N^{-1/2}\frac{\partial}{\partial \xi} + \frac{1}{2}N^{-1}\frac{\partial^2}{\partial \xi^2} + \cdots,$$

and

$$z^{-1} - 1 = -N^{-1/2}\frac{\partial}{\partial \xi} + \frac{1}{2}N^{-1}\frac{\partial^2}{\partial \xi^2} + \cdots.$$

Change time to $\tau = t/N$. Then, the left-hand side of the master equation becomes

$$\frac{\partial P}{\partial t} = N^{-1}\frac{\partial \Pi}{\partial \tau} - N^{1/2}\frac{d\phi}{d\tau}\frac{\partial \Pi}{\partial \xi}.$$

Equating the terms on the two sides of the largest order in N, we arrive at the aggregate dynamic equation

$$\frac{d\phi}{d\tau} = \alpha(x),$$

with

$$\alpha = r_n - l_n.$$

Stationary solutions are obtained as the zeros of the function $\alpha(\phi) = 0$; by substituing the expressions for the transition rates, we find that the zeros are the solutions of

$$\ln \frac{\phi}{1 - \phi} = 2\beta h(g(\phi)).$$

As we remarked earlier, there are at most three solutions when h is cubic in ϕ. Depending on the magnitude of β, a unique locally stable ϕ, two locally stable ϕ's, or a single unstable ϕ is found in the range $0 < \phi < 1$. See Aoki (1996a, Chap. 5; 1998a). We also know that these critical points correspond to those of a double-well potential

$$U(\phi) = -\int^{\phi} h(g(x))\,dx - \frac{1}{2\beta}H(\phi),$$

with $H(\phi) = -\phi \ln \phi - (1 - \phi)\ln(1 - \phi)$ the entropy.

The remainder of the master equation yields

$$\frac{\partial \Pi}{\partial \tau} = \frac{1}{2}(r_n + l_n)\frac{\partial^2 \Pi}{\partial \xi^2} - \alpha'\frac{\partial}{\partial \xi}(\xi \Pi),$$

where r_n and l_n are evaluated at the equilibrium value ϕ^e of the aggregate equation, when we set the left-hand side equal to zero to obtain the stationary Fokker–Planck equation. We obtain a Gaussian distribution for ξ, with mean zero and variance $(r_n + l_n)/4(r'_n - l'_n)$, where the prime indicates differentiation with respect to ϕ, and evaluated at locally stable ϕ-values.

8.6   A new model of fluctuations and growth: Case with underutilized factor of production

We now return to the two-sector model of Section 4.1, and develop it more fully.

As we mentioned there, fluctuations of aggregate economic activities or business cycles have long attracted attention of economists. Here, we discuss dynamics for the two-sector model introduced in Section 4.1, and generalize the model to consist of K sectors.

Resources are stochastically allocated to sectors in response to excess demands or supplied of the sectors. We show that the total outputs of such an economy fluctuate, and that the average level of aggregate production (or GDP) depends on the patterns of demand.[3] Because we assume zero adjustment cost for the sizes of sectors, our model is a model of an economy with underutilized factors of production, such as hours of work of employees.

---

[3] In this sense, the model may be thought of a particular kind of quantity adjustment model. Leijonhufvud (1974, 1993) described a Marshallian quantity adjustment model. He envisioned a representative firm that adjusts outputs to narrow the gap between the supply price and demand prices of the good produced by the firm. Since the demand price schedule is unknown to the firm, the market-clearing price is substituted for it. Aoki analyzed this model in Aoki (1976, pp. 193 ff., 319 ff.) In this paper, sectors are not the same, and sectors adopt stochastic rules of response to gaps between demands and supplies. Sectors are subject to aggregate externalities, as we discuss in the text. See also Leijonhufvud (1993).

In the literature, economic fluctuations are usually explained as a direct outcome of the individual agents behavior. The focus is thus on individual agents. Often, elaborate microeconomic models of optimization or rational expectations are the starting points. The more strongly one wishes to interpret aggregate fluctuations as something "rational" or "optimal," the more one is led to this essentially microeconomic approach.

The model of this section proposes a different approach to explain economic fluctuations. The focus is not on individual agents, nor on elaborate microeconomic optimization modeling. Rather, the focus is on the manner in which a large number of agents interact.

Although studies of macroeconomies with many possibly heterogeneous agents are not new, the dynamic behavior of economies in disequilibrium is not satisfactorily analyzed. Clower (1965) and Leijonhufvud (1968) pointed out that quantity adjustment might be actually more important than price adjustment in economic fluctuations. Although this insight spawned a vast literature of the so-called "non-Walrasian" or "disequilibrium" analysis, this approach suffers from the basically static or deterministic nature of the analysis. See, for example, Malinvaud (1977) or Dréze (1991).

8.6.1   The model

Our model is a simple quantity adjustment model composed of a large number of sectors or agents. Resources are stochastically allocated to sectors in response to excess demands or supplies of the sectors. We show that the total output of such an economy fluctuates, and that the average level of aggregate production (or GDP) depends on the patterns of demand. Because we assume zero adjustment cost for the sizes of sectors, our model is a model of an economy with underutilized factors of production, such as hours of work of employees. For empirical studies of such economies, see Davis et al. (1996).

We assume that sector i has productivity coefficient c_i, which is exogenously given and fixed. Assume, for convenience, that the sectors are arranged in decreasing order of productivity. Sector i employs N_i units of the factor of production. It is a nonnegative integer-valued random variable. We call its value the **size** of the sector. When $N_i(t) = n_i, i = 1, 2, \ldots, K$, the output of sector i is $c_i n_i$, and the total output (GDP) of this economy is

$$Y(t) := \sum_{i=1}^{K} c_i n_i(t). \tag{8.1}$$

Demand for the output of sector i is denoted by $s_i Y(t)$, where $s_i > 0$ is the share of sector i, and $\sum_i s_i = 1$. The shares are also assumed to be exogenously given and fixed.

We denote the excess demand for goods of sector i by

$$f_i(t) := s_i Y(t) - c_i n_i(t), \tag{8.2}$$

$i = 1, 2, \ldots, K$. We keep the cs and demand shares fixed exogenously. Denote the set of sectors with positive excess demands by

$$I_+ = \{i; f_i > 0\},$$

and similarly for the set of sectors with negative demands by

$$I_- = \{j; f_j \leq 0\}.$$

To shorten notation, summations over these subsets are denoted as $\sum_+$ and $\sum_-$. Denote by n_+ the number of n's in the set I_+, that is,

$$n_+ := \sum_+ n_i,$$

where the subscript $+$ is a shorthand for the set I_+, and similarly

$$n_- := \sum_- n_j,$$

for the sum over the sectors with negative excess demands. Let $n = n_+ + n_-$.

Sectors with nonzero excess demands attempt to reduce the sizes of excess demands by adjusting their sizes, up or down, depending on the signs of the excess demands. Section 8.6.3 makes this precise.

8.6.2 Transition-rate specifications

The transition probabilities are such that

$$\Pr(N_i(t + h) = n_i + 1 | N_i(t) = n_i) = \gamma_i h + o(h)$$

for $i \in I_+$, and

$$\Pr(N_i(t + h) = n_i - 1 | N_i(t) = n_i) = \rho_i h + o(h)$$

for $i \in I_-$, where the transition rates, γ and ρ, of the jump Markov process are specified later.

We assume that the γ's and ρ's depend on the total number of sizes and the current size of the sector that adjusts:

$$\gamma_i = \gamma(n_i, n),$$

and

$$\rho_j = \rho(n_j, n).$$

This is an example of applying W. E. Johnson's sufficientness postulate. We have discussed specifications of entry and exit probabilities in Aoki (2000b). See also Costantini and Garibaldi (1979, 1989), who give clear discussions on reasons for these specifications. As explained fully by Zabell (1992), there is a long history of statisticians who have discussed this type of problems. There are good reasons for γ_i to depend only on n_i and n, and similarly for ρ_i. See Zabell for further references on the statistical reasons for this specification.

We specify the entry rate, that is, the rate of size increase, by

$$\gamma_a(n_a, n) = \frac{\alpha + n_a}{K\alpha + n},$$

and that of the exit rate, namely, the rate of size decrease, by

$$\rho_a(n_a, n) = \frac{n_a}{n}.$$

If α is much smaller than K, then $\gamma_i \approx n_i/(\theta + n)$, where we set $\theta := K\alpha$, that is,[4]

$$\gamma_i(n_i, n) \approx \frac{n}{\theta + n} \frac{n_i}{n}.$$

So long as θ is kept constant, the above expression implies that the choices of K and α do not matter, provided α is much smaller than K. It is also clear that γ_i is nearly the same as the fraction n_i/n, which is the probability for exit. Then, the time histories of n_i are nearly those of fair coin tosses. We have K such coin tosses available at each jump. The sector that jumps determines which coin toss is selected from these K coins.

We set $\alpha = 0$ to discuss economies with fixed numbers of sectors, and set it to a positive number to allow for new sectors to emerge. In the latter case, a new sector emerges with probability $\theta/(\theta + n)$, while the size of sector i increases by one when the sector has positive excess demand with probability $(\alpha + n_i)/(\theta + n)$. See Ewens (1972).

8.6.3   Holding times

We assume that the time it takes for sector i to adjust its size by one unit (up or down), T_i, is exponentially distributed:

$$\Pr(T_i > t) = \exp(-b_i t),$$

where b_i is either γ_i or ρ_i, depending on the sign of the excess demand. This time is called the sojourn time or holding time in the probability literature. We

---

[4] There is an obvious interpretation of this approximate expression in terms of the Ewens sampling formula (Ewens 1972).

assume that the random variables T_i of the sectors with nonzero excess demand are independent.

The sector that adjusts first is the sector with the shortest holding time. Let T^* be the minimum of all the holding times of the sectors with nonzero excess demands. Lawler calculates that for $a \in I_+$

$$\Pr(T_a = T^*) = \frac{\gamma_a}{\gamma_+ + \rho_-},$$

where $\gamma_+ = \sum_+ \gamma_i$ and $\rho_- = \sum_- \rho_j$, and if $a \in I_-$, then the probability of a jump in sector a is given by

$$\rho_a / (\gamma_+ + \rho_-),$$

and similarly for the γ's. See Lawler (1995, p. 56), Appendix A.4, or Aoki (1996a, Sec. 4.2)

8.6.4   Aggregate outputs and demands

After a change in the size of a sector, the total output of the economy changes to

$$Y(t + h) = Y(t) + \text{sgn}\{f_a(t)\} c_a,$$

where a is the sector that jumped first by the time $t + h$.[5]
After the jump, this sector's excess demand changes to

$$f_a(t + h) = f_a(t) - c_a(1 - s_a)\,\text{sgn}\{f_a(t)\}. \tag{8.3}$$

Other, nonjumping sectors have the excess demand changed to

$$f_i(t + h) = f_i(t) + \text{sgn}\{f_a(t)\} s_i c_a \tag{8.4}$$

for $i \neq a$.

These two equations show the effects of an increase of size in one sector. An increase by c_a of output increases the GDP by the same amount. However, sector a experiences an increase of its demand by only a fraction s_a of it, while all other sectors experience increase of their demands by $s_i c_a, i \neq a$. Equation (8.3) shows a source of externality for this model that affects the model behavior significantly. The index sets I_+ and I_- also change in general.

Defining $\Delta Y(t) := Y(t + h) - Y(t)$ and $\Delta f_i(t) := f_i(t + h) - f_i(t)$, rewrite (8.1) through (8.4) as

$$\Delta Y(t) = \text{sgn}\{f_a(t)\} c_a,$$
$$\Delta f_a(t) = -(1 - s_a)\,\Delta Y(t),$$

---

[5] For the sake of simplicity, we may think of the skeleton Markov chain, in which the directions of jump are chosen appropriately but the holding times themselves are replaced by a fixed unit time interval. The limiting behavior of the original and that of the skeletal version are known to be the same under certain technical conditions, which hold for this example. See Çinlar (1975).

and

$$\Delta f_i(t) = s_i \, \Delta Y(t)$$

for $i \neq a$.

8.6.5   *Equilibrium sizes of the sectors (Excess demand conditions)*

When the excess demands of all sectors are zero, no section changes its output. We solve K equations of zero excess demands $f_i = 0$, $i = 1, 2, \ldots, K$, and obtain the equilibrium sizes, denoted by superscript e, of the fractions of sector sizes, n_i^e/n^e for $i = 1, \ldots, K$, and the ratio of the total output to the total number of units, Y^e/n^e.

Define K-dimensional column vectors $\mathbf{c} := (c_1, c_2, \ldots, c_K)'$ and $\mathbf{s} := (s_1, s_2, \ldots, s_K)'$. A diagonal $K \times K$ matrix $C := \mathrm{diag}(c_1, c_2, \ldots, c_K)$ is introduced to simplify our discussion.

The output is $Y = \langle \mathbf{c}, \mathbf{n} \rangle$, and the set of zero-excess-demand conditions is expressed by $s_i Y = c_i n_i$, $i = 1, 2, \ldots, K$, which is rewritten compactly as

$$C\mathbf{n} = \mathbf{s}Y = \mathbf{sc}'\mathbf{n},$$

or

$$\Phi\mathbf{n} = \mathbf{0},$$

with $\Phi = C - \mathbf{sc}'$.

Noting that the shares sum to one, the matrix Φ does not have full rank, because $|\Phi| = |C|(1 - \mathbf{c}C^{-1}\mathbf{s}) = 0$. It has rank $K - 1$, and its null space has dimension one and is spanned by the solutions we give next.

The solution is

$$\mathbf{n} = C^{-1}\mathbf{s}Y, \tag{8.5}$$

or

$$\frac{n_i^e}{n^e} = \frac{s_i/c_i}{\sum s_i/c_i}, \qquad i = 1, \ldots, K. \tag{8.6}$$

That is, the fraction is uniquely determined. Multiply it by c_i and sum over i to obtain the relation between Y and n as

$$Y^e = \frac{n^e}{\sum_i s_i/c_i}.$$

Note that $Y_i^e = s_i Y^e$, for all i, as it should.

We later give examples to show that simulation results support the analytical calculations remarkably well. Simulations show that, after the initial transient periods, the model moves around the equilibrium or near-equilibrium values of the sector sizes and outputs, in other words, we have equilibrium cycles when $\alpha = 0$, and growth with cycles with positive α.

8.6.6 *Behavior out of equilibrium: Two-sector model*

The expected level of total output, which is the equilibrium level in a deterministic model of the kind given in the previous subsection, is indeterminate. Here, we explore the behavior of the economy out of equilibrium in a stochastic model.

After a jump by a sector, the patterns of signs of the excess demands in sectors change. The changes are rather complicated to analyze in generality. To gain some insight, we analyze a simple two-sector model, and comment on how the results of that model may generalize. Note that $s_2 = 1 - s_1$ in the two-sector model. This model is characterized then by two parameters s_1 and c_2/c_1. (If you wish, c_1 may be set to one with a suitable choice of unit to measure n_1.)

Equation (8.5) shows that $n_1^e/n_2^e = (s_1/c_1)/(s_2/c_2)$, that is, the sign of $(1 - s_1)/s_1 - c_2/c_1$ determines the relative sizes of the two sectors at equilibrium. Hence, it does matter in the details of stochastic evolution whether n_1^e is larger than n_2^e or not. We describe the model behavior assuming that this sign is positive, that is $n_2^e \geq n_1^e$. The other case may be examined by switching the subscripts.

We suppress time arguments. The nonnegative quadrant of the plane for n_1 and n_2, with the horizontal axis labeled by n_1 and the vertical by n_2, is divided into six regions, denoted by $R_k, k = 1, 2, \ldots, 6$. They are bounded by $n_i \geq 0, i = 1, 2,$ and by five other straight lines with a common slope $\beta :=(c_1/c_2)(1 - s_1)/s_1$. This slope is larger than one for our choice of the parameter values. The intercepts of the five lines are $\beta, 1, 0, -1,$ and $-\beta$. These five lines are denoted by $L_1, L_2, \ldots, L_5$, respectively. Line 3 cuts the n_1 axis at 0, line 4 at 1, and line 5 at -1, and $-\beta$.

In different regions, either the signs of the excess demands, or those after size changes by sector 1 or 2, are different, as detailed below. We note first that the two-sector model is special in that $f_1 + f_2 = 0$. Further, denoting by $f_i'(\pm)$ the value of the excess demand of f_i after a change of n_1 by ± 1, and similarly by $f_i''(\pm)$ the excess demand of f_i after a change in n_2 by ± 1, we note that $f_1'(\pm) + f_2'(\pm) = 0$ and similarly $f_1''(\pm) + f_2''(\pm) = 0$ from (8.1) and (8.2). Recall that only an increase in n_1 is possible when $f_1 > 0$ in sector 1. Similarly, with $f_2 < 0$, $f_1''(+)$ does not happen. To see these facts we note, for example, that in $R_1, R_2,$ and R_3, which are above L_3, $f_1 > 0$. Hence, $f_2 < 0$ in these regions.

Table 8.1. *Excess demand: signs and sign changes.*

| Region | f_1 | Sign of excess demand | | | |
		$f_1'(+)$	$f_1'(-)$	$f_1''(+)$	$f_1''(-)$
R_1	+	+	*	*	+
R_2	+	−	*	*	+
R_3	+	−	*	*	−
R_4	−	*	+	+	*
R_5	−	*	+	−	*
R_6	−	*	−	−	*

* marks non-applicable or theoretically not possible combinations irrelevant situation.

After a change in n_1 by ± 1

$$f_1'(\pm) = s_1 c_2 [n_2 - \beta(n_1 + 1)] > 0$$

above L_1, and so on.

The signs of the excess demands and how the sign changes by a change in size in sector 1 and 2 are summarized in Table 8.1.

The symbol * marks entries that do not apply. Note that signs of f_1 are reversed for regions 4 to 6.

The probability of a size increase in sector 2 is larger than that of a size decrease in sector 2 when

$$\gamma_1(n_1, n_2) \leq \rho_2(n_1, n_2).$$

With $\alpha = 0$, this inequality holds when $n_1 < n_2$.

From a state (n_1, n_2) in R_1, consecutive jumps in sector 1 will bring the state to the boundary L_1 by increasing n_1; then the model state enters R_2, and the nature of the dynamics changes. This is so because f_1 continues to be positive after jumps in sector 1. Similarly, consecutive jumps in sector 2 from a state in R_1 also eventually bring the state to the same boundary by descreasing n_2. In general, we can calculate the various combinations of jumps in sector 1 and sector 2 to bring the state to the boundary, L_1. We thus see that the state leaves R_1 with probability 1. From a state in R_2 consecutive decreases in n_2 are possible until the state enters R_3. From a state on L_2 a jump in sector 2 brings the states to L_3.

The sector that jumps first is determined by the sector with the shortest holding time. Given that sector i changes its size, if $f_i(t)$ is positive, then we assume that n_i will increase by one. If the excess-demand expression is negative, we assume that n_i will decrease by one. Since no adjustment cost is included in the model, the sizes n_i may be interpreted as some measure of the capacity utilization factor in situations where the capacity constraint is not binding. With fixed numbers of employees in each sector, hours worked per period are an example of units of production factor entering and leaving production processes.

We show by simulation that cycles are possible in this model, and that the average level of output responds to demand patterns, that is, larger demand shares for more productive sector outputs tend to produce higher average output of the economy as a whole than smaller demand shares.

8.6.7   Stationary probability distribution: the two-sector model

Here, we derive the stationary probability distribution for the sizes of the two-sector model.

A general discussion of dynamics is conducted via the master (Chapman–Kolmogorov) equation. Here, we report on the derivation of the stationary probability distribution near the equilibrium states represented by L_3.

Table 8.1 in Section 8.6.6 indicates that patterns of signs of excess demands in regions 3 and 4 are such that the state of the model alternates between these two regions, thus exhibiting oscillations in n_i, $i = 1, 2$, and consequently in GDP. The line that defines the region $n_2 \geq n_1$ lies below L_3 and cuts across L_4 and L_5 from left to right. In the regions above this line sector 2 is more likely to jump than sector 1 in R_4. With $\beta > 1$, the lines L_1, L_2, and L_3 are above the line $n_1 = n_2$. Among states below L_3, most will be $n_1 < n_2$.

We show that the sign of the derivative of the expected value of Y with respect to s_1 to be positive near the equilibrium shown in (8.5) in our two-sector model (Sec. 8.6.6). For simpler presentation we just treat the case with $\alpha = 0$.

Suppose that the system enters R_3. We have shown that the state will oscillate in the region $R_3 \cup R_4$. Take the initial state b, which is on or just below L_3. Let $n(b) = (n_1(b), n_2(b))$ be the state, and define two adjacent positions e and c by $n_1(e) = n_1(b) + 1, n_2(e) = n_2(b) + 1, n_1(c) = n_1(b) - 1$, and $n_2(c) = n_2(b) - 1$.

By the detailed-balance conditions between states e and b, and those between b and c, we derive the relations for the stationary probabilities:

$$\frac{\pi(e)}{\pi(b)} = \frac{n_1(b)}{n_1(b) + 1} \frac{n_2(b)}{n_2(b) + 1} \frac{n + 2}{n},$$

where $n := n_1(b) + n_2(b)$, and

$$\frac{\pi(c)}{\pi(b)} = \frac{n_1(b)}{n_1(b) - 1} \frac{n_2(b)}{n_2(b) - 1} \frac{n - 2}{n}.$$

By repeating the process of expressing the ratios of probabilities, we obtain

$$\frac{\pi(b+(k,k))}{\pi(b)} = \left(\frac{n_1(b)}{n_1(b)+k}\right)^2 \frac{n+2k}{n}$$

for $k = 1, 2, \ldots$, where we use $n_2 = \beta n_1$ on or near L_3. Similarly,

$$\frac{\pi(b-(l,l))}{\pi(b)} = \left(\frac{n_1(b)}{n_1(b)-l}\right)^2 \frac{n-2l}{n}$$

for $l = 1, 2, \ldots, \bar{l}-1$, where $\bar{l}$ is the largest positive integer such that $n - 2\bar{l} \geq 0$. Without loss of generality we treat it as an integer. Noting that $n = (1+\beta)n_1$, we write these ratios as

$$\frac{\pi(b+(k,k))}{\pi(b)} = \gamma^{-\mu k},$$

and

$$\frac{\pi(b-(l,l))}{\pi(b)} = \gamma^{\mu l},$$

with $\gamma = \exp(2/n_1(b))$ and $\mu = \beta/(1+\beta)$.

From now on we write b for $n_1(b)$ since there is no ambiguity.

Now, $E(Y) = (c_1 + c_2\beta)E(n_1)$, where

$$E(n_1) = A\left[\sum_{k \geq 1}(b+k)\gamma^{-\mu k} + \sum_{0}^{\bar{l}-1}(b-l)\gamma^{\mu l}\right]$$

for $l = 1, 2, \ldots, \bar{l}-1$, where A is the normalizing constant $A^{-1} = \sum_{0}^{\bar{l}-1}\gamma^{\mu l} + \sum_{k \geq 1}\gamma^{-\mu k} = \gamma^{\mu\bar{l}}/[\gamma^\mu - 1]$. We calculate this sum by means of the generating function,

$$E(n_1) = b + AG'(1),$$

with

$$G(z) = \sum_k (\gamma^{-\mu}z)^k - \sum_l (\gamma^\mu z)^l,$$

with the obvious upper limits of summation, which we drop for simplicity. Note that

$$G(z) = \frac{z}{\gamma^\mu - z} - \frac{\gamma^\mu z - (\gamma^\mu z)^{\bar{l}}}{1 - (\gamma^\mu z)^{\bar{l}}}.$$

Substituting $(1+\beta)b/2$ for $\bar{l}$, we obtain, after some algebra,

$$E(n_1) = \frac{1}{1-\gamma^{-\mu}} + b - \bar{l} = \frac{1}{1-\gamma^{-\mu}} + \frac{b}{2}(\beta - 1).$$

For $\beta = 1$, this is clearly positive. For $\beta > 1$, it is positive if $1/(1 - \gamma^{-\mu}) > (b/2)(\beta - 1)$, which is satisfied for $\beta > \beta^*$ for some β^*. We assume that this condition is satisfied. Then,

$$EY = (c_1 + c_2\beta)E(n_1).$$

Its derivative with respect to s is

$$\frac{dE(Y)}{ds} = \frac{dE(Y)}{d\beta}\frac{d\beta}{ds},$$

where we note that $d\beta/ds = -(c_1/c_2)(1/s^2) \leq 0$, and that

$$\frac{dE(Y)}{d\beta} = [-H(\beta)c_1 - G(\beta)c_2](\gamma^\mu - 1)^{-2},$$

with

$$H(\beta) = \frac{2}{b}\frac{1 + \beta^2}{(1 + \beta)^2} + o(1/b),$$

and

$$G(\beta) = \frac{2}{b}\frac{2\beta^2(\beta - 1)}{(1 + \beta)^2} + o(1/b).$$

Consequently, we have

$$\frac{dE(Y)}{d\beta} \leq 0$$

for all $\beta \geq 1$. This establishes

Proposition. *The expected value of Y will increase as the demand for sector 1 is increased in the range of $\beta > 1$.*

Hence, $E(Y)$ increases with a small inrease in s if and only if $dE(Y)/d\beta < 0$. When this inequality holds, we conclude that $d^2 E(Y)/ds^2) \leq 0$ if $d^2 E(Y)/d\beta^2 < 0$, because of the relation $d^2 E(y)/ds^2 = (d^2 E(y)/d\beta^2)(d\beta/ds)^2 + (dE(y)/d\beta)d^2\beta/ds^2$, which is negative when $dE(Y)/d\beta$ is.

We can also show that $E(Y)$ is concave in s, that is, the increase in $E(Y)$ decreases as s becomes larger. To see this, note that $d^2 E(Y)/d\beta^2 = -c_1 H'(\beta) - c_2 G'(\beta)$, where $c_1 H'(\beta) + c_2 G'(\beta) \geq 0$, with $H' = (4/b)(\beta - 1)/(1 + \beta)^3$ and $G' = (4\beta/b)\beta(\beta^2 + 3\beta - 2)/(1 + \beta)^3$, both expressions are true up to $o(1/b)$.

Hence we have the inequality

$$d^2 E(Y)/d\beta^2 \leq 0.$$

Writing $c_2\beta$ as $c_1 z$, with $z = (1 - s)/s$, and rewriting β as κz where $\kappa = c_1/c_2$, we see that the second derivative of $E(Y)$ with respect to β is negative in the range of z where

$$f(z) := \kappa^2 z^3 + 3\kappa z^2 + (\kappa - 2)z - 1 > 0.$$

For example, with $c_1 = c_2$, $f(z) > 0$ for $z > z^*$ with z^* somewhere between 0.6 and 0.7. This means that for $s \leq 0.5$ so that $\beta \geq 1$, the sign of this second derivative is negative. We can combine this result with that of the first derivative and conclude the following fact.

Fact. $E(Y)$ is a convex increasing function of s in the range $0 < s < c_1/(c_1 + c_2 z^*)$. When $z^* \leq 1$, $\beta \geq 1$ in this range.

Analogous proposition may be established for the range $\beta < 1$ in similar manner.

8.6.8   Emergence of new sectors

Next, suppose that new sectors appear at a rate proportional to $\theta/(\theta + n_+)$. This transition rate may be justified as a limiting case in which the parameter α goes to zero, while $K\alpha$ approaches a positive value θ. More in detail, we assume that either one of the sectors with positive excess demand increases size by one with probability $(\alpha' + n_j)/(K_+\alpha + n_+)$, where K_+ denotes the number of sectors with positive excess demand, and n_+ is the total size of such sectors, or a new sector emerges with rate proportional to $(K_+ - 1)\alpha/(K_+\alpha + n_+)$. In the limit of letting α go to zero, and assuming that $K_+\alpha$ approaches a common positive value for the sake of simplicity, we have a model in which either one of the existing sectors with positive excess demand increases size by one, or a new sector emerges.[6] That is, (8.1) is now modified to read that the conditional change in $Y(t + h)$ given $Y(t)$ consists of two terms, the first conditional on the event of the new sector appearing, which occurs with probability $\theta/(\theta + n_+)$, and the second conditional on the event that no new sector appears.

We assume that a new sector, when it emerges, inherits the characteristics – that is, c and s – of one of the existing sectors with equal probability. That is, if there are L sectors, then with probability $1/L$, the value of c and s of randomly selected sector is inherited. The s's are then renormalized so that they sum to one, including the newborn sector. This is merely for convenience. Other schemes may also be tried.

---

[6] We could assume that $K_+\alpha$ converges to θ_+, which may change each epoch. This would lead to a slight modification of the Ewens sampling formula.

8.6.9 Simulation runs for multi-sector model

This section summarizes our findings of the model's behavior by simulation.

What is most striking is the fact that the production levels, that is, the sizes of the different sectors of the model, are such that high-productivity sectors are constrained by demands. By starting the simulation with the initial condition of equal sizes for all sectors, we see that inflows of production factors into high-productivity sectors are clearly constrained, and the sizes of more productive sectors actually shrink in simulation. This is consistent with the views of Yoshikawa expressed in some of his writings (Yoshikawa 1995, 2000). We keep the total number of sectors at $K = 10$. We have done simulations with $K = 15$ and 20, but do not report them, since we have not observed any substantive differences. As our discussion above indicates, for small value of θ, which ranges from 0.2 to 0.6 in our experiments, there is not much loss of generality in keeping the value of K fixed. We also keep fixed the order of the productivities from $c_1 = 1$ to $c_K = 1/K$ at equal intervals. We start the simulation runs with the initial condition $n_i = 10$ for all sectors, $i = 1, 2, \ldots, 10$. In the graphs below, we skip the first 150 or 200 periods to avoid transient responses.

We vary the demand patterns for the outputs of the sectors as follows. We try five patterns, $P_i, i = 1, \ldots, 5$:

Pattern P_1 has $\mathbf{s} = (5, 5, 4, 4, 3, 1, 1, 1, 1, 1)/26$;
Pattern P_2 has $\mathbf{s} = (5, 3, 2, 1, 1, 1, 1, 1, 1, 1)/17$;
Pattern P_3 has $\mathbf{s} = (2, 2, 2, 2, 2, 1, 1, 1, 1, 1)/15$;
Pattern P_4 has $\mathbf{s} = (1, 1, 1, 3, 3, 3, 3, 1, 1, 1)/18$;
Pattern P_5 has $\mathbf{s} = (2, 2, 2, 1, 1, 1, 1, 1, 1, 1)/13$.

The sum of the shares of the top five sectors are 0.8, 0.7, 0.66, 0.5, and 0.61 respectively. Our analysis of the two-sector model may be adapted to these five patterns by lumping the top five sectors and the bottom five sectors separately to produce a two-sector model. The simulation confirms what the anaysis predicts, that is, the output is the largest for P_1, followed by those of P_2, P_3, and so on.

All patterns were run 200 times for 500 periods with $\theta = 0.6$ except as we note below. Pattern P_2 has also been run with $\theta = 0.2$. Pattern P_5 was also run for 1000 periods 400 times.

Runs of 200 are small for Monte Carlo experiments. Our interest here, however, is not in accurate estimates of any statistical properties of output variations, but rather in exhibiting possibilities of cyclical behavior in this simple model, and showing that output levels respond to demand pattern shifts.

One of the clear effects of different patterns is the dependence of average output levels on the patterns. Mean outputs are approximately in the order of

P_1 to P_5. By putting larger demand shares in higher-productivity sectors, the averge output shifts up. Because the standard deviations of outputs are still large due to the small numbers of runs, effects of different demand patterns on the statistical features of cycles are not so clear cut. Peak-to-peak swings are about 2 percent of the mean levels of outputs.

Figure 8.1 shows outputs, averaged over 200 Monte Carlo runs, with demand shares P_1 through P_5, each for the case of $\theta = 0.6$. Figure 8.2 is the plot of P_2 outputs averaged over 200 runs with $\theta = 0.2$. Figure 8.3 shows 1000 time periods of outputs averaged over 400 runs, with $\theta = 0.6$. Figure 8.4 shows per-unit output Y/n averaged over 200 runs. The equilibrium value is $y^e/n^e = 0.4196$. This value is independent of θ. Figure 8.5 shows the outputs for $\theta = 0.1$ and $\theta = 1$ with P_3 demand share pattern. These two figures are included to give some feel for the effects of the magnitude of θ on the outputs. As is pointed out by Feller (1968, Chap. 3), the random walks generated by fair coin tosses show much counterintuitive behavior. The numbers of periods and runs are not large enough to draw any precise conclusions. These simulation experiments serve to show the existence of equilibrium cycles even in this extremely simple quantity adjustment model.

The four panels of Fig. 8.6 show a sample of how the number of sectors increases, together with the total number of sizes, total output, and output per unit size, for the demand pattern P_3 with $\theta = 0.3$. As the value of θ is increased, the number of new sectors increases more quickly. For small values such as $\theta = 0.01$, new sectors come in much more slowly.

8.6.10   Discussion

Instead of assuming that resources are instantaneously reallocated to equalize productivities in all sectors, the model of this section assumes that (re)allocation of resources takes time. The model calculates the holding times of all sectors, which determine the probability of the sector that actually increases output in response to positive excess demands for goods of sectors of the economy. As parts of this calculation, the probability of a new sector emerging is also determined. The model solves the conceptual problem, in the usual agent-based simulation models, of which agent moves first and by how much.

Without building microeconomic structures into models, this model shows that cyclical fluctuations and growth with fluctuations are possible. What is most striking is the fact that production levels, that is, the sizes of the different sectors of the model, are such that high-productivity sectors are constrained by demands. By starting the simulation with the initial condition of equal sizes for all sectors, we see that inflows of production factors into high-productivity sectors are clearly constrained and sizes of more productive sectors actually

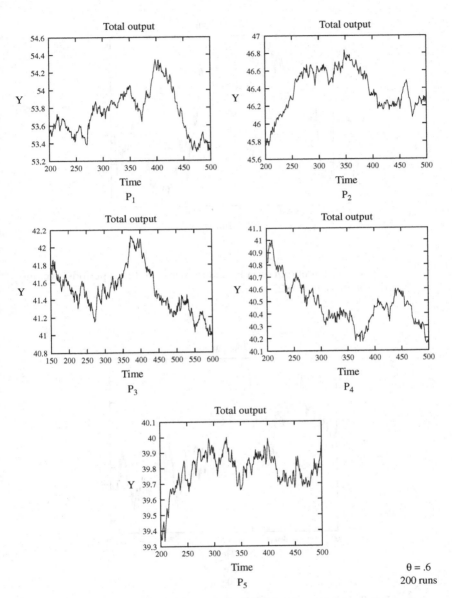

Fig. 8.1. Total outputs of five demand patterns, P_1 through P_5, all for 500 time periods, average of 200 Monte Carlo runs, and $\theta = 0.6$.

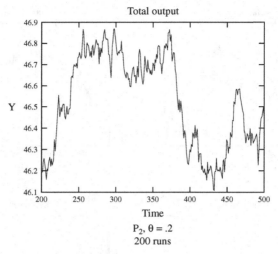

Fig. 8.2. Total output with P_2 pattern with 500 times periods, average of 200 runs, $\theta = 0.2$.

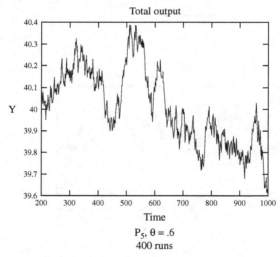

Fig. 8.3. Total output with P_5 pattern with 1000 times periods, average of 400 runs, $\theta = 0.6$.

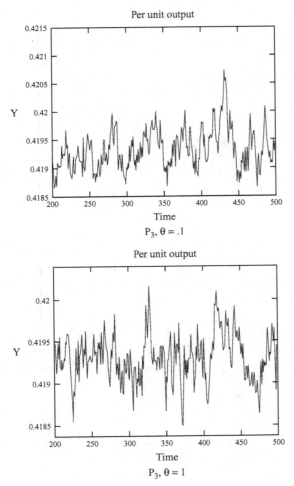

Fig. 8.4. Per unit output, Y/n, with pattern P_3. Upper panel for $\theta = 0.1$ Lower panel with $\theta = 1$.

shrink in simulation. This is consistent with the views in Yoshikawa (2000, 1995). We may also call the reader's attention to Davis et al. (1996, p. 83), which seems to lend support to the kind of modeling described in this section. They complain about downplay between cycles and the restructuring of industries and jobs in the traditional economics literature, and call for going beyond the stress placed on the role of aggregate shocks in business cycles.

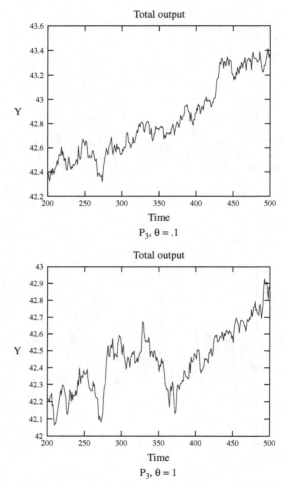

Fig. 8.5. Total output with pattern P_3 . Upper panel $\theta = 0.1$. Lower panel $\theta = 1$.

We have taken the entry and exit probabilities to depend on the sizes of the sectors. An alternative specification will specify them to depend on the excess demands themselves. This possibility is definitely worth pursuing.

Also, we note that changing the outputs from linear ones in (8.1) to concave ones $c_i n_i^\gamma$, with $0 < \gamma \leq 1$, does not change the patterns of the sign changes of excess demands in response to changes in n_i in the two-sector model if we

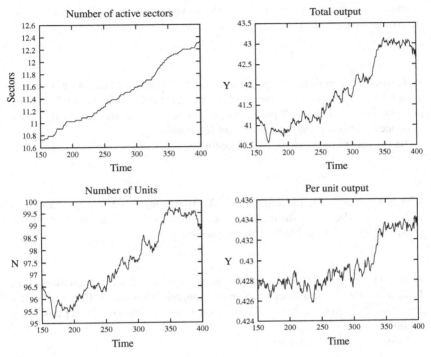

Fig. 8.6. New sectors with $\theta = 0.3$.

replace β with $\beta^{1/\gamma}$. For example, the inequality $n_2 > \beta(n_1 + 1)$ is replaced with $(n_2)^\gamma > \beta(n_1 + 1)^\gamma$, that is, with $n_2 > \beta^{1/\gamma}(n_1 + 1)$.

The regions R_1 through R_6 are analogously defined by lines L_1 through L_5 with slope $\beta^{1/\gamma}$. Arguments to derive the stationary distribution go through with β replaced by $\beta^{1/\gamma}$. Since the Proposition in Section 8.6.7 holds for all values of β, it also holds for economies with $c_i n_i^\gamma$, $i = 1, 2, \ldots, K$.

8.7   Langevin-equation approach

The dynamics of conventional economic models is specified by an n-dimensional deterministic dynamical equation

$$\frac{dx}{dt} = h(x),$$

where x is an n-dimensional state vector. Its stochastic version, especially in econometric models, is often proposed by tacking noises, usually additive, onto deterministic equations. Instead, we consider

$$\frac{dX}{dt} = g(X, \epsilon\xi(t))$$

as its stochastic version, with $g(\cdot, \cdot)$ some smooth function of the two arguments, where $X(t)$ is a stochastic state vector, and $\epsilon\xi(t)$ a vector-valued white noise process. Here, ϵ is a small positive constant, and $\xi(t)$ is standardized to have variance 1. We drop the time argument for simplicity.

Its linearization is called the Langevin equation:

$$\frac{dX}{dt} = b(X) + \epsilon\sigma(X)\xi(t),$$

with $b(X) = g(X, 0)$, and $\epsilon\sigma_{i,j} = \partial g_i(X, 0)/\partial\xi_j$ for $i = 1, 2, \ldots, n$ and $j = 1, 2, \ldots, m$, where m is the dimension of the vector ξ. This equation is usually presented as an Ito stochastic differential equation

$$dX = b(X)\,dt + \epsilon\sigma(X)\,dW(t),$$

where $dW_i(t) = W_i(t + dt) - W_i(t)$ is the Wiener-process increment. See Todorovic (1992) for a brief account of Langevin's approach. Cox and Miller (1965, p. 298) make a brief comment on it as well. Soize (1994) has more details.

Consider a scalar stochastic process

$$dx = b(x)\,dt + \epsilon\sigma(x)\,dW(t)$$

for a twice continously differentiable f on a compact set in the real line, with

$$df(x) = f'(x)\,dx + \frac{1}{2}f''(x)(dx)^2.$$

Substituting dx out, we have

$$df = f'(x)\{b(x)\,dt + \epsilon\sigma(x)\,dW(t)\} + \frac{\epsilon^2 f''(x)}{2}\sigma^2(x)\,dt.$$

Suppose that a probability density function $p(x, t)$ exists. Taking the expectation of the above with this density function, and interchanging the order of differentiation and integration, we evaluate the partial derivative with respect to t of the expectation of $f(x)$ by integration by parts. Noting that f and its partial derivatives have compact support, the resulting expression evaluated at the limits of integrations is zero, e.g., $f(x)b(x)p(x, t)|_{-\infty}^{\infty} = 0$, and so on. The resulting expression is

$$\int f(x)\frac{\partial p}{\partial t} = \int f(x)\left\{-\frac{\partial}{\partial x}[b(x)p] + \frac{\epsilon^2}{2}\frac{\partial^2}{\partial x^2}[\sigma^2(x)p]\right\}dx,$$

so, because f is arbitrary, we derive

$$\frac{\partial p}{\partial t} = -\frac{\partial}{\partial x}[b(x)p] + \frac{\epsilon^2}{2}\frac{\partial^2}{\partial x^2}[\sigma^2(x)p].$$

This is a second-order linear parabolic partial differential equation. To be more precise on the technical conditions, see Soize (1994, Chap. VI), for example. This equation is called Fokker–Planck equation. In addition to the sources cited above, see Cox and Miller (1965, Chap. 5).

We sometimes rewrite the Fokker–Planck equation as

$$\frac{\partial p}{\partial x} = -\frac{\partial J}{\partial x},$$

where

$$J(x) = b(x)p - \frac{1}{2}\frac{\partial p}{\partial x}$$

is defined as the probability current through the point x.

8.7.1 Stationary density function

Setting the left-hand side of the Kolmogorov equation equal to zero, the stationary probability density is obtained. See Soize (1994, Sec. VI.5) for example.

The density must have probability mass 1. In the case of scalar equations defined on the real line and where the positive and negative regions are distinct, and there is no probability flow from one side to the other at the origin, $x = 0$; then the probability current is zero at $x = 0$.

In the steady-state case, the current is constant; hence it is zero throughout if it is zero at any point, such as the origin. Given that $J = 0$ at all x, it follows that

$$b(x)p^e(x) = \frac{1}{2}\frac{\partial p^e(x)}{\partial x},$$

where p^s denotes the stationary probability density. Integrating this equation, we obtain

$$p^e(x) = C \exp -\phi(x),$$

with

$$\phi(x) = \int_x^0 b(u)\, du.$$

8.7.2 The exponential distribution of the growth rates of firms

Let $S(t)$ be a stochastic process of the size of a firm. Here the word "size" is to be interpreted broadly as meaning some quantity related to the scale of firm's activities, such as the number of employees, sales in dollars, or plant and equipment or capitalization in dollar terms. The parameter values of the distributions vary somewhat depending on the S being used, but the functional form of the distribution remains the same. See Amaral et al. (1997) for detail.

Here, we postulate that $s(t) = \ln S(t)$ grows by the rule

$$s(t + \Delta) = s(t) - \text{sgn}[s(t) - s^*]\,(\ln k) + \sigma_\epsilon \xi(t),$$

where σ_ϵ is a positive number, $\xi(t)$ is a mean-zero and variance-one normal random variable, k is some constant greater than 1, and s^* is a parameter assumed to be fixed for now. This equation simply means that a firm has a desired value for its size, S^*, and $S(t)$ grows by the factor $ke^{\sigma_\epsilon \xi(t)}$ if $S(t) < S^*$, and shrinks by the factor $(1/k)e^{\sigma_\epsilon \xi(t)}$ when the reverse inequality holds. With $S(t) = S^*$, it undergoes a random change $e^{\sigma_\epsilon \xi(t)}$.

Later, we describe how it may vary. The expression sgn means a sign function: $\text{sgn}(u) = 1$ for a positive variable u, and $= -1$ if u is negative.

Approximating $s(t + \Delta) - s(t)$ by $\frac{ds}{dt}\Delta$, this dynamics has the Ito representation

$$ds = b(s)\,dt + \sigma\,dW(t),$$

where $W(t)$ is a standard Wiener process, with $b(s) = -\text{sgn}(s - s^*)(\ln k)/\Delta$ and $\sigma = \sigma_\epsilon/\Delta$. Translated into the Fokker–Planck equation for the probability density $p(s, t)$, the equation is

$$\frac{\partial p}{\partial t} = \text{sgn}(s - s^*)\,\frac{\ln k}{\Delta}\frac{\partial p}{\partial s} + \frac{\sigma^2}{2}\frac{\partial^2 p}{\partial s^2}.$$

We next change the variables to put it into a standard form. Define

$$x = \frac{s - s^*}{s_0},$$

with $s_0 = \Delta\sigma^2/\ln k$, and

$$\tau = t/t_0,$$

with $t_0 = (\Delta\sigma)^2/(\ln k)^2$. The Fokker–Planck equation in the new variables is

$$\frac{\partial p}{\partial \tau} = \text{sgn}(x)\,\frac{\partial p}{\partial x} + \frac{1}{2}\frac{\partial^2 p}{\partial x^2}. \tag{8.7}$$

The solution of this equation gives the time-dependent probability density for s or its normalized version x.

The steady-state probability density in the original variable, denoted by $p^e(s)$, is

$$p^e = \frac{1}{s_0}\exp\left(-\frac{|s - s^*|}{2s_0}\right).$$

8.8   Time-Dependent density and heat equation

In nonstationary case, we can further simplify the diffusion equation by eliminating the term $\partial p/\partial x$. Set

$$p(x, \tau) = e^{\alpha x + \beta \tau} V(x, \tau),$$

and choose $\alpha = -\text{sgn}(x)$ and $\beta = -1/2$. Then (8.7) becomes the standard heat-equation form

$$\frac{\partial V}{\partial \tau} = \frac{1}{2} \frac{\partial^2 V}{\partial x^2}.$$

This is a specially simple and well-known parabolic partial differential equation. It is called the heat equation because it arose as a model of the temperature distribution in one-dimensional heat-conducting media in steady heat flow (conduction or diffusion). The book by Sommerfeld (1949) discusses this and other physics examples. As mentioned in the introductory section, the option-pricing equation by Black and Scholes is a slightly more complicated example of this equation, to which it may be reduced by suitable transformation as in Willmot et al. (1993, Sec. 5.4).

The solution of the heat equation is seen to depend on x and t in a special combination $\xi = x/\sqrt{t}$. This is so because the equation and the initial and boundary conditions are invariant under scaling of x by a factor λ, and t by λ^2, for any real number λ. We have

$$\left.\frac{\partial \ln p}{\partial x}\right|_{0+} = -2.$$

We set $V(x, \tau) = \tau^{-1/2} U(\xi)$, as suggested by Willmot et al. (1993, p. 73), to have the integral of U finite. Then, the heat equation for V becomes

$$U'' = -(\xi U)'.$$

The solution is of the form $ce^{-\xi^2/2}$. From the conservation of the probability mass we impose

$$\frac{1}{2} = \int_0^\infty p(x, \tau)\, dx = \int_{-\infty}^0 p(x, \tau)\, dx.$$

The constant c is given by

$$c^{-1} = \sqrt{2\pi}\ [1 - \text{erfc}(\sqrt{\tau}\,)],$$

where

$$\text{erfc}(w) = \sqrt{2\pi} \int_w^\infty e^{-u^2/2}\, du.$$

For large τ the erfc expression is approximately equal to $\tau^{-1/2}e^{-\tau/2}$, with $w = \sqrt{\tau}$. Thus, we recover the steady-state solution discussed above.

8.9   Size distribution for old and new goods

We have described distributions of cluster sizes based on Dirichlet distributions. These are stationary distributions from the viewpoint of random combinatorial analysis. Here, we examine the same subject from a different perspective. We obtain some information on nonstationary distributions this way.

8.9.1   Diffusion-equation approximation

We calculate the probability that there are k clusters formed by n agents at time t starting from n singletons, that is, n individuals initially. We follow the analyses by Derrida and Peliti (1991).

Suppose that there are n agents of either type 1 or 2. Suppose that a Markov chain $X(t)$ is defined by

$$\Pr(X(t+1) = j \mid X(t) = i)) = \frac{n!}{(n-j)!j!}(i/n)^j(1 - i/n)^{n-j},$$

where $X(t)$ is the number of agents of type 1. This process is known to be approximated by a diffusion process with the forward Kolmogorov equation for the density with mean zero and variance $\sigma(x)^2$:

$$\frac{\partial f}{\partial t} = \frac{1}{2}\frac{\partial^2(\sigma^2(x)f)}{\partial x^2},$$

with $\sigma(x)^2 = x(1-x)/n$. This is the equation for the density of the fraction x of the diffusion approximation with a system of n agents. We define $\tau = t/n$ and rewrite the time derivative in terms of τ to remove the $1/n$ in the variance equation. See Ewens (1979, p. 140).

This diffusion equation was first solved by Kimura (1955). We discuss the solution of this equation with the initial condition $\delta(x - p)$.

We posit $f(x, \tau; p) = T(\tau)X(x; p)$ to try the separation of the variables to solve the equation. The equation separates into

$$\frac{T'(\tau)}{T(\tau)} = \frac{1}{2}\frac{\{x(1-x)X(x;p)\}''}{X(x;p)} = \kappa,$$

where κ is a constant.

The function $T(\tau) = T(0)e^{\kappa\tau}$ is immediate, and we change variable from x to $z = 1 - 2x$ in X. It satisfies

$$(1 - z^2)X'' - 4zX' - (2\kappa + 2) = 0,$$

where $'$ denotes differentiation with respect to z now. This differential equation has a solution with $\kappa = -i(i+1)/2$ for any positive integer i. The function that solves the differential equation

$$(1 - z^2)\psi'' - 2(\beta + 1)z\psi' + \alpha(\alpha + 2\beta + 1)\psi = 0$$

is known as the Gegenbauer function, a type of hypergeometric function. See Morse and Feshbach (1953, pp. 547, 731) on the Gegenbauer functions. We see that the case with $\beta = 1$ and $\alpha = i - 1$ is for our function X with $\kappa = -i(i+1)/2$. These values are the eigenvalues, and the corresponding ψ are eigenfunctions. To be explicit, we have

$$X(z) = T^1_{i-1}(z).$$

The class of Gegenbauer polynomials is known to be a system of complete orthogonal polynomials with weight $1 - z^2$ on the interval $[-1, 1]$: For any positive integers m and n,

$$\int_{-1}^{1} (1 - z^2)T^1_m(z)T^1_n(z)\, dz = a_n \delta_{m,n}.$$

Hence the solution of the diffusion equation can be expressed as

$$f(x, \tau; p) = \sum_{i \geq 1} C_i T^1_{i-1}(z)T^1_{i-1}(p)e^{-i(i+1)\tau/2},$$

where $C_i = (2i + 1)(1 - r^2)/[i(i + 1)]$, where $r = 1 - 2p$.

The recursion relations are given by

$$(i + 1)T^1_{i+1}(z) = (2i + 3)zT^1_i - (i + 2)T^1_{i-1},$$

with $T^1_0 = 1$ and $T^1_1 = 3z$. This is obtained from the generating function

$$\sum_{n \geq 0} t^n T^1_n(z) = (1 - 2tz + t^2)^{-3/2}.$$

We note that $T^1_n(1) = (n + 1)(n + 2)/2$ and $T^1_n(-1) = (-1)^n(n + 1)(n + 2)/2$.

8.9.2 Lines of product developments and inventions

We derive joint distributions for shares of old and new goods in a sense we now explain. Pick some past time instant t. Some of the goods or products currently available on the markets were in existence at least t time units or periods ago, that is, when we go back in time t periods, these products were already invented or being produced. Call these goods or products **old** goods or products. The remainder of goods or products that are currently available but were not available t periods in the past have been either invented or improved upon since that time. Call these **new** goods or products.

In this section, we use the theory of coalescents, which was invented by Kingman (1982) and has been applied extensively in the genetics literature, to explain shares of old and new goods (species). See, among others, Watterson (1984), Donnelly and Tavaré (1987), Ewens (1990), and Hoppe (1987) on coalescents and related topics. We describe the distributions of the numbers of old goods and new goods, and the probability density of the shares or fractions of these goods.

At present time, we take a sample of n products or goods, and we examine their histories of developments, going back in time. Some goods can trace their developmental history to an invention or innovation that took place some time ago. Others may have branched out from common prototypes some time in the past.

Pick a time t units in the past, and fix a sample of size n goods out of all goods that are available now in the markets. When the histories of development or improvements, or mere existence in the markets, are traced back in time for these n goods, they can be put in equivalence relations using the notion of **defining events** in the terminology of Ewens (1990, Sec. 7). A defining event is either the emergence of two products from a common prototype, or the invention of a new good or product some time ago. It is assumed that the overall rate at which the former takes place in an interval of length h is $[k(k-1)/2]h + o(h)$ when there are k goods, and the overall rate of invention is specified by $[k\theta/2]h + o(h)$. The rate of arrival of defining events is therefore $k(k+\theta-1)/2$ when there are k products. The mean time of arrival is $2/\{k(k+\theta-1)\}$.

Using the notation in Watterson (1984), at time t ago there were D_t old goods, and their equivalence classes are denoted by $\xi_i, i = 1, 2, \ldots, D_t$. Their sizes are $\lambda_i = |\xi_i|$. New goods are also put into equivalence classes, $\eta_j, j = 1, 2, \ldots, F_t$ (where F_t is the number of the equivalence classes), having the sizes $\mu_j = |\eta_j|$. See the figures in Ewens (1990).

Watterson (1984, (2.9)) has shown

$$\Pr(l; \lambda_1, \lambda_2, \ldots \lambda_k; \mu_1, \mu_2, \ldots, \mu_l | k)$$
$$= \frac{(n-k)!k!}{n!} \frac{\theta^l}{(k+\theta)^{[n-k]}} \prod_i \lambda_i! \prod_j (\mu_j - 1)!,$$

where k is the number of old goods and l the number of new goods. As t recedes into remote past, k will become zero, because all goods coalesce to a single prototype good, and the above simplifies to

$$\Pr(l; \mu_1, \ldots, \mu_l) = \frac{\theta^l}{\theta^{[n]}} \prod_{j=1}^{l} (\mu_j - 1)!.$$

This distribution is related to the Ewens sampling formula. Because there are

$$\frac{n!}{\mu_1! \mu_2! \cdots \mu_l! b_1! b_2! \cdots b_n!}$$

distinguishable ways that the sample can have $D_t = 0$ and $F_t = l$, and new class sizes μ_i, where b_i is the number of classes with size i, we recover the Ewens formula by multiplying the above two expressions.

This can be generalized to the case with nonzero old goods. Let a_i denote the number of old classes of size i. Then, we have

$$\Pr(F_t = l; \lambda_1, \ldots, \lambda_k; \mu_1, \ldots, \mu_l | D_t = k)$$
$$= \frac{(n-k)! k! \theta^l}{(k+\theta)^{[n-k]}} \frac{1}{\prod_j \mu_j \prod_j b_j! \prod_i a_i!}.$$

Noting that $\sum_{i=1}^n a_i = k$, $\sum_{j=1}^n b_j = l$, $\sum_{i=1}^n i(a_i + b_i) = n$, and $\prod_j (\theta/j)^{b_i} = \theta^j / \mu_1 \mu_2 \cdots \mu_l$, we have

$$\Pr(a_1, a_2, \ldots, a_n; b_1, b_2, \ldots, b_n | D_t = k) = \frac{(n-k)! k!}{(k+\theta)^{[n-k]}} \prod_i \frac{1}{a_i!} \prod_j \frac{(\theta/j)^{b_j}}{b_j!}.$$

See Watterson (1984) for proof. Summing this over all l and bs, we derive

$$\Pr(a_1, a_2, \ldots, a_n | D_t = k) = \frac{k!}{a_1! \cdots a_n!} C_{\theta+n-z-1, n-z} / C_{\theta+n-1, n-k},$$

with $z = \sum_i i a_i$.

The process $\{D_t, t \geq 0\}$ is a continuous-time Markov (pure death) process, with $D_0 = n$. Tavaré (1984, (5.5)) has derived its probability,

$$\Pr(D_t = k) = \sum_{j=k}^{\infty} e^{-j(j+\theta-1)t/2} \frac{(-1)^{j-k}(2j+\theta-1)\Gamma(k+\theta+j-1)}{k!(j-k)!\Gamma(k+\theta)},$$

for $k \geq 1$.

Hoppe (1987, Sec. 8) provides related discussions and offers an urn-model interpretation.

Donnelly and Tavaré (1987) characterize the fractions of old goods, x_1, $x_2, \ldots, x_k$, and those of the new goods, $x_{k+1}, x_{k+2}, \ldots$, as follows: the sum $v_k := x_1 + x_2 + \cdots + x_k$ has the density function of Beta(k, θ):

$$f_k(v) = \frac{\Gamma(k+\theta)}{\Gamma(k)\Gamma(\theta)} v^{k-1}(1-v)^{\theta-1},$$

and

$$x_i = v_k u_i,$$

$i = 1, 2, \ldots, k$, where $u_1, \ldots, u_k$ are uniformly distributed on $[0, 1]$ and sum to one, and $x_{k+1} = (1 - v_k)z_1$, $x_{k+2} = (1 - v_k)z_2(1 - z_1)$, and so on, where the z's are i.i.d. with the density of Beta$(1, \theta)$,

$$f(z) = \theta(1 - z)^{\theta - 1},$$

$0 \le z \le 1$. The factor $1 - v_k$ is residually allocated to the shares of new goods, in the order of appearance, that is, in the order of ages of the new goods. See also Ewens (1990).

CHAPTER 9

A new look at the Diamond search model

The search model of Diamond (1982)[1] and its elaboration by Diamond and Fudenberg (1989) have been influential, as evidenced by frequent citations in the search literature. Diamond begins his analysis by assuming infinitely many agents in the model. Consequently, his dynamical analysis is entirely deterministic, and cycles of the model are generated by a set of deterministic differential equations. His model has no room for random fluctuations of the fraction of employed agents.

This is not to fault the model for lack of realism. Nevertheless, one would like to know how his model behaves in a finite-agent version: Does it produce substantial or negligible fluctuations about a locally stable state? Which of the multiple equilibria is chosen?

In this chapter, we recast their model in a framework of the modeling strategy advocated in this book.[2] We have two objectives in recasting their model this way: One is to obtain information on fluctuations about the equilibria, and to provide a simpler explanation than Diamond and Fudenberg did for cyclical behavior. The other is to provide a new and more natural basis for equilibrium selection for models with multiple equilibria than those available in the economic literature on equilibrium selection.

By our reformulation a different view of cycles emerges. We will show that the model has multiple equilibria, and that stochastic fluctuations cause the fraction of the employed to move from one basin of attraction to another with positive probabilities. These stochastic asymmetrical cycles are quite different from the deterministic cycles generated by a set of Diamond–Fudenberg nonlinear differential equations. Even when we take the number of agents to infinity, we show below that we gain new information about the limiting probability distribution over the steady states, and that this provides a

---

[1] This section is based in part on Aoki and Shirai (2000).
[2] This example was suggested by Orszak (1997) as one of his comments on Chapter 5 in Aoki (1996a).

natural basis for considering equilibrium selection in models with multiple equilibria.

The dynamical behavior of the model is now described by the master equation. It determines how the probability for the fraction evolves with time. Then, this master equation is solved approximately to yield two equations: One is an ordinary differential equation for the average or expected value of the fraction of the employed. This is the aggregate dynamical equation for the mean of the employed fraction. The other is a Fokker–Planck equation that governs random deviations, that is, fluctuations of the fraction about the mean.

When we let the number of agents go to infinity, the equation for the mean reproduces the equation for the fraction derived by Diamond. The Fokker–Planck equation is new. The critical points of the ordinary differential equation and the endogenously determined reservation-cost expression jointly yield information on the equilibria. These are the same as in Diamond.

Additionally, we derive information on the asymmetrical cyclical behavior, which is substantially different from his. Fluctuations about aggregate dynamics occur in our analysis because microshocks intrinsic to our models do not vanish when the number of agents in the model is finite.[3] With positive probabilities, net effects of arrivals of production and trading opportunities do not vanish, but accumulate to change the fraction of employed from one basin of attraction to the other.

In Section 9.1, we describe the model as a jump Markov process with the transition rates specified in Section 9.2. The transition rates are endogenously determined, because they depend on the reservation cost for accepting production opportunities, which is determined by comparing value functions for the alternative choices of becoming employed by accepting the production opportunity and of remaining unemployed by rejecting the opportunity as being too costly. Recall our introductory discussion on value functions in Section 6.2. After we discuss the dynamics for the mean of the fraction, and a Fokker–Planck equation for the fluctuations about the mean, in Sections 9.3 and 9.4, the value functions are evaluated in Section 9.5. Then, in Section 9.6, we discuss the expected first-passage times between two locally stable equilibria when the model dynamics have multiple locally stable equilibria. We also discuss our equilibrium selection criterion, which is based on the relative sizes of basins of attractions and the probabilities that the model state is in the basins. The larger the basin of attraction for a stationary state, or the smaller the fluctuation

---

[3] The idea of microshocks creating aggregate risk was proposed by Jovanovic (1987). His main point is that in the nonlinear systems microshocks intrinsic to the model do not vanish. Kirman (1993) discusses a mechanism of stochastic cycles. The focus of his model is on herding effects. See Aoki (1998b, p. 436) for comparison of our method and that of Kirman. Furthermore, our model in this section has optimizing agents. In such a model, fluctuations between two basins of attractions are still possible.

around the stationary state, the more likely it is that such a stationary state will be selected as the equilibrium.

9.1 Model

There are two types of agents: employed and unemployed. Since the model is closed, the fraction of the employed is k/n, where k is the number of employed, and n is the fixed total number of agents. The fraction of the employed, or equivalently k, is used as the state variable.

Each of the $n - k$ unemployed persons independently encounters a production opportunity that appears at the rate of $a \Delta t$ in a small time interval Δt. If the opportunity is accepted, it yields the unit output and at the cost c, which is a nonnegative random number with a known distribution function G. There is a reservation or threshold cost $c^*(k)$, to be determined endogenously later, above which the opportunity is rejected as being too costly. When the opportunity is accepted, the person's status changes from being unemployed to being employed. Each of k employed persons independently encounters a trading opportunity at the rate $b(k/n)$ per unit time. When an employed person encounters a trading opportunity, he forms a pair with another randomly selected employed person, the pair trade, each of the pair consumes the output of the partner to receive instantaneous utility v, and their status changes from being employed to being unemployed. See Diamond (1982) for some explanations for these assumptions.

9.2 Transition rates

Production opportunities arrive to the unemployed at the rate a as a Poisson process. If undertaken, each production opportunity yields a unit of output with cost c. Only production with cost c^* or less will be undertaken. The transition rate from k to $k + 1$ is given by $(n - k)aG(c^*)$, where c^* is the **reservation** cost in the sense that only production with cost $c \leq c^*$ is undertaken. Since this reservation cost is a choice variable and depends on k/n, we write it as $c^*(k/n)$, or as $c^*(k)$ for short, in the following.

For an employed agent, trading opportunities arrive as a Poisson process at the rate $\beta(k/n)$. His probability for being one of the random pair is $1 - C_{k-1,2}/C_{k,2} = 2/k$. We define the arrival rate of trading opportunity for an agent to be $b(k/n) := (2/k)\beta(k/n)$. While an employed agent waits for a trading partner, the probability is $[C_{k-1,2}/C_{k,2}]\beta = [(k - 2)/2]\beta$ that a pair involving other employed agents trade, thus decreasing k to $k - 2$. In aggregate, then, the transition rate from state k to $k - 2$ is given by $(k/2)b(k/n)$.

9.3   Aggregate dynamics: Dynamics for the mean of the fraction

The master equation is

$$dP_k(t)/dt = r_{k-1}P_{k-1}(t) + l_{k+2}P_{k+2}(t) - (r_k + l_k)P_k(t),$$

where l_k is the transition rate for the leftward move from state k, and r_k is that of the rightward move. This is essentially the birth–death equation we have discussed earlier in Chapters 3 through 5. The only difference arises from the fact that the leftward move involves a step of two units, not a single unit, because a matched pair of agents – that is, two agents – change their status.

In Section 9.2, we have described the transition rate for the rightward move to be

$$r_k = (n - k)aG(c^*(k/n)) = n(1 - e)aG(c^*(k/n)),$$

and that for the leftward move rate to be

$$l_k = \frac{k}{2}b\left(\frac{k}{2}\right).$$

Since this equation cannot be solved exactly, we proceed as in Chapters 3 and 4. See also Aoki (1996a, p. 123). The master equation is expanded in Taylor series, and terms of the same order of magnitude are collected. Change the variable as

$$\frac{k}{n} = \phi + \frac{\xi}{\sqrt{n}}.$$

The variable ϕ is the expected fraction of employed, and ξ represents random fluctuations about the mean. This scaling implies that fluctuations are expected to be of the order of $\sqrt{n}$.[4] In this change of the variable, note that $(k+1)/n = \phi + n^{-1/2}(\xi + 1/\sqrt{n})$, and so on. For example, ξ changes by $2/\sqrt{n}$ in l_{k+2}. Let $\Pi(\xi, t) := P_k(t)$. The master equation is now rewritten in terms of Π by noting that

$$\frac{dP_k(t)}{dt} = \frac{\partial \Pi}{\partial t} + \frac{\partial \Pi}{\partial \xi}\frac{d\xi}{dt},$$

where

$$\frac{d\xi}{dt} = -\sqrt{n}\frac{d\phi}{dt}.$$

In the Taylor series expansion, after substituting the change of the variable, we match the left-hand side of order $\sqrt{n}$ with the terms of the same order on

---

[4] That this is the correct order is indicated by the fact that the coefficients of the Fokker–Planck equation for ξ, to be derived below, are independent of n.

the right-hand side. We derive the aggregate dynamic equation for ϕ as

$$\frac{d\phi}{dt} = a\Phi(\phi) := (1 - \phi)aG(c^*) - \phi b(\phi). \tag{9.1}$$

This is in agreement with the dynamical equation for e in Diamond (1982, (1)).

Here we define $\Phi(\phi)$ as above because it is convenient to introduce a natural time unit in terms of the arrival rate of the production opportunity a and define

$$\tau = at,$$

to rewrite the dynamical equation for the mean as

$$\frac{d\phi}{d\tau} = \Phi(\phi) := (1 - \phi)G(c^*) - \phi \hat{b}(\phi).$$

In other words, we measure the arrival rate for trading opportunity relative to that of the production opportunity by defining $\hat{b} = b/a$ as shorthand, because this grouping of terms arises several times below.

9.4 Dynamics for the fluctuations

The rest of the terms are for determining the distribution of ξ. By collecting terms of $O(n^0)$ in the Taylor series expansion this equation is seen to be given by

$$\frac{\partial \Pi}{\partial t} = A\Pi + A\xi \frac{\partial \Pi}{\partial \xi} + C \frac{\partial^2 \Pi}{\partial \xi^2} + O(n^{-1/2}), \tag{9.2}$$

with

$$A = -\Phi'(\phi),$$

and

$$C = \frac{1}{2}[(1 - \phi)G(c^*) + \phi \hat{b}(\phi)].$$

This is a type of Fokker–Planck equation we have encountered earlier in this book. It can be solved as discussed in Aoki (1996a, Sec. 5.13), for example. As we discuss shortly, the local equilibria of the dynamics are the zeros of the function Φ. Its derivative Φ' is negative at those local equilibria that are locally asymptotically stable, i.e., where A is positive. Note that the coefficient C is $2\phi b(\phi)$ at the critical points.

Equation (9.2) can be solved by the method of separation of variables. Let $\Pi(\xi, t) = T(t)X(\xi)$. Then we obtain

$$T'(t)/T(t) = A + A\xi X'(\xi)/X(\xi) + CX''(\xi)/X(\xi) = -\theta,$$

where θ is some constant.

To obtain a stationary solution, set θ equal to zero. Rewriting the equation for X as

$$(C/A)X'' + (\xi X)' = 0.$$

In the case where $X'(0) = 0$, we can solve it as

$$X(\xi) = X(0) \exp\left(-\frac{A}{C}\frac{\xi^2}{2}\right).$$

We have thus shown that this stationary distribution for ξ is normally distributed with mean zero and variance C/A. Its variance is given by

$$\mathrm{var}(\xi) = \frac{C}{A}.$$

With two or more locally stable equilibria, the probability mass around each of the critical points may overlap and assign positive probability to the neighboring critical points. This is one sufficient condition for fluctuations to spill over to the neighboring basins of attraction. Even if this does not happen, we show later that expected first-passage times from one basin to the neighboring ones are finite, i.e., cycles are possible. We show below that the stationary distribution for ξ is normally distributed with mean zero and variance that is a function of ϕ but is independent of n. This is a posteriori justification for the change of the variable we have performed.

9.5   Value functions

Let $W_e(k, t)$ be the present discounted value of the lifetime utility of an employed person in state k at time t. Similarly let $W_u(k, t)$ be that of an unemployed person when the state is k. Because k is a random variable, we take the expectation of these random value functions later, after we derive the stationary distribution of k. We drop t from the argument of the value functions, because dynamic programming involves an infinite horizon and the problem is time-homogeneous.

Denote the discount rate by r. Value functions depend on the fraction k/n rather than on k directly. For shorter notation, however, we denote them by $W_e(k)$ and $W_u(k)$ for the employed and unemployed when the number of the employed is k. For an employed agent, we obtain the relation for the value functions as

$$\begin{aligned}
r W_e(k) = {} & b(k/n)[v + W_u(k-2) - W_e(k)] \\
& + (n-k)aG(c^*(k))[W_e(k+1) - W_e(k)] \\
& + \frac{k-2}{2}b(k/n)[W_e(k-2) - W_e(k)]
\end{aligned}$$

for k between 3 and $n-1$, and for an umemployed agent[5]

$$rW_u(k) = a \int_0^{c^*(k)} [W_e(k+1) - W_u(k) - z]dG(z)$$
$$+ (n-k-1)aG(c^*(k))[W_u(k+1) - W_u(k)]$$
$$+ \frac{k}{2}b(k/n)[W_u(k-2) - W_u(k)]$$

for $k = 2, 3, \ldots, n-1$. There are boundary relations, but we do not use them, so they are not mentioned here. See Aoki and Shirai (2000) for their expressions.

We next take the expected values of these value functions with respect to the stationary distributions of k.

Because the set of value functions is huge, we solve for them approximately, by first obtaining the expressions for the expected values of the value functions and then the expression for the reservation costs as functions of ϕ up to terms of $O(1/n)$.

9.5.1 Expected-value functions

Define

$$W_u(k) := V_u(\phi + \xi/\sqrt{n}),$$

and

$$W_e(k) := V_e(\phi + \xi/\sqrt{n}).$$

The expressions in the square brackets of the value function relations in the previous section become

$$W_u(k+1) - W_u(k) = V_u\left(\phi + \frac{\xi}{\sqrt{n}} + \frac{1}{n}\right) - V_u\left(\phi + \frac{\xi}{\sqrt{n}}\right)$$
$$= \frac{1}{N}V_u'(\phi) + O(1/n),$$

and

$$W_u(k-2) - W_u(k) = -\frac{2}{n}V_u'(\phi) + O(1/n),$$

respectively. Noting that $E\xi = 0$ and $E\xi^2 = \sigma^2$, the expected-value function becomes, after dropping terms of order $1/n$ or smaller,

$$rV_u(\phi) = aG^*[V_e(\phi) - V_u(\phi)] - a\hat{c} + \Phi(\phi)V_u'(\phi).$$

---

[5] The probability intensity for the transition from state k to state $k+1$ is $(n-k)aG^*$, where G^* is shorthand for $G(c^*)$, of which $(n-k-1)aG^*$ is the intensity for other unemployed agents to become employed while he remains unemployed. The intensity for him to become employed is aG^*.

Proceeding analogously with W_e, we obtain

$$rV_e(\phi) = b(\phi)[v + V_u(\phi) - V_e(\phi)] + \Phi(\phi)V_e'(\phi).$$

See Aoki and Shirai (2000) for the details of the calculations.

These two equations correspond with (4a) and (4b) in Diamond and Fudenberg (1989).

Making use of the fact that $\Phi(\phi_e) = 0$, where ϕ_e denote locally stable equilibrium points, these two equations yield equilibrium value functions

$$V_e(\phi_e) = \frac{(\hat{r} + G^*)\hat{b}(\phi_e)v - \hat{b}(\phi_c)\hat{c}}{\hat{r}[\hat{r} + \hat{b}(\phi_e) + G^*]},$$

where $\hat{r} = r/a$, and

$$V_u(\phi_e) = \frac{\hat{b}(\phi_e)G^*v - (\hat{r} + \hat{b}(\phi_e))\hat{c}}{\hat{r}[\hat{r} + \hat{b}(\phi_e) + G^*]},$$

where G^* and $\hat{c}$ are evaluated at ϕ_e.

Setting $c^*(\phi) = V_e(\phi) - V_u(\phi)$, the reservation cost is given implicitly by

$$\hat{r}c^* = \hat{b}(v - c^*) - \int^{c^*} (c^* - c)\,dG(c) + \Phi(V_e' - V_u'),$$

where the last term is recognized as $dc^*/d\tau = (dc^*/d\tau)(d\phi/d\tau)$. Thus, the analogy with the case of an infinite number of agents holds.

We can actually see that this choice of c^* is optimal by differentiating the expected-value functions with respect to c^*, noting that $b(\phi)$ is exogenously specified and its derivative with respect to c^* is zero. Solving for the derivatives of the expected-value functions with respect to c^*, we see that they are both zero. This is the first-order condition for optimality. The second-order condition may be shown to hold by taking derivatives once more.

9.6   Multiple equilibria and cycles: An example

To give the basic idea for dealing with models with several equilibria, here is an example with two locally stable equilibria.

We take $b(\phi) = a\phi$ to simplify algebra. We also let r/a be denoted by r, that is, we normalize both b and r by a. Suppose that there are two possible costs: $0 = c_1 \leq c_2$ – that is, the distribution function $G(c)$ is a step function; $G(c_1) = p > 0$; $G(c_2) = 1$. The right-hand side of the dynamics for the aggregate equation is either $\Phi_1(\phi) = (1 - \phi)p - \phi^2$, or $\Phi_2(\phi) = 1 - \phi - \phi^2$, depending on the range of the argument ϕ. We show below that Φ_1 applies when ϕ is not greater than ψ defined below, and Φ_2 applies otherwise.

There are thus two critical points. They are the roots of $\Phi_i(\phi) = 0, i = 1, 2,$ and are given by

$$\phi_1 = \frac{\sqrt{p^2 + 4p} - p}{2},$$

and

$$\phi_2 = \frac{\sqrt{5} - 1}{2} =: \kappa.$$

We see that $\Phi_i'(\phi_i)$ are negative for $i = 1, 2$, that is, the critical points are locally stable.

From the optimality condition, $c_1^* = c^*(\phi_1)$ is determined by

$$\hat{r} c_1^* = \phi_1(v - c_1^*) - p c_1^*,$$

or

$$c_1^* = \frac{\phi_1 v}{\hat{r} + \phi_1 + p},$$

if $0 < c_1^* < c_2$. The second value $c_2^* = c^*(\phi_2)$ is determined by

$$r c_2^* = \phi_2(v - c_2^*) - c_2^* + c_2(1 - p),$$

or

$$c_2^* = \frac{\phi_1 v + c_2(1 - p)}{\hat{r} + \phi_2 + 1},$$

if $c_2 < c_2^*$.

The two basins of attractions are separated at

$$\psi = \frac{c_2(r + p)}{v - c_2},$$

where we assume that $v > c_2$, that is, the value of Φ undergoes a discontinuous change at this value:

$$\Phi_1(\psi-) < 0,$$

and

$$\Phi_2(\psi+) > 0.$$

Therefore, if there is a large positive disturbance near ϕ_1 that makes the variable ϕ cross the boundary at ψ, then the derivative is positive and the disturbance is amplified, and ϕ is attracted to ϕ_2. Likewise, a large negative disturbance near ϕ_2 will cause the state variable to be attracted to ϕ_1. Figure 1 in Aoki and Shirai (2000, p. 497) plots one example of $\Phi(\phi)$.

The conditions to ensure $0 \leq \phi_1 < \psi < \phi_2 \leq 1$ are

$$c_2 < \frac{\upsilon \kappa}{r + p + \kappa},$$

and

$$\frac{\sqrt{p^2 + 4p}}{2} < \frac{p}{2} + c_2 \frac{r + p}{\upsilon_2 - c_2}.$$

Thus, a small p and not too large c_2 will suffice to satisfy these conditions.

The same construction works with three critical points, although the conditions on the parameters are more complicated to state. The critical points are determined as functions of $p_1 = G(0)$ and $p_1 + p_2 = G(c_2)$, where $0 = c_1 < c_2$. At $c_3 > c_2$, $G(c_3) = 1$. We ensure that $c_i < c^*(\phi_i) < c_{i+1}$ holds, $i = 1, 2$, and $c_3 < c_3^*$.

We now have possibilities of a total of three cycles: not only between ϕ_1 and ϕ_2 and between ϕ_2 and ϕ_3, but also between ϕ_1 and ϕ_3.

9.6.1   Asymmetrical cycles

This section presents several examples to show how we approximately evaluate the mean transition times from one basin of attraction to the other, and calculate the equilibrium probabilities for the model to stay in each of the two basins of attractions, as in the example with two locally stable equilibria.

9.6.1.1   Approximate analysis

First, we recognize that we need to calculate only the event from one of the equilibrium state to the boundary between the two basins of attraction, ψ, which is introduced in connection with the example of the multiple equilibria above. The reason is the same one given by van Kampen (1992), as quoted in Aoki (1996a, p. 151). The time needed for ϕ to reach its equilibrium value (ϕ_1, or ϕ_2, depending on the initial value) is much shorter than the time needed to go from one basin of attraction to the other.

A quick way to see this is to solve the deviational equation for ϕ.[6] To be definite, suppose that ϕ is in the domain of attraction to ϕ_1, and let $x = \phi - \phi_1$. Then x is governed by

$$dx/d\tau = \Phi_1'(\phi_1)x = -A(\phi_1)x,$$

with the initial condition $x(0) = \phi(0) - \phi_1$.

---

[6] In the example of multiple equilibria with discrete and finite support for the distribution function G, one can actually calculate the time to reach a small neighborhood of the equilibrium point by direct integration of the dynamics in the phase plane. This yields a similar results to the deviational analysis.

The solution is $x(\tau) = x(0)e^{-A(\phi_1)\tau}$. Recalling that $e^{-4.5} = 0.01$, it takes about $\tau = 4.5/A(\phi_1)$ to reduce the distance from ϕ_1 to about 0.01 of the original value. In the previous example, $\phi_1 = 0.358$ with $p = 0.2$. In this case, $A(\phi_1) = 0.92$. Thus, it takes about 4.9 or 5 time units to reach the equilibrium point. As we show later, the mean first-passage time for this example is of the order of 10^3. Therefore, we are justified in assuming that ϕ is initially at one of the equilibrium points in calculating the mean first-passage time. The procedure is as outlined by Aoki (1998b, Appendix). We set up a two-state Markov chain, because there are two locally stable equilibria in the example. We then solve

$$d\pi_1/d\tau = W_{2,1}\pi_2 - W_{1,2}\pi_1,$$

where $W_{1,2}$ is the transition rate from ϕ_1 to the boundary ψ of the two basins of attraction, and $W_{2,1}$ is that from ϕ_2 to ψ, and obtain its equilibrium probabilities by

$$\pi_1 W_{1,2} = \pi_2 W_{2,1},$$

and $\pi_2 = 1 - \pi_1$.

The result is

$$\pi_1 = \frac{W_{2,1}}{W_{1,2} + W_{2,1}}$$

for the equilibrium probability that the model stays in basin 1, and the mean first-passage time is given by

$$\tau_{1,2} = \frac{1}{W_{1,2}}.$$

See Aoki (1996a, p. 152).

To calculate $W_{1,2}$ we use

$$W_{1,2} = \Pr(\xi \geq \xi_c),$$

with

$$\phi_1 + \frac{\xi_c}{\sqrt{N}} = \psi.$$

Analogously $W_{2,1}$ is approximated by the probability that ξ is smaller than $\sqrt{N}(\psi - \phi_2)$, or equivalently, that it is larger than $\sqrt{N}(\phi_2 - \psi)$.

9.6.1.2 Example

Let $\hat{r} = 0.1$, $p = 0.3$, and $c_2/v = 0.55$. The boundary of the two basins is located at $\psi = 0.489$.

The variance of ξ in basin 1 is $\Sigma = \phi_1^2/A(\phi_1)$. The standard deviations $sd_1 = 0.374$, and $sd_2 = 0.413$. Thus

$$W_{1,2} = \Pr(\xi \geq \sqrt{N}(\psi - \phi_1)),$$

and

$$W_{2,1} = \Pr(\xi \geq \sqrt{N}(\phi_2 - \psi)).$$

Suppose that $N = 50$. Then $W_{1,2} = 0.00665$ and $W_{2,1} = 0.01375$. We thus estimate the mean first passage times as $\tau_{1,2} = 150.4$, $\tau_{2,1} = 72.7$, $\pi_1 = 0.67$, and $\pi_2 = 0.33$. The ratio of the mean first-passage times is 1.9. If the number of agents is $N = 100$, then $W_{1,2} = 0.00025$, $W_{21} = 0.0009$, $\tau_{1,2} = 4000$, $\tau_{2,1} = 1100$, and $\pi_1 = 0.78$.

This simple example shows that the model can have several locally stable equilibria and that the fraction of the employed agents may fluctuate between the equilibria. We have shown that this leads to a simpler explanations of asymmetrical cycles, among other things. Aoki and Shirai (2000, p. 499) has another example with a similar set of results.

9.7   Equilibrium selection

As we increase the number of agents in the economy to infinity, our model converges to that of Diamond. This can be seen by the fact that the variance of the employed fraction of agents converges to zero as N is taken to infinity, because the density function for e is Gaussian with mean ϕ and variance $\sigma^2(\phi)/N$. This suggests that the stationary (invariant) distribution over the fraction of employed agents in the economy becomes a pair of spikes with probability masses of π_1 and π_2 assigned for employed fractions $e = \phi_1$ and $e = \phi_2$, respectively.

These probability masses for each locally stable critical point provide the criteria for equilibrium selection for the model of multiple equilibria with an infinite number of agents. One can easily check that our special case given in Section 9.5 yields exactly the same stationary fractions of employed agents ϕ_1 and ϕ_2 in Diamond's model if we use the same matching function b and cost distribution function G.

We next calculate π_1 when N is taken to infinity. As suggested earlier, we have

$$W_{1,2} = \Pr[\xi > \sqrt{N}(\psi - \phi_1)]$$

$$= \int_{\sqrt{N}(\psi - \phi_1)}^{\infty} \frac{1}{\sqrt{2\pi\sigma^2(\phi_1)}} \exp\left[-\frac{\xi^2}{2\sigma^2(\phi_1)}\right] d\xi,$$

and

$$W_{2,1} = \Pr[\xi < \sqrt{N}(\psi - \phi_2)]$$

$$= \int_{\sqrt{N}(\phi_2 - \psi)}^{\infty} \frac{1}{\sqrt{2\pi\sigma^2(\phi_2)}} \exp\left[-\frac{\xi^2}{2\sigma^2(\phi_2)}\right] d\xi.$$

It is easy to see that both $W_{1,2}$ and $W_{2,1}$ approach zero as N is taken to infinity. Hence, we can approximate $\lim_{N\to\infty} W_{1,2}/W_{2,1}$ by $\lim_{N\to\infty}(dW_{1,2}/dN)/(dW_{2,1}/N)$. This is given by

$$\lim_{N\to\infty} \frac{W_{1,2}}{W_{2,1}} = \lim_{N\to\infty} \frac{dW_{1,2}/dN}{dW_{2,1}/dN}$$

$$= \lim_{N\to\infty} \exp\left\{\left[\left(\frac{(\phi_2 - \psi)^2}{2\sigma^2(\phi_2)} - \frac{(\psi - \phi_1)^2}{2\sigma^2(\phi_1)}\right) N\right]\right\}$$

$$\times \frac{(\psi - \phi_1)\sigma(\phi_2)}{(\phi_2 - \psi)\sigma(\phi_1)}. \tag{9.3}$$

From this, it is straightforward to see that as N approaches infinity, $W_{1,2}/W_{2,1}$ approaches 0 if and only if $(\psi - \phi_1)/\sigma(\phi_1) > (\phi_2 - \psi)/\sigma(\phi_2)$.

The result is summarized as follows;

$$\lim_{N\to\infty} \pi_1 = \begin{cases} 1 & \text{if } (\psi - \phi_1)/\sigma(\phi_1) > (\phi_2 - \psi)/\sigma(\phi_2), \\ 1/2 & \text{if } (\psi - \phi_1)/\sigma(\phi_1) = (\phi_2 - \psi)/\sigma(\phi_2), \\ 0 & \text{if } (\psi - \phi_1)/\sigma(\phi_1) < (\phi_2 - \psi)/\sigma(\phi_2). \end{cases}$$

The larger the distance between the critical point and the boundary of the basins of attraction, or the smaller the variance of fluctuation around the critical point, the more likely it is that this critical point will be selected as an equilibrium in a model with an infinite number of agents.

9.8 Possible extensions of the model

There are several ways of extending this model. The reader is invited to try some. As an example, we sketch one such extension. This is related to Kiyotaki and Wright (1993), who introduced money traders who each hold a unit of money, which they can exchange with positive probability for a unit of commodity produced by the unemployed. They also work with an infinite number of agents. In their extension, the amount of money, m units, is exogenously fixed, and stays the same throughout the time, even though the identities of agents who hold money change over time. For this reason, the dynamics is basically that of the Diamond model, because m appears in the dynamics as a fixed parameter, not as an additional state variable.

We suggest to the reader that their model be modified so that money traders may hold multiple units of money. This may be accomplished by making the process of changing money for commodities more efficient for agents staying in the cluster of money traders than joining the unemployed each time they exchange a unit of money for commodity. Let a_i be the number of money traders who have exactly i units of money. Then $\mathbf{a} = (a_1, \ldots, a_m)$ is a partition vector and is the state vector for the cluster of money traders. We have

$$\sum_{i=1}^{m} i a_i = m$$

as the total amount of money in the cluster of money traders, and

$$\sum_{i=1}^{m} a_i = K_m$$

is the number of money traders.

See Chapter 10 (Section 10.5 in particular) for the dynamics of such clusters. Specify appropriate transition rates in terms of the partition vector, and establish the corresponding stationary distributions of money stocks among money traders. See Aoki (2000a) for further information and suggestions along this line of model modification.

Interaction patterns and cluster size distributions

Large collections of agents form subgroups or clusters through their interactions. What kinds of distributions of their sizes can we expect to find?
Size distributions have obvious implications for our economic analysis, as one
example in the next chapter illustrates. In this chapter, we import results from
the literatures of population genetics, probability, and combinatorial analysis
to describe the Ewens sampling formula (multivariate Ewens distribution) and
random mappings, and indicate some simple applications.

We first discuss the entry and exit rates of jump Markov processes associated
with three classes of random combinatorial structures we use. They are called
selections, multisets, and assemblies by Arratia and Tavaré (1994), and we use
these names.

We then examine how agents in a large collection interact with each other
and form clusters of various sizes. We derive stationary distributions for cluster
sizes,[1] and use them to draw statistical inferences on various aggregates, that is,
macroeconomic variables. The Ewens sampling formula has not been used in
economic analysis, but we think that it may find important applications there.
The next chapter uses the joint densities for the order statistics of cluster sizes to
discuss situations in which the largest two clusters of agents largely determine
the market behavior. Related materials are found in Aoki (2000b,c).

10.1   Clustering processes

Consider modeling a large number of economic agents or units interacting in
a market. The nature of the agents or units involved varies according to the
context of the model. They could be groups of households, firms or some
sections or divisions of firms, sectors of an economy, or even a collection of
national economies. All are considered to be made up of some basic units
(of capital stocks measured in some basic units, sales measured in millions of

---

[1] In the probability literature, they are called component sizes.

dollars, number of employees in thousands, and so on). These units or agents in a collection, possibly of some fixed size, can be arranged or arrange themselves in a number of ways, and clusters or groupings of basic units of many different sizes may emerge or come to exist in markets, some temporarily and some permanently.

We treat such models as decomposable random combinatorial structures, as we shortly explain. Some existing results, such as the Herfindahl index in the literature on industrial organization, are rephrased in this language. The reader may wish to consult Sutton (1997), for example, for summaries of some of the related topics in the more traditional industrial organization literature.

In this book, we associate types with choices by or characteristics of agents, and speak of agents forming groups by types, by associating types with choices, or by characteristics. The word, "choice" should therefore be interpreted broadly. Choices may be decisions where to buy goods, or what to buy, by households or firms, which algorithms to use for search for employment by unemployed workers, which types of layoff policies to implement by firms, which policy stance to take by central banks, and so on.[2]

As briefly mentioned in earlier sections, we derive probability distributions of the sizes of such clusters or groups and of their growth rates, such as stationary-state or time-dependent probability distributions of firm sizes or market shares. This can be done analytically in simple models, or by simulation otherwise. By having time-dependent distributions we can assess growth rates of developing economies and new industries at initial or later stages, steady-state distributions of market shares of mature markets, and so on.[3]

To derive probability distributions for the numbers of clusters of various sizes, we count the total number of possible configurations of a set of objects of some fixed size and, usually, assign probabilities equally. That is, we treat each basic configuration or pattern as equiprobable. More on this later. We obtain some nonstationary distributions by the method of probability generating functions or cumulant generating functions. In some applications, we translate behavioral models into Fokker–Planck equations via Langevin equations, as in Chapter 8.

Consider economic models in which n agents individually choose, usually subject to some possibly imperfectly perceived externalities or aggregate effects of choices made by others, one of K_n possible alternatives. The number of choices may depend on n, whence the subscript on K. Depending on the context

---

[2] Percolation models are often adapted by physicists to examine clusters in economic models. However, percolation models have different statistical properties than the models based on jump Markov processes discussed in this chapter.

[3] A group of statistical physicists have recently found empirically certain size distributions of firms and growth rates of firms. We later account for their findings by solving certain Fokker–Planck equations to derive nonstationary probability distributions. See also the last section of Chapter 8.

of the model, K_n may be finite, as in binary choice models, such as in Aoki (1996a, pp. 143, 166), or countably infinite. The number of types, that is, the number of choices, may or may not be known in advance, or may be random. Models discussed here are more general than those in the traditional discrete-choice literature. For one thing, we explicitly consider dynamic processes due to the nature of random choices, as will become evident as we proceed.[4]

When a collection of agents falls into distinct groups, there often is no natural way of labeling the groups. The situation is akin to those of occupancy problems in probability textbooks: A large number of indistinguishable balls are placed in a large number of unmarked identical-looking boxes. To produce sensible limiting behavior as the numbers of agents and types become very large, we resort to order statistics, that is, we label groups in order of decreasing size. This is sensible because a rather small number of groups may dominate the aggregate behavior, such as market excess demands for some goods. Such an example will be presented in Chapter 12.

We keep the total number of agents finite, at least in the initial stage of model formulation. We eventually may let the number increase, to link our results with those in the macroeconomic literature. We use the finitary approach in model building in the sense of Costantini and Garibaldi (1999). It is convenient to normalize the number of agents of each type by the number of agents of all types. Then, one speaks of the fractions of agents of various types, where all fractions sum to one. Fractions describe compositions of agents by types. This "demographic" picture of the distribution of agents by types is given by a vector of fractions, which is a point of a simplex of some dimension.[5]

Arratia and Tavaré (1994) have shown that many random combinatorial objects, which are decomposable into some basic units, have a component structure whose joint distribution is equal to, or approximated by, that of a process of independent random variabes, conditional on the value of a weighted sum of the variables. In particular, they have shown that Poisson random variables work for a class of combinatorial structures called assemblies, such as permutations, random mapping functions, and partitions of sets; that negative binomial random variables work for a class of structures called multisets, such as mapping patterns and partitions of integers; and that binomial random variables work for a class called selections.

Partition vectors characterize random exchangeable partitions, and also random combinatorial structures. We use partition vectors as state vectors of these combinatorial objects. More concretely, let n denote the "size," broadly interpreted, of a market to be modeled. The structure of the market is characterized

---

[4] See also Aoki (2000b), Kelly (1979, Chap. 8), and Costantini and Garibaldi (2000).
[5] An alternative and related labeling scheme is called size-biased permutation. In this scheme larger groups are more likely to be labeled first. We return to this scheme later.

by the partition vector

$$\mathbf{a}(n) = \{a_1(n), a_2(n), \ldots, a_n(n)\}.$$

Here, $a_i := a_i(n)$ is the number of components, also called clusters, of size i, so that

$$\sum_{i=1}^{n} a_i(n) = K_n$$

is the number of components or types in the market. For example, a_i may represent the number of firms with i units of sales per year in some industry, the number of sectors of an economy with i firms, or the number of countries that produce i units of some goods. We also note from definition that

$$\sum_{i=1}^{n} i\, a_i(n) = n$$

is the total size of the market, to be interpreted as the total number of participants in the market, or total capitalization in the market, total sales per unit time of a sector of, economy, and so on, depending on particular contexts of models.

The vector **a** is an example of a partition vector, mentioned in Chapter 2, to describe the state of configurations of combinatorial structures.

Our main objective is to derive probability distributions for sizes of clusters. To treat decomposable combinatorial structures randomly, we first count the total number of possible configurations with the same partition vector. This allows us to assign probabilities to each configuration by treating each equally, that is we assign probabilities in proportion to the number of configurations. This is the equiprobable assignment of probabilities referred to earlier. We may also **tilt** probability distributions by weighing configurations not equally but with different weights to allow some features of structures to affect the probability assignment differently. Some examples are in later sections.

10.2　　Three classes of transition rates

Three distinct classes of random combinatorial structures are called assemblies, multisets, and selections by Arratia and Tavaré. We next show how these three types generate three different types of stationary probability distributions.

10.2.1　Selections

Let $N(n, \mathbf{a})$ denote the number of distinct configurations compatible with the partition vector **a** with $\sum i a_i = n$. In closed models, the total number of agents or basic units is fixed at n. Perhaps the simplest and best-known model of agents (in this case particles) separating into two clusters (two urns) is the simple birth-and-death process or Ehrenfest (urn) model found in elementary probability or physics textbooks. See Kelly (1979, Sec. 1.4), or Costantini and Garibaldi (1979) for the urn model. In Aoki (1996a, p. 140), it is used as a basis to build a binary choice model in which each of n agents chooses one of two alternatives subject to aggregate externalities, that is, feedback effects of choices made by all the agents taken together. In this example, there are only two clusters, where $a_k = 1$ and $a_{n-k} = 1$ for $k = 0, 1, \ldots, n$, and cluster sizes change at most by one in a small time interval. The transition rates are specified by

$$w(k, k+1) = \lambda(n - k), \qquad 0 \le k \le n,$$

and

$$w(k, k-1) = \mu k, \qquad 1 < k \le n,$$

where λ and μ are positive parameters. The graph of this simple random-walk model is a tree, and the model satisfies the detailed-balance conditions (Kelly 1979, Lemma 1.5). Hence, the process has a steady-state probability distribution, obtained by solving the first-order difference equation generated by the detailed-balance conditions

$$\pi(k) = B\left(\frac{\lambda}{\mu}\right)^k \binom{n}{k},$$

where B is a normalizing constant, determined by the normalization requirement that the probabilities sum to one, and given by $B = (1 + \lambda/\mu)^{-n}$.

In a slightly more complicated process with K types or categories, consider the entry rate

$$w(\mathbf{n}, \mathbf{n} + \mathbf{e}_i) = \lambda(m_i - n_i),$$

for $0 \le n_i \le m_i$, $i = 1, 2, \ldots, K$, where the state vector is $\mathbf{n} = (n_1, n_2, \ldots, n_K)$. Here, m_i is the maximum number of agents that can occupy a type i box, or cluster. For example, it might be that opportunities that open up in some specific sector can be taken up by at most m_i firms. A similar interpretation is possible in declining sectors of the economy where no more capacity is being added but some may be being, dismantled. See our discussion of multisets in the next subsection.

The exit rate is

$$w(\mathbf{n}, \mathbf{n} - \mathbf{e}_j) = \mu n_j,$$

$i = 1, 2, \ldots, K$. The detailed balance conditions holds,

$$\pi(\mathbf{n})w(\mathbf{n}, \mathbf{n} - \mathbf{e}_j) = \pi(\mathbf{n} - \mathbf{e}_j)w(\mathbf{n} - \mathbf{e}_j, \mathbf{n}).$$

Solving it straightforwardly by assuming that transition rates are simple in the sense of Kingman, that is, assuming that $\pi(\mathbf{n}) = \prod_i \pi(n_i)$, we obtain

$$\pi(\mathbf{n}) = B \prod_j C_{m_j, n_j} \left(\frac{\lambda}{\mu}\right)^{n_j},$$

where $C_{a,b} = a!/[(b!(a-b)!]$ denotes a binomial coefficient, and B is the normalization constant. Here the factor depending on λ/μ may be absorbed into the constant, since it appears with power $n = \sum_j n_j$, which is fixed.

In terms of clusters, out of m_i objects of size i, a_i are chosen for each size $i, i = 1, 2, \ldots, n$, to give the count of configurations in selections:

$$N(n, \mathbf{a}) = I_{\sum_i i a_i = n} \prod_{i=1}^{n} \binom{m_i}{a_i}.$$

Let $p(n)$ be the total number of structures of size n:

$$p(n) := \sum_{w(n)} N(n, \mathbf{a}),$$

where $w(n) = \{\mathbf{a} : \sum_i i a_i = n\}$. Counting each possibility equally, the probability of the partition vector $\mathbf{a}$ is given by $N(n, \mathbf{a})/p(n)$.

10.2.2   Multisets

The next class of random combinatorial structures is called multisets in the combinatorics literature; see Bollobás (1985).[6]

We first discuss the equilibrium distribution using the empirical distribution, that is, by specifying transition rates in terms of $\mathbf{n}$. Then, we describe the distribution in terms of partition vectors.

Suppose that there are K types of agents and $n = n_1 + \cdots + n_K$, where n_i is the number of agents of type i. Agents may change their types as time passes. Assume that the relevant transition rates are given by the entry and exit probability intensities, simple in the sense of Kingman (1969), that is,

$$w(\mathbf{n}, \mathbf{n} + \mathbf{e}_k) = \psi_k(n_k) = c_k(n_k + f_k)$$

for $n_k \geq 0$, with the f's all positive, and

$$w(\mathbf{n}, \mathbf{n} - \mathbf{e}_j) = \phi_j(n_j) = d_j n_j,$$

$n_j \geq 1$. Assume also that the transition intensity for changing types or groups is given by

$$w(\mathbf{n}, \mathbf{n} - \mathbf{e}_j + \mathbf{e}_k) = \lambda_{j,k} d_j n_j c_k(n_k + f_k),$$

---

[6] A multiset is a function μ on a set with K elements, $\{y_1, y_2, \ldots, y_K\}$, with natural numbers as values, $\mu(y_i) = n_i$. The number n_i is called multiplicity of y_i in the literature of random graphs.

with $\lambda_{j,k} = \lambda_{k,j}$, and where $j, k = 1, 2, \ldots, K$. Agents move from cluster j to k at this rate. The constants $\lambda_{j,k}$ are not important, since they cancel out in the difference equation for the equilibrium distribution obtained by applying the detailed-balance conditions. We may think of this transition rate as $w(\mathbf{n}, \mathbf{n} - \mathbf{e}_j)w(\mathbf{n} - \mathbf{e}_j, \mathbf{n} - \mathbf{e}_j + \mathbf{e}_k)$ or $w(\mathbf{n}, \mathbf{n} + \mathbf{e}_k)w(\mathbf{n} + \mathbf{e}_k, \mathbf{n} - \mathbf{e}_j + \mathbf{e}_k)$, corresponding to the event of an agent leaving group j, followed by an agent entering cluster k. Costantini and Garibaldi (2000) specify the transitions in terms of the conditional probabilities as follows. The entry rate is given by

$$P(\mathbf{n} + \mathbf{e}_k | \mathbf{n}) = \frac{f_k + n_k}{\sum_k f_k + n},$$

the exit rate by

$$P(\mathbf{n} - \mathbf{e}_j | \mathbf{n}) = \frac{n_j}{n}.$$

The normalization constant follows from the condition that the conditional probabilities sum to one.

The rate for the joint event is specified by

$$P(\mathbf{n} - \mathbf{e}_j + \mathbf{e}_k | \mathbf{n}) = P(\mathbf{n} - \mathbf{e}_j | \mathbf{n}) P(\mathbf{n} - \mathbf{e}_j + \mathbf{e}_k | \mathbf{n} - \mathbf{e}_j).$$

The vector $\mathbf{n}$ as the conditioning variable in the last term is dropped, by the assumption of Markov processes.

An exit and an entry in either order give the difference equations of the same time structure as the original one in the case of simple probabilities of Kingman:

$$\pi_j(n_j)\pi_k(n_k)w(\mathbf{n}, \mathbf{n} - \mathbf{e}_j + \mathbf{e}_k) = \pi_j(n_j - 1)\pi_k(n_k + 1)w(\mathbf{n} - \mathbf{e}_j + \mathbf{e}_k, \mathbf{n}),$$

except for the time index, which is shifted by one.

Let $\pi(\mathbf{n})$ be the steady-state distribution of $\mathbf{n}$. Since the transition rates are assumed to be simple, we look for the equilibrium distribution in product form as in Pollett (1986). So we posit $\pi(\mathbf{n}) = \prod_{i=1}^{K} \pi_i(n_i)$. The detailed-balance conditions may be written more symmetrically as

$$\pi(\mathbf{n} + \mathbf{e}_j)w(\mathbf{n} + \mathbf{e}_j, \mathbf{n} + \mathbf{e}_k) = \pi(\mathbf{n} + \mathbf{e}_k)w(\mathbf{n} + \mathbf{e}_k, \mathbf{n} + \mathbf{e}_j).$$

Separating out the expressions in the detailed-balance condition into those depending on j and on k, both must equal a constant. Thus, we obtain the relations

$$\pi_j(n_j) = \kappa \frac{n_j - 1 + f_j}{n_j} \pi_j(n_j - 1),$$

where κ is some constant. (We actually obtain relations for $\pi_k(n_k + 1)$ and $\pi_k(n_k)$, which are identical except for the time index. They lead to the same expression for $\pi_k(n_k)$.)

Iterating this recursion, we obtain

$$\pi_j(n_j) = \kappa C_{n_j+f_j-1,n_j} g_j^{n_j} = \kappa C_{-f_j,n_j} (-g_j)^{n_j},$$

with $g_j = c_j/d_j$, and where κ is the normalizing constant, which is determined by the condition $\sum_{n_j \geq 0} \pi_j(n_j) = \kappa(1 - g_j)^{-f_j} = 1$. Here, we use the identity

$$C_{-f_j,n_j} = C_{f_j+n_j-1,n_j} (-1)^{n_j}$$

and the binomial expansion of $(1 - g_j)^{-f_j}$. We obtain the equilibrium probability distribution for the number of type j agents as

$$\pi_j(n_j) = C_{-f_j,n_j} (1 - g_j)^{f_j} (-g_j)^{n_j}.$$

This is a negative binomial distribution.

For simpler demonstration of our procedure, suppose that $g_j = g$ for all j. Then, the product form of $\pi(\mathbf{n})$ can be written as

$$\pi(\mathbf{n}) = \left(-\sum_n f_k \right)^{-1} \prod_{j=1}^{K} \binom{-f_j}{n_j}. \tag{10.1}$$

We see this by expanding $(1 - g)^{-\sum_j f_j} = \prod_j (1 - g)^{-f_j}$. The reader should note that this joint probability distribution is free of the parameters g and the λ's. The latter drop out of the difference equation for the πs.

We can also write the joint probabilities as

$$\pi(\mathbf{n}) = \frac{n!}{f^{[n]}} \prod_{j=1}^{K} \frac{f_j^{[n_j]}}{n_j!},$$

where $f = \sum_j f_j$ and $a^{[b]} = \Gamma(a + b)/\Gamma(a)$. This is called a generalized Pólya distribution.

We may interpret this distribution as a multiset having exactly n_i different objects of size i. In multisets, the parameters f_j are important in specifying the entry transition rates. The f term or (the term containing f) is the immigration term in the birth–death-with-immigration model. More generally, in economic models, it represents effects that encourage entry and that are independent of the number of agents in the cluster. Such effects may be policy-related, or may represent aggregate effects of choices by agents, that is, some kind of field effects generated by the total patterns of decisions at previous periods in discrete-time models, or of niche effects that affect only some sectors of the economies, not the whole economies.

Kelly (1979, Chap. 7) has one genetic example. In his model, one unit dies at random, that is, with equal probability for each type. This specifies the exit rate as

$$\phi_j(n_j) = \mu n_j / n.$$

This unit is replaced with a new units (to keep the total number of units constant), which is chosen at random from the remaining $n - 1$ units. With probability $1 - u$, it is of the same type as the parent that just died. With probability u it is a different type chosen randomly from the remaining $K - 1$ types. This specifies the entry rate as

$$\psi_k(n_k) = \frac{n_k(1 - u) + (n - 1 - n_k)u/(K - 1)}{n - 1},$$

i.e., $c_k = [1 - uK/(K - 1)]/(n - 1)$ and

$$f_k = \frac{(n - 1)u}{K(1 - u) - 1},$$

for all k, i.e., we set $f_k = f$ in this example. Note that it goes to zero as K goes to infinity, while Kf remains finite.

This "story" for the transition rate is not important. What is important is that the entry rate is defined to satisfy the requirement that f_k goes to zero as K tends to infinity, while Kf_k approaches some positive number θ. In the population-genetics example u goes to zero as n tends to infinity in such a way that $n \times u$ approaches some positive constant θ, that is, Kf approaches θ as n becomes very large. In the economic context, when K becomes large, whatever encouragement or inducement there is to enter a particular type of cluster, f, becomes very small, although the total effect of entering some sector, Kf, remains nonzero. We return to this point when we discuss the Ewens distribution. We provide one example of macroeconomic business cycles later in Section 10.5.

As in selections, we can describe the resulting patterns in terms of partition vectors. Let m_i be the number of objects of size i in the multisets. Then the number of configurations is given by

$$N(n, \mathbf{a}) = I_{(\sum_i ia_i = n)} \prod_{i=1}^{n} \binom{m_i + a_i - 1}{a_i},$$

where the binomial coefficient counts the number of ways a_i indistinguishable balls can be put into m_i identical (or delabeled and hence indistinguishable) boxes.[7] For example, this happens in the Bose–Einstein allocation or statistics; see Aoki (1996a, p. 13).

We next sum the numbers of configurations:

$$p(n, k) := \sum_{w(n,k)} \prod_{i=1}^{n} \binom{m_i + a_i - 1}{a_i},$$

---

[7] Note that $\binom{n + f - 1}{n}$ is the number of ways n identical balls can be put into f identical boxes.

where $w(n, k) := \{\mathbf{a} : \sum_i i a_i = n, \sum a_i = k\}$. As in the class of selections the probability of the partition vector $\mathbf{a}$ is given by $N(n, \mathbf{a})/p(n)$, where $p(n) = \sum_{w(n)} N(n, \mathbf{a})$, with $w(n) = \bigcup_{k=1}^n w(n, k)$. More on the method of summation later.

10.2.2.1 Capacity-limited processes

In some circumstances, an opportunity opens up in some submarkets and is taken up by several firms, or by only one firm, as described in Sutton (1997). In such cases, we think of boxes, that is, types, which at most a few economic entities can occupy – say, one, when the capacity of the type is one. This reminds one of Fermi–Dirac allocations or statistics.

Such capacity-limited processes may be modeled in our multiset entry-rate specification by taking integer f_k negative. As an example, suppose that $w(\mathbf{n}, \mathbf{n} + \mathbf{e}_k) = c_k(n_k - d)$, with some $d > 0$. Recalling the parallels with conditional probabilities,

$$\Pr(\mathbf{n} + \mathbf{e}_k | \mathbf{n}) = \frac{n_k - d}{n - Kd},$$

where the denominator is there for normalization. Writing this expression as $(d - n)/(Kd - n)$ with $d \geq n_k$ and $Kd - n > 0$, we arrive at the capacity-limited exit rate. The equilibrium distribution is a hypergeometric distribution.

10.2.3   Assemblies

In the random combinatorial structures called assemblies, m_i is the number of distinct structures of size i. The set of agents is partitioned into blocks, and for each block of size i, one of m_i possible structures is chosen. A simple noneconomic example is permutations of n symbols, in which we decompose a permutation into a product of cycles of length i. For example, with $n = 5$, let the permutation π be such that it rearranges $(1, 2, 3, 4, 5)$ into $(3, 2, 1, 5, 4)$. This is expressed as $\pi(1) = 3, \pi(2) = 2, \pi(3) = 1, \pi(4) = 5$, and $\pi(5) = 4$. It has the cycle decomposition $\pi = (1, 3)(2)(4, 5)$, because it takes 3 into 1, 1 into 3, 4 into 5, and 5 into 4, while 2 is invariant. There is one cycle of length 1, and two cycles of length 2, i.e., $a_1(5) = 1, a_2(5) = 2$, and the other a's are all zero, where $a_i(5)$ denotes the number of cycles of length i of permutations of 5 symbols. A cycle of length i has $(i - 1)!$ structures.

Let $N(n, \mathbf{a})$ be the number of configurations of n agents with partition vector $\mathbf{a}$, having a_i components of size i. For assemblies we have

$$N(n, \mathbf{a}) = I_{(\sum i a_i = n)} n! \prod_{i=1}^n \frac{m_i^{a_i}}{(i!)^{a_i} a_i!}.$$

To understand this expression, recall that the number of ways to partition the

n-set into blocks of specified sizes is given by $n!/\prod_i (i!)^{a_i} a_i!$, and the number of ways to assign the additional structures is equal to $\prod_i m_i^{a_i}$.

As usual, we sum $p(n) = \sum_{w(n)} N(n, \mathbf{a})$, and assign

$$\Pr(\mathbf{a}) = \frac{N(n, \mathbf{a})}{p(n)}.$$

This number is also computed in van Lint and Wilson (1992, Theorem 14.2) by a generating-function method.

In the case of permutations, the cycles are the components, and the number of different structures of cyclic permutations of i items is $m_i = (i - 1)!$. Hence, the expression $m_i^{a_i}/(i!)^{a_i} = 1/(i)^{a_i}$, and we recognize Cauchy's formula

$$\frac{n!}{\prod_j (j)^{a_j} a_j!}$$

for the number of permutations of size n, having cyclical products specified by the partition vector, in the above expression.

10.2.3.1 Internal configurations of assemblies

Denote by π a partition of an n-set, $[n] = \{1, 2, \ldots, n\}$, into parts. For example partition into k parts means that $[n] = \{1, 2, \ldots, n\}$ is partitioned into k blocks or subgroups, $\pi = \{B_1, B_2, \ldots, B_k\}$, such that $B_i \cap B_j = \emptyset$ when $i \neq j$, and $\bigcup B_j = [n]$.

We call the partition π type $\mathbf{a}$, or say that π has partition vector $\mathbf{a}$, when the partition vector associated with the blocks is $\mathbf{a}$. That is, a_i of the blocks have exactly i elements each. We denote by $|\pi|$ the number of blocks in π. We then have $|\pi| = \sum a_i$, and $n = \sum i a_i$.

Suppose that subsets or blocks of size i can be in one of m_i distinct configurations or structures. We say that blocks have **structure M** with the exponential generating function

$$M(x) := \sum_{i \geq 1}^{\infty} \frac{m_i x^i}{i!}.$$

The n set has a **compound structure**, $S(M)$, when it is split into parts and each part has structure of type M. van Lint and Wilson (1992) count the number of internal structure of the n-set as follows. (At the end of this section we discuss an example of Stirling numbers of the second kind, $S(n, k)$, which is the number of partitions of $[n]$ with k blocks.)

For some integer-valued function $f(i)$ such as $f(i) = m_i$, where m_i is the number of labeled (that is, distinguishable) structures on a set of size i, let its generating function be denoted by

$$h(n) = \sum_{\pi} f(1)^{a_1} f(2)^{a_2} \cdots f(n)^{a_n},$$

where the summation is over all partitions with the same partition vector **a**, and define the exponential generating function of this sequence

$$H(x) = \sum_{1}^{\infty} \frac{h(n)x^n}{n!}.$$

Finally, let

$$G(x) = \sum_{1}^{\infty} \frac{x^i}{i!} = \exp x - 1.$$

Then, we have

Proposition. $H[M(x)] = \exp M(x) - 1.$

This is in van Lint and Wilson (1992, Theorem 14.2), and can also be proved by direct calculation of $G[M(x)]$:

$$G[M(x)] = \sum_{k \geq 1} \left[\sum_{i \geq 1} \frac{m_i x^i}{i!} \right]^k \frac{1}{k!}.$$

By comparing the coefficients of $x^n/n!$ we can express $h(n)$ in terms of the ms:

$$N(n, \mathbf{a}) = I_{\sum i a_i = n} n! \frac{m_i^{a_i}}{(i!)^{a_i} a_i!}.$$

The right-hand side of the expression for $G[M(x)]$ is

$$\sum_{k \geq 1} \frac{1}{k!} \sum \frac{m(b_1)m(b_2) \cdots m(b_k)}{b_1! b_2! \cdots b_k!} x^{b_1 + b_2 + \cdots b_k},$$

where we write for convenience $m(i) = m_i$, and the inner summation is over the k-tuples $(b_1, b_2, \ldots, b_k)$ with the same partition vector. Noting that $\sum_1^k b_i = \sum_1^n i a_i = n$, the inner sum becomes

$$x^n \frac{c(\mathbf{a})}{(1!)^{a_1}(2!)^{a_2} \cdots (n!)^{a_n}} m(1)^{a_1} m(2)^{a_2} \cdots m(n)^{a_n},$$

where $c(\mathbf{a})$ is the number of distinct k-tuples $(b_1, \ldots, b_k)$ with exactly the same partition vector **a**, that is,

$$c(a_1, \ldots, a_n) = \frac{k!}{a_1! a_2! \cdots a_n!}.$$

Therefore, the coefficient of $x^n/n!$ is given by $N(n, \mathbf{a})$ of the theorem.

Example.   Let the structure M be $m_i = \gamma$ for all i. Recall that the number of k-part unordered partitions of n is given by the Stirling number of the second kind, $S(n, k)$. Therefore, we have $h(n) = \sum_{k \geq 1} S(n, k) \gamma^k$. The theorem of van Lint and Wilson says that

$$1 + \sum_{n \geq 1} \frac{S(n, k) x^n \gamma^k}{n!} = \exp\left[\gamma \sum_{n \geq 1} \frac{x^n}{n!}\right].$$

Set γ to 1, then we obtain

$$1 + \sum_{n \geq 1} \sum_{k \geq 1} \frac{S(n, k) x^n}{n!} = \exp(e^x - 1),$$

or

$$\frac{(e^x - 1)^k}{k!} = \sum_{n \geq k} \frac{S(n, k) x^n}{n!}.$$

This recursion relation is obtained in another way in Section A.5.

10.3   Transition-rate specifications in a partition vector

When an agent leaves a group of j agents, the number of clusters of size j is reduced by one and that of size $j - 1$ increases by one, that is, a_j is reduced by one and a_{j-1} increases by one. Unlike the transition-rate expressions in terms of $\mathbf{n}$, an entry of one agent into a cluster of size i in terms of the partition vector is denoted by $w(\mathbf{a}, \mathbf{a} + \mathbf{u}_i)$, with $\mathbf{u}_i := \mathbf{e}_i - \mathbf{e}_{i-1}$, where $\mathbf{e}_0$ is vacuous. Exit from a cluster of size j by one agent is expressed by $w(\mathbf{a}, \mathbf{a} - \mathbf{u}_j)$. The next example illustrates this.

In Section 10.5.1, we describe the transition rate of a type change which we specify as a composite event of

$$P(\mathbf{a} - \mathbf{u}_j | \mathbf{a}) = \frac{j a_j}{n},$$

and

$$P(\mathbf{a} - \mathbf{u}_j + \mathbf{u}_i | \mathbf{a} - \mathbf{u}_j) = \frac{f + (i - 1) a_{i-1}}{K f + n - 1}.$$

See the Ewens sampling formula description in Section 10.5.2.

10.4   Logarithmic series distribution

In this section, we connect the (ordered) market-share distributions with Zipf's distributions and the like used in the economics literature on size distributions.

Kelly (1979) used a birth-and-death process with immigration to study family sizes and clustering of agents in social environments such as at cocktail parties. His models may be reinterpreted in terms of agents of different types in the spirit of this chapter. The state space of a continuous-time Markov process is $\mathbf{a} = (a_1, a_2, \ldots)$, where only a finite number of components are nonzero.

A birth in a collection of categories with j agents may be interpreted as one agent changing his type, i.e., moving from a category that contains j agents to form a new category with $j + 1$ agents, i.e., $\mathbf{a}$ changes into

$$\mathbf{a} + \mathbf{u}_{i+1} = (a_1, \ldots, a_{j-1}, a_j - 1, a_{j+1} + 1, \ldots).$$

A death in a category with j agents means that $\mathbf{a}$ changes into

$$\mathbf{a} - \mathbf{u}_i = (a_1, \ldots, a_{j-1} + 1, a_j - 1, a_{j+1}, \ldots).$$

The boundary condition is $\mathbf{a}$ changing into $(a_1 + 1, a_2, \ldots)$ when an agent of a new type enters and when a single agent departs $(a_1 - 1, a_2, \ldots)$.

In a simple case of constant birth rate λ and death rate μ with immigration rate $\lambda\nu$, Kelly has established that the equilibrium distribution is given by

$$p(\mathbf{a}) = \text{const} \times \prod_{j=1}^{\infty} \frac{\beta_j^{a_j}}{a_j!},$$

where

$$\beta_j = \nu \frac{x^j}{j}, \qquad x = \lambda/\mu,$$

and where x is assumed to be less than one, is a stationary distribution for $\mathbf{a} = (a_1, a_2, \ldots)$, where a_j is either the number of types containing exactly j agents, or the number of agents of type j, depending on the interpretation. Note that

$$E(a_j) = \beta_j.$$

The random variable a_j is Poisson with a mean that is inversely related to j, and is called a logarithmic series distribution in Watterson (1976).

To extend this model to market-share models, we follow Watterson in part, and assume that the components a_i of the partition vector are independent Poisson random variables with mean

$$E(a_i = j) = \theta \frac{x^j}{j},$$

where $\theta^{-1} = -\ln(1 - x)$, with x less than one.

From the assumption, we have

$$P\{a_1, a_2, \ldots, a_n\} = \exp\left\{-\theta \sum_{i=1}^{n} \frac{x^i}{i}\right\} \prod_{j=1}^{n} \left(\frac{\theta x^j}{j}\right)^{a_j} \frac{1}{a_j!},$$

subject to the constraints

$$\sum_{j=1}^{n} a_j = K,$$

and

$$\sum_{j=1}^{n} ja_j = n.$$

Using the dummy variable s_j, the joint probability generating function of these random variables is

$$E\left\{\prod_{j=1}^{n} s_j^{a_j}\right\} = \prod_{j=1}^{n} \exp\left\{\frac{\theta x^j}{j}(s_j - 1)\right\}.$$

Set $s_j = s^j$. Then

$$E(s^n) = \exp\left(-\theta \sum \frac{x^j}{j}\right) \exp\left(\theta \sum \frac{(xs)^j}{j}\right),$$

since $\sum_j ja_j = n$. We can use $(1 - xs)^{-\theta}$ for the second exponential expression, since the powers of s match up to the nth in our generating-function calculations. The coefficient of s^n yields

$$P\left(\sum ja_j = n\right) = \exp\left(-\theta \sum \frac{x^j}{j}\right)_{n+\theta-1}C_n x^n,$$

where we use the relation between the negative binomial and binomial coefficients

$$_{-\theta}C_n(-x)^n = {}_{n+\theta-1}C_n x^n.$$

We thus recover the Ewens formula by dividing the joint probability by the above:

$$P\{a_1, a_2, \ldots, a_n | n\} = \frac{1}{_{n+\theta-1}C_n} \prod \left(\frac{\theta x^j}{j}\right)^{a_j} \frac{1}{a_j!}.$$

By setting s_j to s, we obtain

$$E(s^K) = \exp\left(-\theta \sum \frac{x^j}{j}\right)(1 - x)^{-\theta s}.$$

After replacing s_j by $s\phi^j$ and proceeding analogously, we use

$$E(s^K \phi^n) = \exp\left(-\theta \sum \frac{x^j}{j}\right)(1 - x\phi)^{-\theta s}$$

to obtain

$$E(s^K|n) = \frac{\Gamma(n + \theta s)}{\Gamma(\theta s)} \frac{\Gamma(\theta)}{\Gamma(n + \theta)}.$$

By taking the derivative with respect to s, and setting it equal to one, we can extract the expression for $E(K = k)$ in terms of the unsigned Stirling number of the first kind. See Hoppe (1987).

By replacing s_j with $s_j \phi^j$ in the probability generating function of the as, differentiating k_j times $E(\prod(s_j)^{a(j)} \phi^{ja(j)}|N)$ with respect to s_j, and setting the result equal to 1, we have

$$E\{(a(j))_{k_j}|n\} = \phi^M \prod \frac{(\theta/j)^{k_j} \exp(\theta \sum \phi^j/j)}{{}_{n+\theta-1}C_n},$$

where $M = \sum jk_j$, and where $(m)_k = m(m - 1)\cdots(m - k + 1)$. Up to terms of degree n in ϕ, the exponential term agrees with $(1 - \phi)^{-\theta}$, in which ϕ^{n-M} has the coefficient ${}_{n-M+\theta-1}C_{n-M}$. Note that $k_1 + 2k_2 + \cdots + nk_n = M \leq n$.

10.4.1   Frequency spectrum of the logarithmic series distribution

A special case is obtained by setting $k_j = 1$, all other ks being zero:

$$E(a_j|n) = \frac{\theta}{j} \frac{{}_{n-j+\theta-1}C_{n-j}}{{}_{n+\theta-1}C_n}.$$

When we evaluate the right-hand side by approximating the factorials by the Stirling's formula, it is seen to be approximately equal to

$$\frac{\theta}{j}\left(\frac{1 - \frac{j}{n+\theta-1}}{1 - \frac{j}{n}}\right)^{n-j}\left(\frac{n}{n+\theta-1}\right)^j\left(1 - \frac{j}{n+\theta-1}\right)^{\theta-1}.$$

The second and the third factors converge to 1 as n become large. The last factor converges to $(1 - j/n)^{\theta-1}$. Therefore we recover an approximate expression for the frequency spectrum, which is defined to be the expected value of the clusters of size j,

$$E(a_j|n) \approx \theta x^{-1}(1 - x)^{\theta-1}\,dx,$$

where x is the relative frequency j/n and dx is approximated by $1/n$. See further discussions in Section 10.8.

10.5   Dynamics of clustering processes

An organization in category i may move up or down to category j in some small time interval. Transition rates $w(i, j)$ specify the probability intensity of such a move. Once such transition rates are specified for all possible moves, all the machinery in connection with the master-equation solutions can, in principle, be employed to calculate probability densities for stationary or nonstationary accumulation or decumulation processes. This is how one would address growth problems. Examples of growth processes described in terms of the partition vectors are found in Kelly (1979, Chap. 8). Some basic elements of this approach have already been explained. We add further detail and explanations next.

10.5.1   Examples of clustering-process distributions

The first example is in Kelly (1979). Instead of the biological interpretation he gives, we think of it as a model of a sector of the economy in which an opportunity for a submarket opens up and a firm of size one enters. This is modeled by a transition rate

$$w(\mathbf{a}, \mathbf{a} + \mathbf{e}_1) = \nu\lambda,$$

with positive constants ν and λ, that is, all entrants are scaled to be of unit size. In addition, an organization of size j may grow by a unit to become size $j + 1$. The probability intensity of this event is modeled as

$$w(\mathbf{a}, \mathbf{a} + \mathbf{u}_{j+1}) = \lambda j a_j,$$

where we define $\mathbf{u}_{j+1} := \mathbf{e}_{j+1} - \mathbf{e}_j$, because an agent joining a cluster of size j causes the number of clusters of size $j + 1$ to increase by one, and that of size j to decrease by one. The vector $\mathbf{u}_1$ is the same as $\mathbf{e}_1$.

The organization also may become smaller by a unit. Assume that

$$w(\mathbf{a}, \mathbf{a} - \mathbf{u}_j) = \mu j a_j$$

for $j \geq 1$, where $\mathbf{e}_0 = 0$.

The equilibrium probability distribution is obtained, as usual, by the application of the detailed-balance conditions to be

$$\pi(\mathbf{a}) = \left(1 - \frac{\lambda}{\mu}\right)^\nu \prod_{j=1}^\infty \frac{\beta_j^{a_j}}{a_j!},$$

where

$$\beta_j = \frac{\nu}{j}\left(\frac{\lambda}{\mu}\right)^j.$$

The identity due to Kendall (1967),

$$(1 - x)^{-\theta} = \prod_{j}^{\infty} \exp \left(\frac{\theta x^j}{j} \right),$$

is used again to calculate the normalizing constant. This expression shows that the random variables $a_1, a_2, \ldots$ are independent, each with Poisson distribution with mean β_j.

Instead of organizations growing or decaying by unit amounts, we may model the process of merger, acquition, or breakups of large firms more directly. Here, we refer to a cluster of size r as an r-cluster.

For the conditional-probability setup, we follow Costantini and Garibaldi (1979, 1989) and posit

$$P(\mathbf{a} - \mathbf{u}_j + \mathbf{u}_i | \mathbf{a} - \mathbf{u}_j) = \frac{f + (i - 1) a_{i-1}}{Kf + n - 1},$$

where we assume that all additive parameters f_i above are the same f, and set $\theta = Kf$. We note as before that

$$P(\mathbf{a} - \mathbf{u}_j | \mathbf{a}) = \frac{j a_j}{n},$$

and for the composite event

$$P(\mathbf{a} - \mathbf{e}_i + \mathbf{e}_1 | \mathbf{a}) = \frac{\theta i a_i}{n(\theta + n - 1)}.$$

The detailed-balance conditions yield the equilibrium distribution as

$$\pi(\mathbf{a}) = \frac{n!}{\theta^{[n]}} \prod_{k} \left(\frac{\theta}{k} \right)^{a_k} \frac{1}{a_k!}.$$

This is the justly famous Ewens sampling formula (Ewens 1972, 1990), taken up in the next subsection.

Next, we adapt some examples from Kelly (1979) and Watterson (1976). There are n basic units partitioned into distinct clusters or collections, with a_i being the number of groups consisting of i units. Recall that we mean by units some basic building blocks from which objects that cluster are made up.

The transition rate $w(\mathbf{a}, \mathbf{a} + \mathbf{e}_i) = f$ represents the process in which a basic unit, or **singleton** (called an isolate in Kelly (1979, Chap. 8)) joins a group of size i at rate f, $i = 1, 2, \ldots$. The transition rate $w(\mathbf{a}, \mathbf{a} - \mathbf{e}_i) = \beta$ refers to the rate at which a unit leaves that group to become an isolate. Call a cluster of size i an i-cluster.

We assume $\mathbf{a}$ is a Markov process in which the transition rate is $w(\mathbf{a}, \mathbf{a} - \mathbf{e}_1 - \mathbf{e}_i + \mathbf{e}_{i+1}) = \alpha a_1 a_i$, $i \geq 2$. This refers to the rate at which an isolate joins an i-cluster, hence forming one more $i + 1$-cluster. For two isolates to form a new group of size 2, the transition rate is $w(\mathbf{a}, \mathbf{a} - 2\mathbf{e}_1 + \mathbf{e}_2) = \alpha a_1(a_1 - 1)$. The rate at which an i-cluster breaks up into an isolate and a cluster of size $i - 1$ is represented by $w(\mathbf{a}, \mathbf{a} + \mathbf{e}_1 + \mathbf{e}_{i-1} - \mathbf{e}_i) = i\beta a_i$, $i \geq 2$. The transition rate $w(\mathbf{a}, \mathbf{a} + 2\mathbf{e}_1 - \mathbf{e}_2) = 2\beta a_2$ refers to one cluster of size 2 dividing into two isolates. See Kelly (1979, Chap. 8)[8].

In a more general setting, consider the transition rate for one r-cluster and one s-cluster to form one u-cluster. It is written as

$$w(\mathbf{a}, \mathbf{a} - \mathbf{e}_r - \mathbf{e}_s + \mathbf{e}_u) = \lambda_{rsu} a_r a_s,$$

when $r \neq s$. When $r = s$, we specify the transition rate by

$$w(\mathbf{a}, \mathbf{a} - 2\mathbf{e}_r + \mathbf{e}_u) = \lambda_{rru} a_r(a_r - 1).$$

Finally,

$$w(\mathbf{a}, \mathbf{a} - \mathbf{e}_u + \mathbf{e}_r + \mathbf{e}_s) = \mu_{rsu} a_u$$

is the transition rate for one u-cluster breaking up into one r-cluster and one s-cluster. In the simple example described above, we have

$$\lambda_{1,i,i+1} = \alpha,$$

and

$$\mu_{1,i-1,i} = i\beta$$

for $i \geq 2$.

Assume that $\lambda_{rsu} = \lambda_{sru}$ and $\mu_{rsu} = \mu_{sru}$. We check the detailed-balance conditions and verify that the equilibrium distribution is of the form

$$\pi(\mathbf{a}) = B \prod_r \frac{c_r^{a_r}}{a_r!},$$

where B is a normalizing constant, provided there exist positive numbers $c_1, c_2, \ldots$ satisfying

$$c_r c_s \lambda_{rsu} = c_u \mu_{rsu}.$$

This is seen to be true by verifying the detailed-balance conditions

$$\pi(\mathbf{a}) w(\mathbf{a}, \mathbf{a} - \mathbf{a}_r - \mathbf{a}_s + \mathbf{a}_u) = \pi(\mathbf{a} - \mathbf{a}_r - \mathbf{a}_s + \mathbf{a}_s, \mathbf{a}).$$

---

[8] We use a_i rather than m_i used by Kelly because we use m_i to denote the number of structures later. See Arratia and Tavaré (1994).

We can easily verify that the detailed-balance conditions are satisfied. In the simple example, we note that

$$c_r = \frac{\beta}{\alpha r!}$$

satisfies the detailed-balance conditions.

For a closed model with n fixed, the equilibrium distribution

$$\pi(\mathbf{a}) = B \prod_{i=1}^{n} \frac{1}{a_i!} \left(\frac{\beta}{\alpha i!} \right)^{a_i}$$

is an example of the assemblies analyzed by Arratia and Tavaré (1994). Here $m_i = \beta/\alpha$ serves as the number of labeled structures on a set of size i, that is, the number of labeled structures in this example is independent of the size of the block. In the more general development that follows the example, if we set

$$c_r = \frac{m_r}{r!},$$

then m_r is the number of labeled structures on a set of size r.

Associate the generating function $F(x) = \sum_{r \geq 1} c_r x^r$ with this closed model, and let $G(x) = \exp F(x)$. Calculating the coefficient of x^N, we obtain

$$B_n^{-1} = \sum \prod_r \frac{c_r^{a_r}}{a_r!},$$

where the summation is over the partition vectors subject to the constraint $\sum_r r a_r = n$. A recursion for the normalizing constant is obtained by comparing the coefficients of $x G'(x) = \sum_r r c_r G(x)$, that is,

$$n B_n^{-1} = \sum_{r=1}^{n} r c_r B_{n-r}^{-1},$$

with $B_0 = 1$.

The expected number of clusters of size i is given by

$$E(a_i) = \sum a_i B_n \prod_r \frac{c_r^{a_r}}{a_r!} = \sum a_j B_n \frac{c_j^{a_j}}{a_j!} \prod_{r \neq j} \frac{c_r^{a_r}}{a_r!}$$

$$= B_n c_j \frac{c_j^{a_j-1}}{(a_j-1)!} \prod_{r \neq j} \frac{c_r^{a_r}}{a_r!} = B_n c_j B_{n-j}^{-1},$$

because $\sum_{r \neq j} r a_r + j(a_j - 1) = n - j$.

To open this model, that is, to treat n as a random variable, let an entrant be of unit size,

$$w(\mathbf{a}, \mathbf{a} + \mathbf{e}_1) = \nu,$$

and

$$w(\mathbf{a}, \mathbf{a} - \mathbf{e}_1) = \mu a_1.$$

Then, if there exist positive numbers $c_1, c_2, \dots$ such that

$$\nu = c_1 \mu,$$

and

$$c_r c_s \lambda_{rsu} = c_u \mu_{rsu},$$

then

$$\pi(\mathbf{a}) = \prod_r e^{-c_r} \frac{c_r^{a_r}}{a_r!}.$$

This shows that $\mathbf{a}$ is reversible in equilibrium, and the partition variables $a_1, a_2, \dots$ are independent Poisson random variables with mean c_r. Again, we see the truth of this by verifying the detailed-balance conditions $\pi(\mathbf{a})\nu = \pi($ $\mathbf{a} + \mathbf{e}_1)\mu(a_1 + 1)$. These are Kelly's Theorems 8.1 and 8.2.

Suppose that we have $u = r + s$, and abbreviate λ_{rsu} by λ_{rs} and similarly μ_{rsu} by μ_{rs}. Suppose also that r clusters enter or leave, instead of firms of unit size. This is modeled by

$$w(\mathbf{a}, \mathbf{a} + \mathbf{e}_r) = \nu_r,$$

and

$$w(\mathbf{a}, \mathbf{a} - \mathbf{e}_r) = \mu a_r.$$

Example. Suppose that $\lambda_{rs} = \alpha$ and $\mu_{rs} = \beta C_{r+s,r}$. The latter probability intensity reflects the number of ways a firm of size $r + s$ may break up into r- and s-clusters. From the entry we must have

$$\nu_r = c_r \mu_r$$

in addition to the usual $c_r c_s \lambda_{rs} = c_{r+s} \mu_{r,s}$.

Define the positive constants c_r by

$$c_r = \frac{\beta}{\alpha} \frac{\theta^r}{r!}.$$

Then, the relation $c_r c_s \lambda_{rs} = c_{r+s} \mu_{rs}$ is satisfied for arbitrary θ. The value of θ is determined for the open model by the relation $\nu_r = c_r \mu_r$, where r is the size of the clusters of the entrants and the breakaways.

Suppose that $\lambda_r := \lambda_{1,r-1,r} = \alpha r$ and that $\mu_r := \mu_{1,r-1,r} = \beta r$. Then

$$c_r = \beta / \alpha r,$$

and in the closed model $\sum_r r a_r = n$, the equilibrium distribution is

$$\pi(\mathbf{a}) = B_n^{-1} \prod_r \frac{1}{a_r!} \left(\frac{\beta}{\alpha r} \right)^{a_r},$$

where the normalizing constant is $B_n = C_{\beta/\alpha+n-1,n}$. This is the same as the process of birth and death with immigration discussed earlier, which becomes the Ewens distribution in the limit of N becoming infinite. Here is then another way to approach the Ewens sampling formula from the clustering process.

Other simple combinations of constant or linear expressions for λ's and μ's can be analogously analyzed.

10.5.2 Example: Ewens sampling formula

We have seen that the number of selection structures with a given partition vector $\mathbf{a}$ is given by

$$N(n, \mathbf{a}) = I_{\{\sum i a_i = n\}} \prod_i C_{m_i + a_i - 1, a_i}.$$

Let $p(n)$ be the sum of the above over all possible $\mathbf{a}$ subject to the constraint $\sum i a_i = n$, and assign probability $N(n, \mathbf{a}) / p(n)$ to this $\mathbf{a}$.

As Kelly, Ewens, and others point out, letting K go to infinity causes the probability that any given type is present in the model (samples of agents) to tend to zero. One way to avoid this is to work with order statistics, to which we return later. Here, we restate the Ewens formula in terms of the partition vector before letting K go to infinity.

To express (10.1) in terms of the a's, we note that among $n_1, n_2, \ldots, n_n$, a number a_i are equal to i, $i = 1, 2, \ldots, n$. Put differently, the product $n_1 n_2 \cdots n_n = 1^{a_1} 2^{a_2} \cdots n^{a_n}$. Also, there are $K! / a_1! a_2! \cdots a_n!$ many ways of satisfying the constraint. We rewrite the equilibrium distribution (10.1), which is written in terms of the state vector $\mathbf{n}$, in terms of the partition vector. For simplicity, take $f_k = f$ for all k. Thus, we have[9]

$$\pi(\mathbf{a}) = \frac{K!}{a_1! a_2! \cdots a_n!} C_{-Kf,n}^{-1} C_{-f,1}^{a_1} C_{-f,2}^{a_2} \cdots C_{-f,n}^{a_n}.$$

[9] If the sum of a's is $k < K$, then $K!$ in the numerator is replaced with $K!/(K-k)!$, which is the number of ways of selecting k types out of K.

If K goes to infinity and f to zero in such a way that the product Kf approaches a nonnegative constant θ, then noting that $C_{-f,j} \to (f/j)(-1)^j$, the terms involving negative binomials approach

$$\binom{\theta + n - 1}{n} \prod_j (f/j)^{a_j}.$$

In the above, the factor $(-1)^n$ combined with $\prod_j (-1)^{ja_j}$ becomes one, and we obtain

$$\pi_n(\mathbf{a}) = C_{\theta + n - 1, n}^{-1} \prod_{i=1}^{n} \left(\frac{\theta}{i}\right)^{a_i} \frac{1}{a_i!}.$$

This form was conjectured by Ewens (1972). Since then this distribution has been found in many different models. That this is a well-defined probability distribution can be verified by seeing that the expression sums to one. In verifying this we use the identity $-\ln(1 - x) = \sum_j x^j / j$, or

$$(1 - x)^{-\theta} = \prod_j e^{\theta x^j / j},$$

and compare the coefficients of x^n on both sides.

See Section 11.2, and Hoppe (1987) as well. He uses the device of urn models. In particular, after sampling n agents, the probability that the next draw is a new type, that is, the entry rate for an agent of a type not represented in the sample, is $\theta/(\theta + n - 1)$. Costantini and Garibaldi (1989, 2000) have a natural way of deriving this. Their approach is sketched in Appendix A.3.1. Kelly (1977) has derived that in a sequential sample of size n, the probability that the type of the first-drawn agent has representative i in this sample of size n is

$$\Pr(S_1 = i \,|\, n) = \frac{\theta}{n} \frac{C_{n,i}}{C_{\theta + n - 1, i}}.$$

Hoppe observes that the first agent observed carries label (type) 1. Its future occurrence in the sample can be described by a two-type Pólya urn of binomial type with success probability Beta$(1, \theta)$. Hence

$$\Pr(S_1 = i \,|\, n) = \int_0^1 C_{n-1, i-1} p^{i-1} (1 - p)^{n-i} \theta (1 - p)^{\theta - 1} \, dp.$$

When n is large, by the Stirling approximation of $n!$ and $(n - i)!$, the ratio of the binomial coefficient is approximated by $(1 - i/n)^{\theta - 1}$; hence we derive an approximate expression for this probability as

$$\Pr(S_1 = i \,|\, n) \approx \theta(1 - i/x)^{\theta - 1}.$$

10.5.3 *Dynamics of partition patterns: Example*

Here is a simple Markovian dynamics, expressed in terms of partition vectors in Kelly (1979). See also Aoki (1996a, Sec. 4.5.5) for details. Recall that a partition vector defined by

$$\mathbf{a} = \{a_1, a_2, \ldots\}$$

indicates that a_j is the number of subgroups with exactly j agents in each of them. Only a finite number of elements of $\mathbf{a}$ are nonzero, as in Shepp and Lloyd (1966), and thus the set of all partition vectors is countable. Assume that the transition rates are specified by

$$w(\mathbf{a}, \mathbf{a} + \mathbf{e}_1) = \nu\lambda(n),$$
$$w(\mathbf{a}, \mathbf{a} + \mathbf{u}_{j+1}) = ja_j\lambda(n),$$

and

$$w(\mathbf{a}, \mathbf{a} - \mathbf{u}_j) = ja_j\mu(n),$$

where ν is a constant and λ and ν are functions of n. Note that when one agent leaves a group with j people in it to join another subgroup with j people, the net effect is to reduce the number of subgroups with j agents by one and increase the number of subgroups with $j + 1$ agents in each of them. It has been suggested in the last part of Chapter 9 that this scheme may be applied to modify the model of Kiyotaki and Wright (1993) to allow money traders to hold several units of money.

In this example, n is also a random variable and has the transition rates

$$w(n, n + 1) = (\nu + n)\lambda(n),$$

and

$$w(n, n - 1) = n\mu(n).$$

These are obtained from the basic transition rates specified above by appropriate additions.

In this case there is an equilibrium probability distribution for n verifying the detailed-balance condition

$$P(n) = C^{-1} \binom{\nu + n - 1}{n} \prod_{k=1}^{n} \frac{\lambda(k - 1)}{\mu(k)},$$

where we assume that

$$C = \sum_{n=0}^{\infty} \binom{\nu + n - 1}{n} \prod_{k\geq 1} \frac{\lambda(k - 1)}{\mu(k)}$$

is finite. As an example suppose that there is a constant $\omega < 1$ such that the ratio $\lambda(k-1)/\mu(k) \leq \omega$ for $k \geq 1$. Then, the product of the ratios is bounded from above by ω^N, and $C \leq (1-\omega)^{-\nu} \leq \infty$. For simplicity, we may assume that λ and μ are constant and the ratio λ/μ is less than one.

The equilibrium probability distribution for the partition vector also exists in a similar form:

$$\Pr(\mathbf{a}) = C^{-1} \prod_{j \geq 1} \left(\frac{\nu}{j}\right)^{a_j} \frac{1}{a_j!} \left(\frac{\lambda}{\mu}\right)^{ja_j},$$

where we use the relation $\sum_i i a_i = n$. That this is a bona fide probability distribution is verified by the sum becoming one. To see this use the Kendall–Kelly identity. The detailed-balance conditions are easily verified to show the existence of the equilibrium distribution.

Note that this shows that the structure is an assembly with $m_i = (i-1)!$ $\nu(\lambda/\mu)^i$ members.

This probability has the form of the product of Poisson random variables with mean $\lambda_j = (\lambda/\mu)^j(\nu/j)$, $j = 1, 2, \ldots, N$. The products of Poisson distributions are not as special as they may at first appear. Some models in the next section have this type of equilibrium distributions. Actually, distributions of Poisson random variables, conditional on their weighted sums, arise in a fairly general context, as shown by Arratia and Tavaré (1992).

10.6   Large clusters

When a large number of agents interact in a market and form clusters or groups, the number of groups formed often depends crucially on the correlation among agents. As the level of aggregation increases, namely, as the number of agents over which averages are being formed increases, the range of correlations increases. The higher the probability that two randomly chosen agents are of the same type (use the same strategy, share the same view of the future, and so on), the smaller the number of groups in general.

A simple scalar parameter θ specifies this degree of correlatedness of two randomly chosen agents in the Ewens distribution, which we use in some of our later analysis. The closer the value of θ to zero, the larger is the probability that two randomly chosen agents are of the same type. The larger the value of θ, the more likely that two randomly chosen agents are not of the same type. We derive expressions for the expected number of clusters as a function of this parameter θ.

In the rest of this section, we treat θ as exogenously fixed, although it may quite possibly be endogenously generated in some models.

10.6.1   Expected value of the largest cluster size

Now, we assume that exchangeable agents have many choices. Denote the number of agents by n, and by K the number of choices, types, categories, or subgroups as the modeling context dictates. We regard both n and K as large. Here, they are kept fixed for ease of explanation, even though they are actually random variables in many applications.

Suppose that fractions $X_1, X_2, \ldots$ describe the population composition by types of exchangeable agents. Subscripts 1, 2, and so on have no intrinsic meaning, but are a mere convenience in referring to different clusters. Denote the largest fraction by $X_{(1)}$. Here, we follow Watterson and Guess (1977) to show how to calculate its expected value. An entirely analogous procedure, given later, can calculate the joint probability density for r order statistics of the fractions. From now on we use xs as realized values instead of X's.

By exchangeability we can assume that x_K is $x_{(1)}$, i.e., assume without loss of generality that

$$0 \leq x_i \leq x_K = 1 - x_1 - \cdots - x_{K-1}$$

for $i = 1, \ldots, K - 1$. We assume that the x's are jointly distributed on the K-dimensional simplex with a symmetric Dirichlet distribution. Readers may be puzzled by the sudden introduction of this distribution here. The use of the Dirichlet distribution is based on the deep connection of this distribution with the representation of random exchangeable partitions introduced by Kingman (1978a,b), and later expounded by Zabell (1992). We do not stop here to explain these facts, but go directly to calculate the expected size of the largest fraction governed by the Dirichlet distribution. See also Costantini and Garibaldi (2000) as well as Appendices A.7 and A.10.4 for further explanations of the connections.

Change variables from the x's to

$$y_i = x_i/(1 - x_1 - x_2 - \cdots - x_{K-1}) \leq 1.$$

Then, we have

$$E(X_{(1)}) = K \int \cdots \int x_K \phi(x_1, \ldots, x_K) \, dx_1 \, dx_2 \cdots dx_{K-1},$$

where ϕ is the symmetric Dirichlet distribution with parameter ϵ,

$$\phi(p_1, p_2, \ldots, p_K) = \frac{\Gamma(K\epsilon)}{(\Gamma(\epsilon))^K} \prod_{i=1}^{K} p_i^{\epsilon-1}.$$

See Appendix A.10 for details.

Noting that $1 - x_1 - \cdots - x_{K-1} = \left(1 + \sum_{j=1}^{K-1} y_j\right)^{-1}$, and that the Jacobian is

$$\frac{\partial \mathbf{x}}{\partial \mathbf{y}} = \left(1 + \sum_j y_j\right)^{-K}$$

by straightforward calculation, we rewrite the expectation as

$$E(X_{(1)}) = \frac{K\Gamma(K\epsilon)}{(\Gamma(\epsilon))^K} \int \cdots \int \prod_{j=1}^{K-1} y_j^{\epsilon-1} \left(1 + \sum_j y_j\right)^{-1-K\epsilon} dy_1 \cdots dy_{K-1},$$

where the range of integration is over the cube $0 \leq y_j \leq 1$, $j = 1, \ldots, K-1$. On multiplying the numerator and denominator by ϵ^{K-1}, we can regard this integral as the expected value of $(1 + Z_{K-1})^{-1-K\epsilon}$ with respect to Y_j, $j = 1, \ldots, K-1$, which are independent and identically distributed with the density $\epsilon^{K-1} \prod_{j=1}^{K-1} y_j^{\epsilon-1}$. The random variable Z_{K-1} is the sum of these independent random variables Y_j.

Although we cannot express its expected value in closed form, we can give the Laplace transform of Z_{K-1} and obtain its limit as K goes to infinity. From the independence of the Y's, it is equal to

$$E(e^{-sZ_{K-1}}) = \{E(e^{-sY_1})\}^{K-1} = \left\{ \int_0^1 e^{-sy} \epsilon y^{\epsilon-1} dy \right\}^{K-1}.$$

Write the integrand as

$$\epsilon e^{-sy} y^{\epsilon-1} = \epsilon\{y^{\epsilon-1} + (e^{-sy} - 1)y^{\epsilon-1}\},$$

and let K go to infinity and ϵ to zero while the product goes to a nonnegative value θ. We see then

$$E(e^{-sZ_{K-1}}) \rightarrow \exp\left\{ \theta \int_0^1 (e^{-sy} - 1)y^{-1}\, dy \right\}.$$

We recognize the right-hand side as the Lévy–Khinchin formula for an infinitely divisible random variable. Denote by Z the limiting random variable with the Laplace transform specified above. Thus, we arrive at the expression we are after,

$$E(X_{(1)}) = e^{\gamma\theta}\Gamma(\theta + 1)E\{(1 + Z)^{-1-\theta}\}.$$

In deriving this expression, we note that $\Gamma(K\epsilon) \rightarrow \Gamma(\theta)$, $\Gamma(\epsilon) = \Gamma(1+\epsilon)/\epsilon$, and that $\Gamma(1 + \epsilon) \approx \Gamma(1) + \Gamma'(1)\epsilon = 1 - \gamma\epsilon$, where $\gamma = -\Gamma'(1)$ is Euler's constant. See Abramovitz and Stegun (1968, (5.1.1), (5.1.11)).

Differentiate Ee^{-sZ} with respect to s and set it equal to zero to see that $E(Z) = \theta$. By Jensen's inequality we have a bound

$$E(1 + Z)^{-1-\theta} \geq (1 + \theta)^{-1-\theta},$$

from which we obtain a lower bound

$$EX_{(1)} \geq e^{\gamma\theta} \frac{\Gamma(1+\theta)}{(1+\theta)^{1+\theta}} \approx 1 - (1-\gamma)\theta,$$

where the last expression is approximately good for small θ.

The marginal probability density of the largest fraction is

$$f(x) = \theta x^{-1}(1-x)^{\theta-1}$$

for $1/2 < x \leq 1$. When x is not greater than $1/2$, the expression is more complex:

$$f(x) = \Gamma(\theta + 1)e^{\gamma\theta}x^{\theta-2}g(x^{-1} - 1),$$

where $g(\cdot)$ is the density of the random variable Z introduced above, and characterized in terms of its Laplace transform. These formulas are derived in Watterson and Guess (1977). Using them, we can give an alternative expression for the expected value of the largest fraction as

$$E(X_{(1)}) = G\Gamma(\theta)e^{\gamma\theta},$$

where

$$G := \int_0^\infty g(z)(1+z)^{-1-\theta}\, dz.$$

This follows by splitting the range of integration to calculate the expected value from 0 to $1/2$ and from $1/2$ to 1, and noting that

$$g(z) = z^{\theta-1}/\Gamma(\theta)e^{\gamma\theta},$$

where $z = (1 - x)/x$ in the range of $0 \leq x \leq 1/2$, or from zero to 1 in z.

10.6.2 *Joint probability density for the largest r fractions*

We next derive the joint probability density for the largest r fractions on the K-dimensional simplex $x_{(1)} \geq x_{(2)} \geq \cdots \geq x_{(r)}$, where x_i, $i = 1, 2, \ldots, K$, are the fractions. Denote the Dirichlet probability density on the simplex by $\phi(x_1, x_2, \ldots, x_k) = \mathcal{D}(\epsilon, K)$. Then the probability density for the first r order statistics is given by

$$f(x_1, x_2, \ldots, x_r) = K(K - 1)(K - 2) \cdots (K - r + 1)$$
$$\times \int \phi(x_1, x_2, \ldots, x_k)\, dx_{r+1} \cdots dx_{K-1},$$

where $1 \geq x_1 \geq x_2 \geq \cdots \geq x_r > 0$, and where we subsitute $x_K = 1 - x_1 - \cdots - x_{K-1}$. Carrying out the integration, we have

$$f(x_1, \ldots, x_r) = \frac{K!}{(K-r)!} \frac{\Gamma(K\epsilon)}{\Gamma(\epsilon)^K} (x_1 \cdots x_r)^{\epsilon-1} x_r^{(K-r)\epsilon-1} I,$$

where

$$I = \int \cdots \int \prod_{r+1}^{K-1} y_j^{\epsilon-1} [1 - a - x_r(y_{r+1} + \cdots + y_{K-1})]^{\epsilon-1} dy_{r-1} \cdots dy_{K-1},$$

in which the integration is carried out over the area

$$A = \{0 \leq y_j \leq 1, r + 1 \leq j \leq K - 1;$$
$$(1 - a - x_r)/x_r \leq y_{r+1} + \cdots + y_{K-1} \leq (1 - a)/x_r\},$$

where $a := x_1 + x_2 + \cdots + x_r$.

As in the case of the largest fraction, introduce a random variable Z with the density function g_{K-r-1}, which is the $(K - r - 1)$-fold convolution of the density $\epsilon y_j^{\epsilon-1}$, $j = r + 1, \ldots, K - 1$. The integral is approximately given by

$$I = \frac{\epsilon^{-(K-r)}}{x_r} g_{K-r-1} \left(\frac{1 - a}{x_r} \right).$$

Letting $K\epsilon$ approach θ, while K goes to infinity and ϵ to zero, we note that $K(K - 1) \cdots (K - r + 1)$ approaches K^r, and

$$\Gamma(\epsilon)^K = \left[\frac{\Gamma(1 + \epsilon)}{\epsilon} \right]^K,$$

which approaches $\epsilon^{-K} e^{-\gamma\theta}$, where we use the fact

$$\Gamma(1 + \epsilon) \approx 1 - \gamma\epsilon,$$

where γ is Euler's constant, $\gamma = 0.5772\ldots$.

Putting all together, we arrive at

$$f(x_1, x_2, \ldots, x_r) = \theta^r e^{\gamma\theta} \Gamma(\theta) x_r^{\theta-1} g\left(\frac{1 - a}{x_r} \right) (x_1 x_2 \cdots x_r)^{-1}$$

in the range $1 \leq x_1 \leq \cdots \leq x_r > 0$, and $\sum_1^r x_i \leq 1$.

We know from our result for the largest fraction that $f(x_1) = \theta x_1^{-1}(1 - x_1)^{\theta-1}$ for x_1 between $1/2$ and 1, that is,

$$\Gamma(1 + \theta) e^{\gamma\theta} g\left(\frac{1 - x_1}{x_1} \right) = \theta \left(\frac{1 - x_1}{x_1} \right)^{\theta-1}$$

for x_1 between $1/2$ and 1. To obtain the expression for the density in the range

$0 \leq x \leq 1/2$, we follow Watterson (1976) and differentiate the Laplace transform for the random variable Z:

$$E(e^{-sZ}) = \exp\left[\theta \int_0^1 (e^{-sz} - 1)z^{-1}\, dz\right],$$

with respect to s. Recall that this transform is derived in connection with the largest fraction. Then, divide the result by $-\theta$ to see

$$\frac{1}{\theta} \int_0^\infty e^{-sz} z g_\theta(z)\, dz = \int_0^\infty I_{(0,1]}(y)e^{-sy}\, dy \int_0^\infty e^{-sz} g_\theta(z)\, dz.$$

The right-hand side is the product of two Laplace transforms. Hence the integrand of the left-hand side is the convolution of the uniform function on the unit interval and g_θ:

$$\frac{1}{\theta} z g_\theta(z) = \int_{z-1}^z g_\theta(y)\, dy.$$

Setting z to 1, we obtain

$$g_\theta(1) = e^{-\gamma\theta} / \Gamma(\theta).$$

Differentiating the integral equation with respect to z, we derive the differential equation that determines the function recursively:

$$z g'_\theta(z) + (1 - \theta)g_\theta(z) = -\theta g_\theta(z - 1),$$

where $z \geq 0$. In the range $z \in [0, 1)$, this integro-differential equation yields the result we obtained above. In the next range $z \in [1, 2)$ we have

$$g_\theta(z) = z^{\theta-1}\left[g_\theta(1) - \theta \int_1^z g_\theta(u - 1)u^{-\theta}\, du\right].$$

Changing variable of integration to $v = 1/u$, we note that the integration above becomes

$$\int_{1/z}^1 v^{-1}(1 - v)^{\theta-1}\, dv.$$

The joint density for the two largest fractions is given by

$$f_\theta^{(2)}(x, y) = \frac{e^{\gamma\theta}\theta^2\Gamma(\theta)y^{\theta-1}}{xy} g_\theta\left(\frac{1 - x - y}{y}\right) = \frac{\theta^2}{xy}(1 - x - y)^{\theta-1}.$$

This expression is valid for the range $0 < y < x < 1$, $0 < x + y < 1$, and $x + 2y > 1$, that is, $y > (1 - x)/2$.

We know that

$$g(z) = \frac{z^{\theta-1}}{\Gamma(\theta)e^{\gamma\theta}}$$

for z between 0 and 1. For other values of z, we have a recursion

$$\frac{zg(z)}{\theta} = \int_{z-1}^{z} g(y)\, dy;$$

see Watterson and Guess (1977). Alternatively put, we have

$$g(z) = z^{\theta-1}\left[g(n)n^{1-\theta} - \theta \int_{n}^{z} g(y-1)y^{-\theta}\, dy \right]$$

in the range $n \le z < n+1$. This can be verified by direct substitution into the differential equation for g_θ.

10.7   Moment calculations

Having the joint density, we can calculate moments such as

$$J = E\left[x_{(1)}^{l} x_{(2)}^{m} \right]$$

for some positive integers l and m. Using the density expression with $r = 2$,

$$J = \theta^2 \Gamma(\theta)e^{\gamma\theta} \int\int g\left(\frac{1 - x_1 - x_2}{x_2} \right) x_1^{l-1} x_2^{m+\theta-2}\, dx_1\, dx_2.$$

Changing variables to $u = x_1$ and $v = (1 - x_1 - x_2)/x_2$,

$$J = \theta^2 \Gamma(\theta)e^{\gamma\theta} \int\int g(v)(1 + v)^{-m-\theta} u^{l-1}(1 - u)^{m+\theta+1}\, du\, dv$$

over the region $u > (1 - u)/(1 + v) \ge 0$ and $v \ge 0$.

Let $w = \max(0, (1 - 2u)/u)$. In the range of $u > 1/2$, $w = 0$. Then, a lower bound on J is obtained as

$$J \ge H\theta^2 \Gamma(\theta)e^{\gamma\theta} \int_{1/2}^{1} u^{l-1}(1 - u)^{m+\theta-1}\, du,$$

where H is a constant defined by

$$H = \int_{0}^{\infty} g(v)(1 + v)^{-m+\theta}.$$

See Watterson and Guess (1977) for approximate evaluations of these moment expressions.

10.8   Frequency spectrum

The expression of the marginal density for x larger than $1/2$ appears often in dealing with distributions of fractions, such as the Ewens distribution. The notion of frequency spectrum was introduced by Ewens (1972) as a way of expressing the average number of clusters of sizes between two specified limits, and is quite useful in calculating some possibly complicated expressions of cluster sizes in a straightforward way.

Here is a typical example of how this notion arises. Suppose we have a function of fractions

$$S = \sum_{j=1}^{K} h(x_i),$$

say, where h is some bounded and continuous function, and wish to evaluate its expected value. Its expectation is

$$E(S) = \sum E(h(x_j)) = K E h(x_1),$$

where the last equality follows by exchangeability of the random variables.

Since the marginal distribution of x_j of a Dirichlet distribution $\mathcal{D}(a_1, \ldots, a_K)$ is Beta $(a_j, \sum_{i \neq j} a_i)$, we have the marginal density for x_1 as

$$f(x_1) = \frac{\Gamma(K\epsilon)}{\Gamma(\epsilon)\Gamma((K-1)\epsilon)} x_1^{\epsilon-1}(1-x_1)^{(K-1)\epsilon-1}.$$

We use it to evaluate the expected value in a straightforward calculation. Using the relation $\Gamma(\epsilon) = \Gamma(1 + \epsilon)/\epsilon$, and letting $K\epsilon$ go to θ as ϵ goes to zero and K to infinity, we see that the expected value of S is evaluated by

$$E(S) \to \theta \int_0^1 h(x) x^{-1} (1-x)^{\theta-1} \, dx.$$

This clearly exhibits $\theta x^{-1}(1-x)^{\theta-1}$ as the probability density of x in $h(x)$. It is known as the frequency spectrum in the literature of population genetics. The same expression appears in discussions of relative sizes of basins of attraction of certain random dynamics in the physics literature with $\theta = 0.5$ (Derrida and Flyvbjerg 1987) and in the statistics literature (Aldous 1985), apparently independently. Donnelly et al. (1991) show how to obtain this as the limit of a discrete frequency spectrum with n points in random mappings of $\{1, 2, \ldots, n\}$ onto itself, where the discrete frequency spectrum is the expected value of the clusters of specified size. They show how the random mappings with $\theta = 0.5$ and the Ewens sampling formula with $\theta = 0.5$ give nearly the same order statistics for large n.

10.8.1   Definition

The expected number of types with fractions in the interval $(x, x + dx)$ is called the **frequency spectrum**. It is important in that the expected values of many variables of interest can be calculated readily in terms of it.

The mean number of types with fractions between α and β then is given by

$$\int_{\alpha}^{\beta} f(x)\, dx.$$

The particular frequency spectrum we have seen above is

$$f(x) = \theta x^{-1}(1 - x)^{\theta-1}.$$

For small x, it behaves like x^{-1}, which indicates that there are many types with small fractions. This function is not normalizable, but

$$g(x) = xf(x) = \theta(1 - x)^{\theta-1}$$

is normalizable. This function is interpreted as the probability that a randomly chosen sample is of the type with fractions between x and $x + dx$. This function is normalizable:

$$\int_{0}^{1} g(x)\, dx = 1.$$

10.8.2   Herfindahl index of concentration

In many situations, a set of fractions $\{x_i\}_1^n$, that is, a set of positive-valued variables that sum to one, $\sum_i x_i = 1$, arises naturally. For example x_i could be the "share," broadly interpreted, of firm i in some industrial sector, or the relative size of a basin of attraction.

We discuss the distribution $\Pi(Y)$ of the quantity $Y = \sum_i x_i^2$. This is called the Herfindahl index of concentration in the older industrial-organization literature. See Scherer (1980), for example. In the population-genetics literature, it is called the homozygosity and is the probability that two randomly selected genes at a given locus are identical. In ecology, the relative abundances of different species within a community are of interest. Here Y is the probability that two randomly selected individuals are of the same species. A similar interpretation is available in the industrial-organization literature: The probability that two randomly selected economic agents are of the same type is given by $\Pi(Y)$. Recall that agent types may refer to size of firms, size of shares, or other characteristics. It is also interesting that this same variable Y is treated in the physics literature by Derrida and Flyvbjerg (1987) when they discuss distributions of the relative sizes of basins of attraction of random mappings of a set of n points onto itself. Aldous (1985) also discusses this distribution.

We have earlier calculated the mean of Y, $E(Y) = 1/(1 + \theta)$, using the frequency spectrum $\theta x^{-1}(1 - x)^{\theta-1}$. The variance is obtained by calculating

$$E(Y^2) = \frac{6}{(1 + \theta)(2 + \theta)(3 + \theta)},$$

and

$$\text{var } Y = \frac{2\theta}{(1 + \theta)^2 (2 + \theta)(3 + \theta)}.$$

A simple heuristic derivation of the notion of frequency spectrum is given first. See Kingman (1978b) or Aldous (1985) for rigorous derivations.

10.8.3   A heuristic derivation

Suppose that a partition vector is distributed as the Ewens distribution. The expected value of a_j is

$$E a_j = \sum a_j \pi_n(\mathbf{a}; K_n) = \frac{n!}{\theta^{[n]}} \sum \prod_j a_j \left(\frac{\theta}{j}\right)^{a_j} \frac{1}{a_j!}.$$

We note that the terms in the summand may be rewritten as $(\theta/j) \cdot (\theta/j)^{a_j-1} \cdot [1/(a_j - 1)!]$, and—defining $\mathbf{a}' = (a_1, \ldots, a_j - 1, \ldots a_n)$, and noting that the constraints change to $\sum' i a_i = n - j$, and $\sum' a_i = K_n - 1$, where $\sum'$ indicates the summation subject to these constraints—we have

$$\sum' \prod_i \left(\frac{\theta}{i}\right)^{a'_i} \frac{1}{a'_i} = \frac{\theta^{[n-j]}}{(n - j)!},$$

and hence

$$E a_j = \frac{\theta}{j} \frac{n!}{(n - j)!} \frac{\Gamma(\theta + n - j)}{\Gamma(\theta + n)} = \theta C_{n,j} B(\theta + n - j, j),$$

where

$$B(\alpha, \beta) = \frac{\Gamma(\alpha)\Gamma(\beta)}{\Gamma(\alpha + \beta)} = \int_0^1 x^{\alpha-1}(1 - x)^{\beta-1} \, dx$$

is the Beta function. We rewrite this as

$$E a_j = \int_0^1 C_{n,j} p^j (1 - p)^{n-j} \theta p^{-1} (1 - p)^{\theta-1} dp.$$

Here, we recognize the frequency spectrum

$$f(p) := \theta p^{-1}(1 - p)^{\theta - 1}$$

in this integral.

We can justify our interpretation of the frequency spectrum given in the definition above by calculating the expected number of types in the population

$$E K_n = \sum_{j=1}^{n} E a_j = \int_{\epsilon}^{1} \sum_{j} C_{n,j} p^j (1 - p)^{n-j} f(p) \, dp$$

$$= \int_{\epsilon}^{1} f(p) \, dp,$$

where the lower limit of integration is denoted by $\epsilon = 1/n$. Note also that the summation over j equals one in the integrand. In words, the integral of the frequency spectrum from 0 to 1 gives the expected (i.e., average) number of types. We may thus interpret the expression $f(p) \, dp$ as the probability that a type exists in the population with relative frequency (fraction) between p and $p + dp$, or in $(p, p + dp)$. The expression $p f(p) = \theta(1 - p)^{\theta}$ may be interpreted as the probability that an agent drawn at random from population is of a type with fraction in $(p, p + dp)$.

To illustrate the use of this notion, suppose that type i agents constitute a fraction p_i of the whole population of agents. Then, the probability that the $(j + 1)$th draw of the agents from the population is a new type not so far sampled is given by

$$E \left[\sum_{i} (1 - p_i)^j p_i \right] = \int_{0}^{1} (1 - x)^j x \theta x^{-1} (1 - x)^{\theta - 1} \, dx = \frac{\theta}{\theta + j}.$$

This gives an interpretation of the parameter θ: The probability that the next draw from the population is a new type is smaller, the smaller the value of θ.

We describe several ways this frequency spectrum arises. One way is in connection with the residual allocation process.

To interpret the parameter θ in the frequency spectrum, we introduce sequential sampling into the relationship between the sample sizes and the numbers of different types of agents contained in the samples. Suppose we take two samples. The probability that they are of the same type is given by

$$E \left(\sum_{i} x_i^2 \right) = \theta \int^{1} x^2 x^{-1} (1 - x)^{\theta - 1} \, dx = \frac{1}{\theta + 1}.$$

Thus, the larger the value of θ, the smaller the probability that two samples are of the same type. In this sense, the parameter θ represents correlatedness of samples. For $k > 1$, we compute

$$E\left(\sum_j x_j^k\right) = \theta \int_0^1 x^k x^{-1} (1-x)^{\theta-1} \, dx = \theta \frac{\Gamma(k)\Gamma(\theta)}{\Gamma(k+\theta)}.$$

This is the probability that first k samples are all of the same type. The next expression,

$$E\left(\sum_i (1-x_i)^k x_i\right) = \theta \int_0^1 x(1-x)^k x^{-1}(1-x)^{\theta-1} \, dx = \frac{\theta}{\theta+k},$$

is the probability that the $(k+1)$st draw is a new type; hence $1 - \theta/(\theta+k) = k/(\theta+k)$ is the probability that the $(k+1)$st draw is one of the types already drawn.

10.8.4   Recursion relations

Let

$$q_{n,i} = \Pr(K_n = i).$$

We know from the above that the probability that the first j draws produce the same type is

$$q_{j,1} = \frac{\theta(j-1)!}{\theta^{[n]}},$$

where $\theta^{[n]} = \theta(\theta+1)\cdots(\theta+n-1)$. The probability that the first j samples are all of different types is

$$q_{j,j} = \frac{\theta^j}{\theta^{[n]}}.$$

The random variables $q_{n,i}$ are governed by the recursion relation

$$q_{j+1,i} = \frac{j}{\theta+j} q_{j,i} + \frac{\theta}{\theta+j} q_{j,i-1}.$$

It can be represented by

$$q_{n,i} = c(n,i) \frac{\theta^i}{\theta^{[n]}},$$

where $c(n,i)$ is the unsigned Stirling number of the first kind, because

$$c(n+1,k) = nc(n,k) + c(n,k-1),$$

which agrees with the recursion for the qs. It is the number of cycles of size k in permutations of n symbols.

10.8.5 Examples of applications

Take a sample of size n, and let K_n be the number of different types in the sample. This number may be represented as

$$K_n = \xi_1 + \xi_2 + \cdots,$$

where the random variable ξ_i is one if type i is present in the sample and zero otherwise.

Denote by p_i the relative frequency, or the fraction, of type i in the population. Then the expected number of types present in the sample of size n is

$$E(K_n) = \sum_i E(\xi_i) = \sum_i E[1 - (1 - p_i)^n | \mathbf{p}],$$

where $\mathbf{p}$ stands for the vector with components p_i. This is evaluated in terms of the frequency spectrum as

$$E(K_n) = \theta \int^1 [1 - (1 - x)^n] x^{-1} (1 - x)^{\theta - 1} \, dx.$$

We return to this expression later.

10.8.6 Discrete frequency spectrum

Donnelly et al. (1991) showed that the expected number of components of random mappings from $[n] = \{1, 2, \ldots, n\}$ to $[n]$ is

$$q_n(j) := E(K_j) = C_{n,j}(j/n)^j (1 - j/n)^{n-j} p(j),$$

where

$$p(j) = \sum_{i=1}^{j} C_{j-1,i-1}(i - 1)! j^{-i}$$

is the probability that a random mapping from $[j]$ to itself is indecomposable, i.e., has a single component. (See Katz (1955, p. 515).)

We note that $(j/n)^j$ is the probability that $\{1, 2, \ldots, j\}$ maps onto $\{1, 2, \ldots, j\}$. The factor $(1 - j/n)^{n-j}$ is the probability that $\{j + 1, \ldots, n\}$ maps onto this set. We call $q_n(j)$ the discrete frequency spectrum in direct analogy with our previous development.

As n goes to infinity, we see that

$$q_n(j) \to r(j) := j^{-1}e^{-j} \sum_{i=0}^{j-1} \frac{j^i}{i!}.$$

Note that $jr(j)$ is the probability of a Poisson random variable with mean j having values less than its mean.

If we keep $x = j/n$ fixed, and let j and n go to infinity, then

$$nq_n(j) \to \frac{1}{2}x^{-1}(1-x)^{-1/2},$$

which shows that the frequency spectrum of the random map has $\theta = 1/2$. This has been derived by Aldous (1985) and is noted also by Derrida and Flyvjberg (1987).

10.9   Parameter estimation

Ewens (1972, 1990) has shown that the number of types observed in a finite sample can serve as a sufficient statistics for the parameter θ. This can be seen by calculating $\Pr(\mathbf{a}|K_n)$ from the Ewens distribution $\Pr(\mathbf{a})$, and $\Pr(K_n = k) = c(n, k)\theta^k/\theta^{[n]}$ to be

$$\Pr(\mathbf{a}|k) = \frac{n!}{c(n, k)\prod_j j^{a_j}a_j!}.$$

Guess and Ewens (1972) have explored estimating θ.

Ewens (1972) showed that with $n = 250$, $E(K_n) \approx 4.1$ with variance about 2.9, while with $\theta = 0.4$, $E(K_n) \approx 3.5$ with variance about 2.4. These numbers are relevant to our example in Chapter 12. See his Tables I and II for more detail.

To interpret the parameter θ in the frequency spectrum, we introduce sequential sampling into the relationship between the sample sizes and the number of different types of agents contained in the samples. Suppose we take two samples. The probability that they are of the same type is given by

$$E\left(\sum_i x_i^2\right) = \theta \int_0^1 x^2 x^{-1}(1-x)^{\theta-1}\, dx = \frac{1}{\theta+1}.$$

Thus, the larger the value of θ, the smaller the probability that two samples are of the same type. In this sense, θ represents correlatedness of samples. For $k > 1$, we compute

$$E\left(\sum_j x_j^k\right) = \theta \int_0^1 x^k x^{-1}(1-x)^{\theta-1}\, dx = \theta\frac{\Gamma(k)\Gamma(\theta)}{\Gamma(k+\theta)}.$$

This is the probability that first k samples are all of the same type. The next expression,

$$E\left[\sum_i (1 - x_i)^k x_i\right] = \theta \int_0^1 x(1 - x)^k x^{-1}(1 - x)^{\theta-1}\, dx = \frac{\theta}{\theta + k},$$

is the probability that the $(k + 1)$st draw is a new type; hence $1 - \theta/(\theta + k) = k/(\theta + k)$ is the probability that the $(k + 1)$st draw is one of the types already drawn.

CHAPTER 11

Share market with two dominant groups of traders

As an application of the cluster size distribution, this chapter models the behavior of price differences in a share market in which a large number of shares of a holding company are traded.[1]

Agents in the market employ various strategies or trading rules. When we put into the same group or cluster all agents with the same strategy, trading rule, excess demand function, or the like, there typically will be many clusters in the market. For convenience of reference, we identify agents with the rules they employ, and say that agents of the same type form a **group** or **cluster**.

Clusters evolve over time as agents enter or exit the market, and also as they switch their decision rules or behavioral patterns in response to changing economic environments, such as changing market sentiments. In modeling markets, it is important to realize that it is impossible to say in advance how many clusters are going to be present in the market at any given time. We can only sample agents, that is, take a snapshot or freeze the time, and sample some numbers of agents and count the number of different strategies being used at that particular time. There can be, in principle, an infintely many potential strategies. For example, random combinations of two basic algorithms in different proportions, say, produce different strategies, because they will have different expected performance and variances or risk characteristics. New decision or trading rules will be invented in the future, and so on. This problem of not knowing the types of agents present in a market is exactly the same as the so-called sampling-of-species problem faced by statisticians in species sampling. See Zabell (1992).

To analyze the behavior of such markets, we consider order statistics of shares of types, that is, we derive distributions of the normalized sizes of the clusters in nonincreasing order, and concentrate on the largest several clusters of agents, if the size distributions are such that most probabilities are concentrated

---

[1] A preliminary version was presented at the Workshop on Economics of Heterogenous Interacting Agents, University of Genoa, Italy, June, 1999.

on the first few order statistics. Examining a few such large clusters will give us the approximate behavior of markets as a whole, as we show later in this chapter. This claim is especially true when agents are positively correlated in a sense we make precise later.

In Chapter 10, the distribution of the partition vector, which describes random partition patterns of agents over the set of trading rules, is shown to converge to the Ewens sampling formula as the number of available rules becomes very large. We examine conditions under which a large number of participants in the market form two groups on opposite sides of the market. We derive stationary distributions of clusters of agents, and look for conditions under which two dominant subgroups nearly occupy 100 percent of the shares of the market. We assume a certain entry and exit rates for a jump Markov process, and use the order statistics of the sizes of clusters, and their distributions, derived in Chapter 10 to calculate the expected shares and other macroeconomic variables.

These distributions are used, then, to infer behavior of the price differences by assigning specific trading rules for the dominant subgroups. By switching assignment of the rules to the two dominant groups, we also explain switches of the behavior of volatilities of the price differences.

We then concentrate on situations where market participants are positively correlated, which corresponds to small values of the parameter θ in the Ewens distribution. In these cases about 95 percent of the market participants belong to two largest subgroups of agents with two trading rules. Contributions of the remaining 5 percent or so of participants are ignored in examining the market behavior as a whole.

In this way, we can examine market excess demand, and price dynamics. At the end of this chapter a possibility for the existence of a power law is raised.

Our approach thus provides a stochastic generalization of a deterministic model of a share market such as Day and Huang's (1990),[2] by providing a microscopic probabilistic process for agents, changing their strategies.

11.1   Transition rates

We use both empirical distributions and partition vectors to describe the state of the market. This section employs empirical distributions. We first give the transition rates in terms of the state vector.

Suppose that there are potentially a large number K of types of agents who participate in a market. For the moment, suppose that the value of K is known. Then the vector $\mathbf{n} = (n_1, n_2, \ldots, n_K)$ describes how n agents are distributed over K types, $n = n_1 + n_2 + \cdots + n_K$. In this section we use this

---

[2] Their model is deterministic and discrete-time with two types of agents of fixed number, namely, one of each.

vector as state vector, then switch to the partition-vector description in the next section.

Suppose that we use the same set of transition rates as these in Sections 7.4 and 10.2,

$$w(\mathbf{n}, \mathbf{n} + \mathbf{e}_k) = c_k(n_k + h_k)$$

for $n_k \geq 0$, where $\mathbf{e}_k$ is the vector with unit element in the kth position and zero elsewhere,

$$w(\mathbf{n}, \mathbf{n} - \mathbf{e}_j) = d_j n_j,$$

$n_j \geq 1$, and

$$w(\mathbf{n}, \mathbf{n} - \mathbf{e}_j + \mathbf{e}_k) = \lambda_{jk} d_j n_j c_k(n_k + h_k),$$

with $\lambda_{jk} = \lambda_{kj}$, where $j, k = 1, 2, \ldots K$. We assume that $d_j \geq c_j > 0, h_j > 0$, and $\lambda_{jk} = \lambda_{kj}$ for all j, k pairs. The first transition rate specifies the entry rate to the market by agents of type k, the second the exit or departure rate from the market by type j agents, and the last the transition intensity of changing types by agents from type j to type k, that is, switching of trading rules by agents. In the specification of the entry transition rate, the term $c_k n_k$ stands for attractiveness of a large group, such as a network externality that makes it easier for others to join the cluster or group. The other term, $c_k h_k$, represents new entry to the market, which is independent of cluster size. It represents the attractiveness of the strategy to outsiders, irrespective of the number of agents who are currently using it.

The jump Markov process thus specified has the steady state or stationary distribution

$$\pi(\mathbf{n}) = \prod_{j=1}^{K} \pi_j(n_j),$$

where

$$\pi_j(n_j) = (1 - g_j)^{-h_j} \binom{-h_j}{n_j} (-g_j)^{n_j},$$

where $g_j = c_j/d_j$. These expressions are derived straightforwardly by applying the detailed-balance conditions to the transition rates.

For simplicity, suppose that $g_j = g$ for all j. Then, as we show in Chapter 10, the joint probability distribution is expressible as

$$\pi(\mathbf{n}) = \left(\frac{-\sum h_k}{n} \right)^{-1} \prod_{j=1}^{K} \binom{-h_j}{n_j}. \tag{11.1}$$

11.2   Ewens distribution

Now, we introduce the partition vector $\mathbf{a} = (a_1, a_2, \ldots, a_n)$, where a_k is the number of types or clusters with exctly k agents. Consequently, we have an inequality

$$\sum_i a_i = K_n \leq K,$$

where K_n is the number of groups or clusters formed by n agents, and

$$\sum_i i a_i = n,$$

which is an accounting identity.

To further simplify our presentation, let us suppose that $h_j = h$ for all j in (11.1). Then

$$\pi(\mathbf{n}) = \binom{-Kh}{n}^{-1} \prod_{j=1}^{K} \binom{-h}{j}^{a_j}.$$

This is so because there are a_j of the n's that equal j.

Now let K become very large to allow for the possibility of indefinitely many types. To keep the mean finite we make h very small, so that the product Kh approaches a positive constant θ. We note that the negative-binomial expression

$$\binom{-h}{j}^{a_j}$$

approaches $(h/j)^{a_j}(-1)^{j a_j}$ as h becomes smaller. Suppose $K_n = k < K$. Then, there are

$$\frac{K!}{a_1! a_2! \cdots a_n!(K-k)!}$$

many ways of realizing the vector $\mathbf{a}$. Hence,

$$\pi_n(\mathbf{a}) = \binom{-\theta}{n}^{-1} (-1)^n \frac{K!}{a_1! a_2! \cdots a_n!(K-k)!} \prod_j \left(\frac{h}{j}\right)^{a_j}. \qquad (11.2)$$

Noting that $[K!/(K-k)!] \times h^k$ approaches θ^k in the limit of K becoming infinite and h approaching 0 while keeping Kh at θ, we arrive at the Ewens distribution

$$\pi_n(\mathbf{a}) = \frac{n!}{\theta^{[n]}} \prod_{j=1}^{n} \left(\frac{\theta}{j}\right)^{a_j} \frac{1}{a_j!},$$

where $\theta^{[n]} := \theta(\theta + 1) \cdots (\theta + n - 1)$. This distribution is very well known in the genetics literature; see Ewens (1972), Kingman (1978a,b), or Johnson et al. (1997). This distribution has been investigated by Arratia and Tavaré (1992) and Hoppe (1987) among several others. Kingman (1980) states that this distribution arises in many applications. There are other ways of deriving it; see Costantini and Garibaldi (1999). We next examine some of its properties, following Watterson (1976).

11.2.1   The number of clusters and value of θ

The Ewens sampling formula has a single parameter θ, which was introduced in the previous section as the limit of Kh as K goes to infinity while h goes to zero. We introduce another interpretation here. Its value influences the number of clusters formed by the agents. Smaller values of θ tend to produce a few large clusters, while larger values produce a large number of smaller clusters.

To obtain quickly some intuitive understanding of the effects of the value of θ on the cluster size distributions, take $n = 2$ and $a_2 = 1$. All other as are zero. Then,

$$\pi_2(a_1 = 0, a_2 = 1) = \frac{1}{1 + \theta}.$$

This shows that two randomly chosen agents are of the same type with large probability when θ is small, and with small probability when θ is large.

Two extreme situations also reveal connections between the value of θ and the number of clusters. We note that the probability of n agents forming a single cluster is given by

$$\pi_n(a_j = 0, 1 \leq j \leq n - 1, a_n = 1) = \frac{(n - 1)!}{(\theta + 1)(\theta + 2) \cdots (\theta + n - 1)},$$

while the probability that n agents form n singletons is given by

$$\pi_n(a_1 = n, a_j = 0, j \neq 1) = \frac{\theta^{n-1}}{(\theta + 1)(\theta + 2) \cdots (\theta + n - 1)}.$$

With θ much smaller than one, the former probability is approximately equal to 1, while the latter is approximately equal to zero. When θ is much larger than n the opposite is true.

We can show that the probability of n agents forming k clusters is given by

$$\Pr(K_n = k) = \frac{1}{\theta^{[n]}} c(n, k)\theta^k,$$

where $c(n, k)$ is a signless Stirling number of the first kind, introduced in Appendix A.5, and is defined by

$$\theta^{[n]} = \sum_{1}^{n} c(n, k)\theta^k.$$

See Hoppe (1987) for the derivation. This number is the number of permutations of n symbols with exactly k cycles. Hoppe's urn model of the Ewens distribution makes the occurrence of this number natural.

We can use this formula to verify that the expected number of types increases with θ. As θ goes to infinity, the expected number of types approaches n, namely, total fragmentation of agents in the sample by types. For small values of θ, Ewens has shown that

$$E(K_n) = \sum_{j=0}^{n-1} \frac{\theta}{\theta + n - j} \approx 1 + \theta[\ln(n-1) + \gamma],$$

where $\gamma = 0.577$ is Euler's constant.

11.2.2 Expected values of the fractions

The expected value of a_j is given earlier in Section 10.8.3 by

$$E(a_j) = \sum_{w(n)} a_j \pi_n(\mathbf{a}) = \frac{\theta}{j} \frac{n!}{(n-j)!} \frac{\theta^{[n-j]}}{\theta^{[n]}}, \tag{11.3}$$

where $w(n) := \{\mathbf{a} : \sum_j ja_j = n\}$. We can evaluate the effects of increasing correlations or mutual dependence on the size of Ea_j by taking the partial derivative of it with respect to θ: As θ increases, Ea_j for j much smaller than n increases linearly in θ.

We explain how to calculate moments in Section 10.7, following Watterson (1976). For example the variance and covariances are computed by using the relation

$$E\{a_j(a_j - 1)\} = \left(\frac{\theta}{j}\right)^2 \frac{n!}{(n-2j)!} \frac{\theta^{[n-2j]}}{\theta^{[n]}},$$

and for $i \neq j$

$$E\{a_i a_j\} = \frac{\theta^2}{ij} \frac{n!}{(n-i-j)!} \frac{\theta^{[n-i-j]}}{\theta^{[n]}}.$$

Note that the standard deviations of the as are of the same order of magnitude as the means.

Let $x_i = ia_i/n$. This is the fraction of agents of type i. This fraction is in the infinite-dimensional simplex $\sum_i x_i \leq 1$. Its expected value is

$$E(x_j) = E(ja_j/n).$$

The order statistics of the fractions, $x_{(1)} \geq x_{(2)} \geq \cdots$, are important in markets with highly correlated agents. With θ smaller than 1, the sum of two or three largest fractions can be shown to be nearly one. See Table III of Watterson and Guess (1977), where numerical values of the expected values of the largest fraction are listed for different values of θ. For example, with $\theta = 0.3, 0.4$, and 0.5, the expected value of the largest fraction is $E(x_{(1)}) = 0.84, 0.79$, and 0.76. They calculated these figures numerically. We describe some theoretical background in the next section.

11.2.3   The largest two shares

Next, we calculate the joint distribution of largest two shares, by setting r to 2 in Section 10.6.2 as outlined in Watterson and Guess (1977).

Let x and y be the largest two fractions. Their joint density is

$$f(x, y) = \theta^2(xy)^{-1}(1 - x - y)^{-1/2}$$

in the region $x + 2y \geq 1$ and $x + y \leq 1$. Its partial derivative with respect to y vanishes on the line $2x + 3y = 2$, which is located in the region where the expression given above holds. This line is a ridge along which the most probable values of y, given x are located. With $\theta = 0.5$, $E(x) = 0.758$ by Table III of Watterson and Guess. Approximating y by the most probable value, $y \approx 2/3 - 2x/3$, we calculate Ey. We also know that $Ey \approx Ex\theta(\ln 2 - \theta/2)$. They both give the value $Ey \approx 0.16$. We may approximate y by the equation for the most probable y without too much error.

The marginal probabilty density of the largest fraction is

$$f(x) = \theta x^{-1}(1 - x)^{\theta-1}$$

for $1/2 < x \leq 1$. When x is not greater than $1/2$, the expression is more complex:

$$f(x) = \Gamma(\theta + 1)e^{\gamma\theta}x^{\theta-2}g(x^{-1} - 1),$$

where $g(\cdot)$ is the density of the random variable Z introduced in Section 10.6.2, and is characterized in terms of its Laplace transform.

11.3 Market volatility

Here we show that our model has nonvanishing volatility as the number of participants goes to infinity, unlike some simulation models, which specify an exogenously fixed numbers of agents.

Let $E(x)$ and $E(y)$ be the expected values of the largest two fractions, x and y. Watterson (1976) shows that

$$E(y) \geq \theta E(x) B_{1/2}(0, \theta + 1) \approx \theta E(x)(\ln 2 - \theta/2),$$

where $B_{1/2}$ is an incomplete beta function; see Abramovitz and Stegun (1968, 26.5). Using this formula, $E(y) \approx 0.16$ with $\theta = 0.4$; hence $E(x) + E(y) \approx 0.95$. Similarly, we have $E(x + y) = 0.97$ and 0.92 for $\theta = 0.3$ and 0.5, respectively. We may therefore suppose θ is about 0.4. With $\theta = 0.4$, the expected numbers of clusters are $E(K_{10}) = 2.1$, $E(K_{100}) = 3.0$, $E(K_{1000}) = 4.0$, $E(K_{10^5}) = 5.8$, and $E(K_{10^7}) = 7.7$. These figures indicate that there are several small fractions in addition to the two large ones when the number of participants is $n \geq 100$.

Watterson also has bounds for other moments with k and l nonnegative integers:

$$E(x^k y^l) \geq G\theta^2 \Gamma(\theta) e^{\gamma\theta} B_{1/2}(k, l + \theta),$$

with $G = E(x)/\theta \Gamma(\theta) e^{\gamma\theta}$, and where $B_{1/2}(a, b)$ is the incomplete beta function. The inequality comes from an approximation he used to evaluate some integrals. Abramovitz and Stegun have some series expansions for the incomplete beta functions. Unfortunately, the bounds are not sharp enough to give precise bounds on the variances of x. If we use $y \approx 0.95 - x$, then

$$\frac{E(xy)}{E(x)} = \theta B_{1/2}(1, 1 + \theta) \approx \frac{\theta}{1+\theta}\left[1 - \left(\frac{1}{2}\right)^{1+\theta}\right] \tag{11.4}$$

may be used to estimate

$$\sqrt{\text{var}(x)}/E(x) \approx 0.21.$$

In other words, the standard deviation of the largest fraction is about $1/5$ of its mean. See Watterson (1976) and Watterson and Guess (1977) for more precise calculation procedures.

What is most remarkable about the patterns of clusters of agents when n is large is that some small subsets of configurations account for a majority of possible patterns. That is, some small number of configurations are most likely to be realized or observed. This feature has been noticed in other contexts as well. Mekjian (1991) compares genetics and physics examples.

11.4   Behavior of market excess demand

We derive approximate expression for the market excess demands with two large fractions x and y, which approximately sum to 1. In the previous section, we have shown that about 95 percent of the total market participants belong to the largest two subgroups of agents by types, when the parameter θ is about 0.4. With the largest two clusters, there are two regimes: one in which a cluster of agents with strategy 1 is the largest share, and the other in which a cluster of agents using strategy 2 is the largest. For ease of comparison, we use the same formulas for the individual excess demand functions as in Day and Huang (1990). The agents with strategy 1 have the excess demand

$$d_1(P) = (u - P)h(P),$$

and the agents with strategy 2 have the excess demand

$$d_2(P) = -(u - P),$$

with $h(P) = [(P - m)(M - P)]^{-1/2}$, where we have set $a = b = 1$ in Day and Huang's specification and set $u = (M + m)/2$ without loss of generality. In the language of Day and Huang, agents with strategy 1 are **fundamentalists** and those with strategy 2 are **chartists**. We note that the two excess demands are of opposite sign, i.e., the two types of agents are on opposite sides of the market.

Let P denote the price of the shares, and let $d_x(P)$ denote the individual excess demand of the type that happens to have fraction x. Similarly for $d_y(P)$.

11.4.1   Conditions for zero excess demand

The market excess demand D is then given by summing over individual excess demands:

$$D(P)/n = xd_x(P) + yd_y(P).$$

We have divided the excess demand by the total number of market participants so that we can express it in terms of fractions. Set the right-hand side equal to zero to find the critical prices at which the condition of zero market excess demand is realized. In the case where the agents in the largest cluster are using strategy 1, there are three prices at which the market excess demand is zero if the inequality $(M - m)/2 \geq (x/y)$ holds. One is $P = u$, and the other two are given by the roots of

$$h(P) = y/x, \tag{11.5}$$

or $P^2 - 2uP + Mm = (x/y)^2$. Denote them by P^*, and P_*, where $P_* < u < P^*$. These critical values depend on x and y, although we omit the arguments not to clutter the notation.

If $(M - m)/2 \leq x/y$, then $P = u$ is the only price that produces zero excess demand. To be definite, we assume that $(M - m)/2$ is sufficiently large for the three critical prices to exist.[3] In the other regime, where the agents in the largest cluster are using strategy 2, there are also three critical points if the condition holds with y/x replacing x/y. We proceed to examine the case with three critical prices in both regimes.

Noting that $P^* = u + \sqrt{(M - m)^2/4 - (x/y)^2}$ in the first regime and $P^* = u + \sqrt{(M - m)^2/4 - (y/x)^2}$ in the second regime, the two critical prices P^* and P_* are further apart in regime 2 than in regime 1: $m < P_*(2) < P_*(1) < u < P^*(1) < P^*(2) < M$, where we use notation such that $P^*(2)$ denotes the largest critical price under regime 2, and so on.

The derivative of the market excess demand with respect to P is

$$D'(P) = y - \left(\frac{M - m}{2}\right)^2 h(P)^3 x$$

in regime 1, and in particular

$$D'(u) = -f(u)x + y = -\frac{2}{M - m}x + y$$

in regime 1, which is positive and less than 1, that is, the critical price $P = u$ is locally stable. The derivative is positive in regions where P satisfies

$$\left(\frac{M - m}{2}\right)^2 h(P)^3 < \frac{y}{x}.$$

The other two critical prices at which the market excess demand vanish are locally unstable in both regimes in difference equation approximation:

$$D'(P^*) = -(u - P^*)^2 h(P^*)^3 < -1,$$

and

$$D'(P_*) = -(u - P_*)^2 h(P_*)^3 < -1.$$

11.4.2   Volatility of the market excess demand

Watterson (1976) and Watterson and Guess (1977) have shown how to derive the probability density for x and y, $1 \geq x \geq y \geq 0$ and $x + y \leq 1$. The expressions for the densities are simple for certain ranges of the variables but are complicated

---

[3] If $y/x \leq (M - m)/2 \leq x/y$, then regime 1 has a unique $P = u$, but in regime 2 there are three critical points. Because $x \geq y$ by construction, $\max\{x/y, y/x\} = x/y$.

for the rest. We have

$$f(x) = \theta x^{-1}(1 - x)^{\theta-1}$$

for $1/2 < x$, and

$$g(x, y) = \theta^2 x^{-1} y^{-1}(1 - x - y)^{\theta-1}$$

for $0 \leq y \leq x \leq 1$ and $x + 2y \geq 1$. In the regions $x < 1/2$ and $x + 2y < 1$ more complicated formulas obtain and we must resort to numerical determination of the density. With θ small, it is likely that both the inequalities $x > 1/2$ and $x + 2y \geq 1$ hold. We proceed on this assumption in evaluating the expected values.

The upper and lower market-clearing prices are functions of the fractions x and y. To investigate the effects of the fractions deviating from their means on the critical prices, let $\delta P^* = P^* - P^*(Ex, Ey)$ denote the deviation of the upper critical price from that when the fractions are at their mean values, where the dependence of P^* on x and y is not explicitly shown. We have

$$\delta P^* = -B \left(\frac{\delta x}{Ex} - \frac{\delta y}{Ey} \right),$$

where $B := (Ex/Ey)^2/(\bar{P} - u)$ with $\bar{P} = P^*(Ex, Ey)$ is a constant. This is the expression in regime 1. In regime 2, the roles of x and y are interchanged. The expression for δP_* in regime 2 is the negative of this.

From this, we obtain the variance of δP^* in terms of variances and covariance of x and y. We note that only the coefficient B varies with changes of regime.

Proposition.   *Volatilities of prices near the upper and lower critical values are greater under regime 1 than under regime 2 if* $(M - m)^2/4 > [(Ex/Ey)^2 + (Ey/Ex)^2]^{-1}$.

11.4.3   *Approximate dynamics for price differences and power law*

In this subsection, we discuss the behavior of large price changes, and returns, in heuristic terms. We fix the time interval Δ and write the recurrence equation for share price as

$$P_{t+\Delta} = P_t + \kappa D(P_t, \xi_t),$$

where $\kappa = c \times \Delta$ is an adjustment constant, and ξ_t stands for the two-dimensional vector with components x_t and y_t.

Let ρ_t be the price difference $P_t - P_{t-\Delta}$ for some small Δ. Then the price difference is governed by the difference equation

$$\rho_{t+\Delta} = A_t \rho_t + B_t,$$

with $A_t = 1 + \kappa D'(P_{t-\Delta}, \xi_{t-\Delta})$, where the prime indicates the partial derivative with respect to P, and $B_t = \kappa D_\xi(P_{t-\Delta}, \xi_{t-\Delta})(\xi_t - \xi_{t-\Delta})$, where the subscript ξ indicates the gradient vector with respect to x and y.

In the mathematical literature, we do not find theory to examine the behavior of this difference equation, since the existing theory requires that (A_t, B_t) be i.i.d.; see Kesten (1973), Vervaat (1979), Letac (1986), Goldie (1991), or de Haan et al. (1989). In particular, the condition of identically distributed pairs of random variables may not be valid in general. However, the condition holds approximately in the neighborhood of $P = u$ or P_* or P^*. Alternatively, we may appeal to Brandt (1986), who derives the conditions under the assumption of ergodic stationarity for (A_t, B_t), rather than the i.i.d. conditions used by other writers.

We assume that, under certain technical conditions, a stationary distribution exists for $\rho_\infty = A_1 \rho_\infty + B_1$. See also Sornette and Cont (1997), Takayasu and Sato (1997), or Blank and Solomon (2000), among others.[4] We know that the distribution of the price differences will have a stationary statistical distribution with power law, that is, the expression

$$\Pr(|\rho_\infty| > z) = cz^{-\gamma}$$

holds with some constants c and γ, under some technical conditions. In particular the index γ is determined by

$$E(A_1^\gamma) = 1.$$

This condition, if satisfied, will determine γ by

$$\gamma = 1 + \frac{2}{\kappa} \frac{E(-D')}{E(D'^2)},$$

where

$$\frac{E(-D')}{E(D'^2)} = \frac{\Theta E(x) - E(y)}{\Theta^2 E(x^2) - 2E(xy)\Theta + E(y^2)}$$

$$\approx \frac{\Theta - 0.18}{0.18\left(\Theta + \frac{2}{3}\right)^2 - \frac{4}{3}\Theta - 0.35},$$

with $\Theta = (\frac{2}{M-m})^2 h(\rho_\infty)^3$. Then, with a large Θ we have an approximate expression $\gamma \approx 1 + 10/\kappa\Theta$. Recall that κ measures the adjustment speed of the price dynamics in reducing the magnitude of excess demands. Faster adjustment, other things being equal, will give smaller γ-values.

Returns may be similarly analyzed.

---

[4] Blank and Solomon point out an error in Gabaix (1998).

11.4.3.1 Simulation experiments

We have established that for a small value of θ, there are two or three groups in a market, and the largest two occupy about 95 per cent or more of the market share. For example, We have seen that $E(x) = 0.8$, $E(y) = 0.16$, and $E(K_{100}) = 3$ for $\theta = 0.4$, where x and y are largest two cluster sizes.

Having seen this, we conduct a simulation experiment in which only two groups of agents are in the market, and agents of the two types arrive at Poisson rates m_1 and m_2. We pick $m_1 = 5$ and $m_2 = 1$. We assume that prices are adjusted by a trading specialist who buys and sells at prices he posts. He attempts to maintain the market excess demand near zero. When the price deviates beyond the limits he sets, he adjusts the posted price by the rule

$$P_{t+1} = P_t + \kappa D(P_t) I(|D(P_t)| \geq L),$$

where $I(\cdot)$ is the indicator function, and where L is the limit, which is taken to be the same for upper and lower limits.

Returns are defined by $x_t = \ln(P_t/P_{t-1})$. In the range where the specialist adjusts prices, they are governed approximately by the stochastic difference equation

$$x_{t+1} = A_t x_t + B_t.$$

Depending on the initial conditions, there may be one or three equilibrium points of the dynamics. Conditions under which stationary distributions exist as solutions of $x_\infty = A x_\infty + B$ for some A, B pair have been examined in several papers; see Brandt (1986), de Haan, et al. (1989), Letac (1986), Goldie (1991), and Vervaat (1979), among others. de Haan et al. discuss the case where the A's and B's are uncorelated and i.i.d. Vervaat and Letac discuss the existence of stationary solutions. Goldie gives a nice discussion of power laws. Brandt does not require the i.i.d. condition.

Using the same excess-demand specifications for the two groups as above, in the neighborhood of P^* where $f(P^*) = m_2/m_1$, which is the price at which the expected excess-demand is zero, we have $A_t \approx \kappa(u/P^*)m_2[n_2/m_2 - \Lambda(P^*)n_1/m_1]$, with $\Lambda(P) = u/(M - P) - (P - u)/u$, which approaches 1 as M becomes large, and $B_t \approx \kappa(1 - u/P^*)m_2[n_2/m_2 - n_1/m_1]$. These are the case where agents of type 1 are the larger group and use the fundamentalist strategy. In the case, where they use the chartist strategy, subscripts 1 and 2 are interchanged.

We estimate the distribution function $F(\cdot)$ of the returns by the histogram constructed from the simulation runs, and plot $1 - F(y) + F(-y)$ against y, where y is the standardized return, positive in the log–log plot.

Figures 11.1 and 11.2 are the results of the 100 simulations of the last 100 time steps of a total of 300 time steps. This is done to ensure that the returns

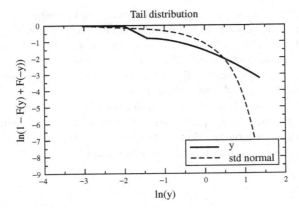

Fig. 11.1. Tail distribution, with that of normal distribution superimposed (dashed line).

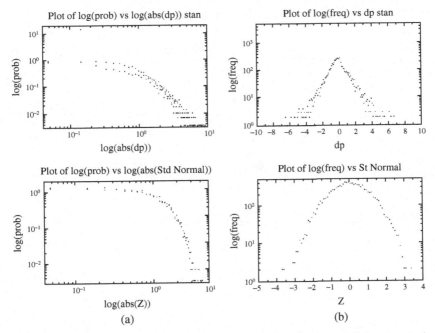

Fig. 11.2. Left upper panel: Plots of $\ln P$ vs $\ln |dP|$, left lower panel that of standard normal for comparison.

Right upper panel: Plot of $\ln(\textit{frequency})$ vs dP, where dP is standardized. Left lower panel that of normal distribution for comparison. Note the differences in scale.

are approximately stationary. Figure 11.1 plots the tail distribution with that of the standard normal distribution superimposed for comparison.

The right-hand panel of Fig. 11.2 compares the simulation result with the normal distribution. It shows that tails are much larger in the returns. Its left-hand panel indicates the exponent of the power law as the negative slope of the top plot. It appears that γ is definitely less than 2, about 1.7 or 1.8.

The bottom panel shows the normal distribution for comparison. Various choices of adjustment-speed parameters affect the rate of convergence and the choice of local equilibria, but do not affect the tail behavior. These simulation runs are not conclusive, but are indicative of the tail behavior of the model.

Appendix

A.1 Deriving Generating Functions via Characteristic Curves

We follow Hildebrand (1976, Chap. 8) in summarizing the method for deriving generating functions defined by quasilinear partial differential equations.

We only consider equations with two independent variables, x and y, and a dependent variable z, of the form

$$P(x, y, z)\frac{\partial z}{\partial x} + Q(x, y, z)\frac{\partial z}{\partial y} = \tilde{R}(x, y, z).$$

An important special case is

$$P(x, y)\frac{\partial z}{\partial x} + Q(x, y)\frac{\partial z}{\partial y} = \tilde{R}(x, y)z + S(x, y).$$

We put this into a more symmetrical form. Suppose that $G(x, y, z) = c$ defines a solution implicitly, i.e., this equation determines z as a function of x and y that satisfies the partial differential equation. Assume that $\partial G/\partial z \neq 0$. Then,

$$\frac{\partial z}{\partial x} = -\frac{\partial G/\partial x}{\partial G/\partial z},$$

and

$$\frac{\partial z}{\partial y} = -\frac{\partial G/\partial y}{\partial G/\partial z}.$$

Substituting these into the original equation, we arrive at

$$P\frac{\partial G}{\partial x} + Q\frac{\partial G}{\partial y} + R\frac{\partial G}{\partial z} = 0.$$

We can interpret this equation geometrically as saying that the vector (P, Q, R) is orthogonal to the gradient ∇G, i.e., the vector lies in the tangent plane to $G(x, y, z) = \text{const}$. At any point on the solution (integral) surface, the

195

vector (P, Q, R) is tangent to any curve on the surface passing through at the point. Such curves are called **characteristic curves** of the differential equation.

A characteristic curve has the same direction as the vector (P, Q, R); hence the tangent vector (dx, dy, dz) is such that

$$\frac{dx}{P} = \frac{dy}{Q} = \frac{dz}{R},$$

because $P = \mu \, dx/ds$, $Q = \mu \, dy/ds$, and $R = \mu \, dz/ds$, where s represents arc length along the curve. This is equivalent to two ordinary differential equations. When $R = 0$, we take $dz = 0$. This and $dx/P = dy/Q$ constitute the two equations.

Let the solutions of the two independent differential equations be

$$u_i(x, y, z) = c_i$$

for $i = 1, 2$, where c_1 and c_2 are two independent constants. These represent two families of surfaces such that the intersections of the two surfaces are the characteristic curves. The two constants are related by

$$F(c_1, c_2) = 0,$$

that is,

$$F[u_1(x, y, z), u_2(x, y, z)] = 0$$

is an integral surface of the original partial differential equation for any differentiable function F. Alternatively, we may use

$$u_2(x, y, z) = f[u_1(x, y, z)].$$

The function F or f may be chosen to include a specified curve on the integral surface.

In the special case in which P and Q do not depend on z, we can treat

$$\frac{dy}{dx} = \frac{Q}{P}$$

as an ordinary differential equation independent of z. If it can be solved in the form $u_1(x, y) = c_1$, then we use it to express y, say, in terms of x and c_1. Since we are looking for a second expression $u_2(x, y, z) = c_2$ such that $F(c_1, c_2) = 0$, we keep c_1 constant. For example, the second equation becomes

$$\frac{dz}{dx} = \frac{R}{P}$$

after y is substituted out. When this is solved as

$$z = c_2 A(x, c_1),$$

we have $u_2 = z/A(x, c_1) = c_2$, and using $u_2 = f(u_1)$, we derive

$$z = A(x, u_1(x, y) f[u_1(x, y)].$$

A.2   Urn models and associated Markov chains

A.2.1   Pólya's urn

A two-type Pólya urn is an urn containing balls of two colors, b black and y yellow balls, say. Each time a ball is drawn, it is returned to the urn together with c balls as the same color the one just drawn. The probability of getting black balls on the first m draws and then yellow on the next $l = n - m$ draws is

$$\frac{b}{b+y} \cdot \frac{b+c}{b+y+c} \cdots \frac{b+(m-1)c}{b+y+(m-1)c} \cdot \frac{y}{b+y+mc} \cdots \frac{y+(l-1)c}{b+y+(n-1)c}.$$

Note that any other outcome of the first n draws with m black and l yellow balls drawn has the same probability, because the factors in the denominator increases by c per draw, and the numerators are just permutations of the ones shown above. The fraction of black balls after the nth draw, X_n, is a martingale and nonnegative. It converges to X_∞ by the martingale convergence theorem. Durrett (1991, p. 209) shows that it has the Beta distribution $B(b/c, y/c)$. With $\theta := y/c$ and $b/c = 1$, it reduces to $B(1, \theta)$, that is, the density is given by $\theta(1-x)^{\theta-1}$. See also Feller (1968, pp. 119–121).

A.2.2   Hoppe's urn

An application of this to a model with a partition vector as a state vector is given in Hoppe (1987). Suppose that we wish to compute the expected value of the number of types with exactly j agents, denoted by a_j. In the context of size distribution of firms, this is the number of firms in category j, i.e., the number of firms with j units, given the total of n units in the model. Draw the first sample and label it type 1. Its future occurrences in the sample are described by a two-type Pólya urn just discussed. See also Appendix A.9.2. The probability that type 1 is observed i times in a sample of size n is

$$\Pr(S_1 = i) = \int_0^1 C_{n-1,i-1} x^{i-1} (1-x)^{n-i} \theta (1-x)^{\theta-1} \, dx,$$

where S_1 is the number of times type 1 units are observed. There are $i a_i$ type 1 units in the total n units; hence

$$\Pr(S_1 = i \mid a_1, a_2, \ldots, a_n) = \frac{i a_i}{n}.$$

By integration

$$E(a_i) = \frac{n}{i} \Pr(S_1 = i) = \frac{\theta}{i} \frac{(n)_i}{(\theta + n - 1)_i},$$

where $(n)_i := n(n-1)\cdots(n-i+1)$.

Hoppe (1984) also shows how to derive the Ewens sampling formula from a generalized Pólya urn. Consider an urn that contains one black ball of weight $\theta > 0$, and various numbers of nonblack balls, each of weight one. Initially the urn contains only the black ball. At the nth drawing, a ball is drawn at random in proportion to its weight. If a nonblack ball is drawn, then it is returned together with one more ball of the color drawn. If the black ball is drawn, then the black ball is returned together with one ball of a color not previously drawn, that is, this returned ball has a new color. This event occurs with probability $\theta/(\theta + n)$. This is the entry probability for a ball of a color not previously observed. For convenience of reference label the nonblack colors as $1, 2, \ldots, K$ in the order of appearance when there are K nonblack colors, that is, the black ball has been drawn K times by the end of the nth drawing.

Define the random variable $Y_n = i$ when a ball of color i is returned after the nth drawing, $1 \le i \le K$. A partition of n balls into K colors is the same as an allocation of n balls into K labeled boxes.

Let n_i be the number of balls of color i, $1 \le i \le K$. We note that $n_1 + n_2 + \cdots + n_K = n$. Here, we have a random partition of a set $\{1, 2, \ldots, n\}$ into K subsets. The partition vector $\mathbf{a} = (a_1, a_2, \ldots, a_K)$ is such that a_i is the number of colors with exactly i balls, or the number of times i appears in $\{n_1, n_2, \ldots, n_K\}$. The sequence of random variables $\{Y_k\}_{k=1}^{n}$ partitions the set $\{1, 2, \ldots, n\}$ randomly.

A sample path $\{Y_i = y_i, i = 1, 2, \ldots, n\}$ has the probability

$$\Pr(Y_1 = y_1, \ldots, Y_n = y_n) = \frac{\theta^K \prod_{i=1}^{K}(n_i - 1)!}{\theta^{[n]}},$$

because the black ball is drawn K times. In between, $n_i - 1$ nonblack balls are drawn, and the denominator has the factors increasing by one by each drawing. Here $\theta^{[n]} = \theta(\theta + 1)\cdots(\theta + n - 1)$.

We next count the number of such sample paths consistent with the partition vector $\mathbf{a}$. We observe two constraints: (a) balls of color 1 preceeds those of color 2, and so on, and (b) the number of each color is not fixed. We merely know the sizes of different colors or clusters are given by n_j, $j = 1, 2, \ldots, n_K$. There are $n! / \prod_j n_j!$ ways of such clusters. Given the partition vector, there are

$$\frac{K!}{\prod_i a_i!}$$

ways of distributing the ns.

In total then, there are

$$\frac{1}{K!} \frac{K!}{\prod_j a_j!} \frac{n!}{\prod_j n_j!}$$

many sample paths consistent with the partition vector, where the first factor is there because there are $K!$ disjoint classes of permutations given by the first integer and these are all equally likely. When the above is multiplied by the sample probability given above, we obtain the Ewens sampling formula.

A.2.3 *Markov chain associated with the urn*

Hoppe (1987) associates a Markov chain with the partition process $\{\Pi_n\}$ having one-step transition probabilities

$$\Pr(\mathbf{a}, \mathbf{b}) = \Pr[\Pi_{r+1} = \mathbf{b} \mid \Pi_r = \mathbf{a}]$$

from a partition vector $\mathbf{a}$ of dimension r to a partition vector $\mathbf{b}$ of dimension $r + 1$, with Π_0 the empty partition.

Transition probabilities are specified to make a familiy of distributions on partitions satisfy the Kingman consistency relation. Define

$$\Pr(\mathbf{a}, \mathbf{b}) = \frac{\theta}{\theta + r}$$

if $\mathbf{b} = (a_1 + 1, a_2, \ldots, a_r, 0)$. If $\mathbf{b} = (a_1, \ldots, a_i - 1, a_{i+1} + 1, \ldots, 0)$, then define

$$\Pr(\mathbf{a}, \mathbf{b}) = \frac{i a_i}{\theta + r},$$

and finally, if $\mathbf{b} = (a_1, \ldots, a_r - 1, 1)$, then

$$\Pr(\mathbf{a}, \mathbf{b}) = \frac{r a_r}{\theta + r}.$$

Define the time-reversed probabilities by

$$\Pr(\Pi_r = \mathbf{a} \mid \Pi_{r+1} = \mathbf{b}) = \frac{\Pr(\Pi_{r+1} = \mathbf{b} \mid \Pi_r = \mathbf{a}) \Pr(\Pi_r = \mathbf{a})}{\Pr(\Pi_{r+1} = \mathbf{b})}.$$

Using the Ewens sampling formula, we verify that

$$\Pr(\Pi_n = \mathbf{a} \mid \Pi_{n+1} = \mathbf{b}) = \frac{a_1 + 1}{n + 1},$$

if $\mathbf{b} = (a_1 + 1, a_2, \ldots, a_n, 0)$,

$$\Pr(\Pi_n = \mathbf{a} \mid \Pi_{n+1} = \mathbf{b}) = \frac{(r + 1)(a_r + 1)}{n + 1},$$

if $\mathbf{b} = (a_1, \ldots, a_r - 1, a_{r+1} + 1, \ldots, a_n, 0)$, and the conditional probability is 1 if $\mathbf{b} = (a_1, a_2, \ldots, a_n - 1, 1)$.

Define $T_n(\mathbf{a}) = \Pr(\Pi_n = \mathbf{a} \mid \Pi_0 = \emptyset)$, and compute

$$T_n(\mathbf{a}) = \sum_{\mathbf{b}} \Pr(\Pi_n = \mathbf{a} \mid \Pi_{n+1} = \mathbf{b}) T_{n+1}(\mathbf{b}).$$

This result is exactly the consistency relation of Kingman with a family $\{P_n\}$ of distributions on partitions identified with T_n.

Just as $\Pr_n$ satisfy $\Pr_m = \sigma_{mn} \Pr_n$ for $m < n$, where σ_{mn} is a family of linear transformations that satisfy the relation $\sigma_{ln} = \sigma_{lm}\sigma_{mn}$, $l < m < n$, we have $T_m = \Sigma_{mn} T_n$, where Σ_{mn} is the matrix with components $\Sigma_{mn}(\mathbf{a}, \mathbf{b}) = \Pr(\Pi_m = \mathbf{a} \mid \Pi_n = \mathbf{b})$ and where $\Sigma_{ln} = \Sigma_{lm} \Sigma_{mn}$.

A.3   Conditional probabilities for entries, exits, and changes of type

A.3.1   Transition probabilities

We follow Costantini and Garibaldi (1989) in this section to examine the conditional probability of the next sample type, given data (that is, the entry probability and exit probability), and describe the concept of relevance coefficients.

Given that there are K types of exchangeable agents, the probability that the next observed or sampled agent is of type j is denoted by

$$\Pr(j \mid \mathbf{n}) := \Pr(X_{n+1} = j \mid X_1 = j_1, X_2 = j_2, \ldots, X_n = j_n),$$

where the X's are exchangeable random variables that denote the types of the sampled agents, $j = 1, 2, \ldots, K$. Because the agents are exchangeable, the vector $\mathbf{n} = (n_1, n_2, \ldots, n_K)$, with n_i the number of agents of type i in the sample, can serve as a state vector.

More formally, define the random variable Y_i^k to be the indicator random variable of the event that the ith observation is of type k, and define

$$\mathbf{X}_n = \left(X_n^1, X_n^2, \ldots, X_n^K \right) = \sum_{i=1}^n \left(Y_i^1, \ldots, Y_i^K \right).$$

Then,

$$\Pr(j \mid \mathbf{n}) = \Pr\left(Y_{n+1}^j = 1 \mid \mathbf{X}_n = \mathbf{n} \right).$$

Assume that $\Pr(j \mid \mathbf{n}) \geq 0$, that $\sum_{j=1}^K \Pr(j \mid \mathbf{n}) = 1$, and that the probability is symmetric in its arguments. This reflects the assumption that agents are exchangeable.

We also assume that because of the exchangeability of agent types,

$$\Pr\left(Y_{n+1}^j = 1 \mid \mathbf{X}_n = \mathbf{n} \right) \Pr\left(Y_{n+2}^k = 1 \mid \mathbf{X}_{n+1} = \mathbf{n} + \mathbf{e}_j \right)$$
$$= \Pr\left(Y_{n+1}^k = 1 \mid \mathbf{X}_n = \mathbf{n} \right) \Pr\left(Y_{n+2}^j = 1 \mid \mathbf{X}_{n+1} = \mathbf{n} + \mathbf{e}_k \right).$$

This last statement is written more compactly as

$$\Pr(j \,|\, \mathbf{n})\,\Pr(k \,|\, \mathbf{n} + \mathbf{e}_j) = \Pr(k \,|\, \mathbf{n})\,\Pr(j \,|\, \mathbf{n} + \mathbf{e}_k)$$

for j and k from 1 to K.

Costantini and Garibaldi (1989) emphasized the importance of the notion of (hetero) relevance coefficient. They cite Keynes (1973, pp. 150–155) as one of the instances of this notion. Intuitively, this notion compares the conditional probabilities, $\Pr(X_{n+1} = j \,|\, \mathbf{n})$ and $\Pr(X_{n+2} = j \,|\, \mathbf{n}, X_{n+1} = i)$. In words,[1] two probabilities conditional on the data $\mathbf{n}$ are compared: that the next sample is of type j, and that the next sample turns out to be of a different type ($X_{n+1} = i$, $i \neq j$), and the sample X_{n+2} is of type j. In other words, we ask how $X_{n+1} \neq j$ affects the probability of $X_{n+2} = j$.

One would think that in sampling without replacement from an urn, say, the event that $X_{n+1} \neq j$ would increase the probability that $X_{n+2} = j$, while in sampling with replacement, this probability would be reduced. That is to say, the ratio of these two probabilities should carry information on the correlation between the two consecutive sample values. If the ratio is one, then the samples X_{n+1} and X_{n+2} should be independent.

Formally, define for a pair $i \neq j$

$$Q^i_j(\mathbf{n}) = \frac{\Pr(j \,|\, \mathbf{n} + \mathbf{e}_i)}{\Pr(i \,|\, \mathbf{n})}.$$

Recall our notation that $\mathbf{n} + \mathbf{e}_i$ means that there are $n_i + 1$ agents of ith type. This expression is for exchangeable samples.

The heterorelevance coefficient is said to be **invariant** if

$$Q^i_j(\mathbf{n}) = Q^l_k(\mathbf{n}')$$

for all $i \neq j, k \neq l$, and all state vectors $\mathbf{n}$ and $\mathbf{n}'$ with the same numbers of samples.

Costantini and Garibaldi (1989) show that the invariant heterorelavance coefficient is such that the probability depends on data only through n_i and n:

$$\Pr(j \,|\, \mathbf{n}) = \Pr(j \,|\, n_j, n),$$

where $n = n_1 + n_2 + \cdots + n_K$ is the total number of samples in $\mathbf{n}$, and that

$$\Pr(j \,|\, n_j, n) = \frac{n_j + \lambda/K}{n + \lambda},$$

with $\lambda = \eta/(1 - \eta)$, where

$$\eta = \Pr(j \,|\, \mathbf{0}) = \frac{\Pr(j \,|\, 0, 1)}{\Pr(j \,|\, 0, 0)}.$$

---

[1] I owe this to Costantini (private communication).

They prove this by induction, first for $\Pr(j|0, n)$, and then for $\Pr(j|m, n)$ with $m \le n$.

In the above, $\Pr(j|0, 0)$ is the probability of type j in the absence of any observation. For example, if all types are equally probable with no additional data, then it has the probability $1/K$.

The rate at which agents leave a cluster is often specified by

$$\Pr(\mathbf{n} - \mathbf{e}_j|\mathbf{n}) = \frac{n_j}{n}.$$

When agents change their mind, they leave the group to which they have belonged and enter a new one:

$$\Pr(\mathbf{n} - \mathbf{e}_i + \mathbf{n}_j|\mathbf{n}) = \Pr(\mathbf{n} - \mathbf{e}_i|\mathbf{n}) \Pr(\mathbf{n} - \mathbf{e}_i + \mathbf{n}_j|\mathbf{n} - \mathbf{e}_i).$$

The reverse transition probabilities are given by

$$\Pr(\mathbf{n}|\mathbf{n} - \mathbf{e}_i + \mathbf{n}_j) = \Pr(\mathbf{n}' - \mathbf{e}_j + \mathbf{e}_i|\mathbf{n}'),$$

where $\mathbf{n}' = \mathbf{n} - \mathbf{e}_i + \mathbf{e}_j$.

Suppose that $\Pr(\mathbf{n} + \mathbf{e}_k|\mathbf{n}) = (n + k + \beta_k)/(n + \beta)$, with $\beta = \sum_{j=1}^{K}$. Earlier we used the notation λ/K for β_k as a special case of equiprobable assignment of probability to $\Pr(k|0, 0)$. The detailed-balance conditions lead to the expression for the equilibrium distribution

$$\pi(\mathbf{n}) = B \prod_{j=1}^{K} \frac{\beta_j^{[n_j]}}{n_j!},$$

where the normalizing constant is $B = n!/\beta^{[n]}$.

A.3.2 *Transition rates*

The rates and probabilities may be defined in parallel, as Kelly (1979) does. Let Δ be a small positive time increment. Then, the transition rate $w(\mathbf{n}, \mathbf{n}')$ is converted to the conditional probabilities $\Pr(\mathbf{n}(t + \Delta) = \mathbf{n}') = w(\mathbf{n}, \mathbf{n}')\Delta + o(\Delta)$.

A.4 **Holding times and skeletal Markov chains**

Let $Y = \{Y_t; t \ge 0\}$ be a time-homogeneous jump Markov process, i.e.,

$$\Pr\{Y_{t+s} = j \mid Y_u, u \le t\} = \Pr\{Y_{t+s} = j \mid Y_t\} = \Pr\{Y_s = j \mid Y_0\}.$$

Sample paths of the process are right-continuous and have a countable number of jumps of finite sizes. We call

$$\Pr\{Y_{t+s} = j \mid Y_s = i\} = P_t(i, j)$$

the **transition function**. Because of the assumed time homogeneity, it depends on t but not on s.

Let $t_0, t_1, \ldots$ be the instants of transitions for the process Y, and let $X_0, X_1, \ldots$ be the sucession of states visited by Y. Suppose $X_n = i$. The time interval $[t_n, t_{n+1})$ is the called the **holding** or **sojourn interval**, and $W_n = t_{n+1} - t_n$ the **sojourn** (waiting) **time**, i.e.,

$$W_t = \inf\{s : Y_{t+s} \neq Y_t\}.$$

This has an exponential distribution. To see this, consider $f(u + v) := \Pr(W_t > u + v \mid Y_t = i)$. By first rewriting $\Pr(W_t > u + v \mid Y_t = i)$ as $\Pr(W_t > u, W_{t+u} > v \mid Y_t = i)$, and expressing the latter as the product of $\Pr(W_t > u \mid Y_t = i)$, and $\Pr(W_{t+u} > v \mid W_t > u, Y_t = i) = \Pr(W_{t+u} > v \mid Y_{t+u} = i)$ [because $Y_t(\omega) = i$ and $W_t(\omega) > u$], we have $Y_{t+u} = i$ and $\Pr(W_{t+u} > v \mid Y_{t+u} = i) = f(v)$. So we derive a functional equation

$$f(u + v) = f(u)f(v).$$

It is known that its solution is exponential, i.e.,

$$\Pr\{W_t > u \mid Y_t = i\} = e^{-q_i u},$$

for some nonnegative q_i. See Breiman (1969, Theorem 15.28), for example.

State i is called absorbing if $q_i = 0$, stable if q_i is finite and positive. We do not consider processes with states for which q_i is ∞. (Such states are called instantaneous states.)

Jump Markov processes have the strong Markov property Norris (1997, p. 93).

Knowledge of $X_0, X_1, \ldots, X_n, t_0, t_1, \ldots, t_n$ is equivalent to knowledge of $\{Y_t, t \leq t_n\}$. Denote $T := t_n$. It is a stopping time. Note that $W_T = t_{n+1} - t_n$ and $X_{n+1} = Y_{T+W_T}$.

We have

$$\Pr\{X_{n+1} = j, t_{n+1} - t_n > u \mid Y_t, t \leq T\}$$
$$= \Pr\{Y_{T+W_T} = j, W_T > u \mid Y_t; t \leq T\}.$$

Denote the right-hand side by $g(Y_T) = g(X_n)$, where the strong Markov property is used. The function g is defined by

$$g(i) = \Pr(Y_{W_0} = j, W_0 > u \mid Y_0 = i)$$
$$= \Pr(W_0 > u \mid Y_0 = i)\Pr(Y_{W_0} = j \mid Y_0 = i, W_0 > u).$$

Since $\{Y_0 = i, W_0 > u\} = \{Y_s = i, s < u\}$, we see that

$$g(i) = q(i, j)e^{-q_i u},$$

where

$$\Pr(Y_{u+W_u} = j \mid Y_u = i) = \Pr(Y_{W_0} = j \mid Y_0 = i) := q(i, j),$$

and we recall that $\Pr(W_0 \geq u \mid Y_0 = i) = e^{-q_i u}$. The sequences of states X_0, $X_1, \ldots$ together with the transition probability matrix $Q := \{q(i, j)\}$ defines a Markov chain X, which mimics Y except for the fact that time is now discrete, i.e., sojourn intervals are of the same length. We call this X the **skeletal** Markov chain of the jump Markov process Y. Many of the properties of Y are related to those of X.

We write $\Pr(Y_t = j \mid Y_0 = i)$ as $P_i(Y_t = j)$ for short. Using this notation,

$$P_t(i, j) = P_i(Y_t = j, t_1 \geq t) + P_i(Y_t = j, t_1 \leq t).$$

If $t_1 \geq t$, then $Y_t = Y_0 = i$, and

$$P_i(Y_t = j, t_1 \geq t) = P_i(t_1 \geq t)\delta_{ij} = e^{-q_i t}\delta_{ij}.$$

When the alternative $\{t_1 \leq t\}$ occurs, then by the strong Markov property

$$P_i(Y_t = j, X_1, t_1) = P_{t-t_1}(X_1, j),$$

and hence

$$P_i(Y_t = j, t_1 \leq t) = \int_0^t q_i e^{-q_i s} \sum_k q(i, k) P_{t-s}(k, j)\, ds.$$

Adding the two terms, the transition function is given by

$$P_t(i, j) = e^{-q_i t}\left[\delta_{i,j} + \int_0^t q_i e^{q_i u} \sum_k q(i, k) P_u(k, j)\, du\right].$$

To interpret the qs we differentiate this with respect to t and set t to zero:

$$\left.\frac{d P_t(i, j)}{dt}\right|_{t=0} = -q_i \delta_{i,j} + q_i q(i, j),$$

because of the relations $P_0(i, j) = \delta_{i,j}$ and $P_0(k, j) = \delta_{k,j}$. In this book, we use the name in the physics literature, and call it the **master equation**. In the probability literature it is known as the backward (Chapman–)Kolmogorov equation.

We define a matrix A by $A := \{a(i, j)\}$ with

$$a_{i,j} = q_i q(i, j)$$

for $i \neq j$, and

$$a_{i,i} = -q_i.$$

This matrix is called a **generator**. Then we can write the above differential equation compactly as

$$\frac{dP_t}{dt} = AP_t.$$

This equation can be solved as $P_t = e^{tA}P_0$. In terms of the elements of the generator, we obtain

$$q(i, j) = \frac{a(i, j)}{\sum_{j \neq i} a(i, j)}$$

for $i \neq j$, and

$$q_i = \sum_{j \neq i} a(i, j).$$

A.4.1   Sojourn-time models

Suppose we have a model Y and $Y_0 = i$. How long does the model state stay at i, and where does it jump to next? Each state has associated with it the exponential waiting random variable. Lawler (1995, p. 56) uses an analogy with alarm clocks. The process jumps to the state whose alarm clock rings first. Let $T = \min\{T_1, T_2, \ldots, T_K\}$, where T_j is the independent waiting time in state j for the alarm clock to ring, and where K is the number of states of the state space for Y. The random variable T is also exponentially distributed, because

$$\begin{aligned} \Pr(T > t) &= \Pr(T_1 > t, T_2 > t, \ldots, T_K > t) \\ &= \Pr(T_1 > t)\Pr(T_2 > t)\cdots\Pr(T_K > t) \\ &= \exp\{-(q_1 + \cdots + q_K)t\} \end{aligned}$$

The state jumps to the state with the minimal waiting time, so it jumps to state 1, say, with probability

$$\begin{aligned} \Pr(T_1 = T) &= \int_0^\infty \Pr(T_2 > t, T_3 > t, \ldots, T_K > t)\, d\Pr(T_1 = t) \\ &= \int_0^\infty e^{-(q_2 + \cdots + q_K)t} q_1 e^{-q_1 t}\, dt = \frac{q_1}{q_1 + q_2 + \cdots + q_K}. \end{aligned}$$

Thus, it jumps from state i with probability $q_i / \sum_j q_j$, after waiting for a random period with exponential distribution with rate $\sum_j q_j$.

A.5   Stirling numbers

To count the number of possible states of a model composed of a large number of agents, when they have at most countably many decision rules or behavioral patterns, is to count the number of random combinations of their choices. Stirling numbers of first and second kinds invariably appear in such counting situations.

The Stirling numbers can be introduced in at least two ways: by counting the number of distinct combinatorial structures as mentioned above, or by algebraic recursions. We use both ways; see Van Lint and Wilson (1992, p. 104). Other and older references are Jordan (1947), Riordan (1958), and David and Barton (1962, p.13). See also Sachkov (1996, Sec. 3.2). Abramovitz and Stegun (1968, p. 824) provides a useful summary of the properties of the Stirling numbers we develop below. We selectively discuss their properties in this section.

A.5.1   Introduction

In one sense, the simplest definition of the Stirling numbers is by identitites. Expand a descending factorial

$$(x)_n := x(x-1)(x-2)\cdots(x-n+1)$$

into power series, that is, into Taylor series, as

$$(x)_n = \sum_{k \geq 1} s(n,k)x^k. \tag{A.1}$$

The coefficients of the expansion define the Stirling numbers of the first kind. They are recovered by repeated differentiation as

$$s(n,k) = \left\{ \frac{1}{k!} D^k (x)_n \right\}_0,$$

and $s(n, 0) = 0$, where the symbol D represents differentiation with respect to x. The subscript means that the derivative is evaluated at 0. This definition is valid for nonnegative integers n and $k \leq n$; see Jordan (1947, p. 142) and Riordan (1958, p. 33).

Equation (A.1) shows that $(x)_n$ is the generating function of the Stirling numbers of the first kind.

The Stirling numbers of the second kind appear as coefficients of expansion of x^n in terms of the descending factorials:

$$x^n = \sum_{k \geq 1} S(n,k)(x)_k.$$

These numbers are defined for nonnegative integer values of n and k. They are zero for k greater than n.

We next use a Newton series expansion, which expresses $f(x)$ in terms of its value and the values of finite differences expressed at a point (taken to be zero here), to relate the Stirling numbers of the second kind to finite-difference expressions. Let

$$\Delta = E - 1,$$

with

$$Ef(x) = f(x + 1).$$

This is the familiar lead operator in econometrics. We have

$$f(x) = E^x f(0) = (1 + \Delta)^x f(0).$$

By expanding the right-hand side using the binomial coefficients, we have for $f(x) = x^n$

$$x^n = \sum_k \frac{1}{k!}(x)_k \Delta^k 0^n = \sum_k S(n, k)(x)_k, \qquad (A.2)$$

where we see that the Stirling numbers of the second kind are given by

$$S(n, k) = \frac{1}{k!}\{\Delta^k x^n\}_0. \qquad (A.3)$$

A.5.2 Recursions

Noting that $(x)_{n+1} = (x - n)(x)_n$, the comparison of the coefficient of x^m in

$$\sum s(n + 1, k)x^k = (x - n) \sum s(n, k)x^k$$

immediately leads to the recursion relation for the Stirling numbers of the first kind,

$$s(n + 1, m) = s(n, m - 1) - ns(n, m).$$

By subsituting $-x$ for x we can turn descending factorials into ascending ones:

$$(-x)_n = (-1)^n x^{[n]},$$

where we define an **ascending factorial** by

$$x^{[n]} := x(x + 1)(x + 2) \cdots (x + n - 1).$$

Then, the Taylor series expansion (A.1) becomes

$$x^{[n]} = \sum_k (-1)^{n-k} s(n, k)x^k,$$

and on defining

$$c(n, k) = (-1)^{n-k} s(n, k),$$

the recursion relation becomes that for $\{c(n, k)\}$:

$$c(n + 1, k) = nc(n, k) + c(n, k - 1). \tag{A.4}$$

These are sometimes called signless or unsigned Stirling numbers of the first kind. This recursion relation has a natural interpretation in terms of the number of cycles of length k in random permutations of n objects or symbols, to which we return shortly. Equation (A.1) is now the generating function of the signless Stirling numbers of the first kind,

$$x^{[n]} = \sum_{1}^{n} c(n, k) x^k.$$

We have the exponential generating function for $x^{[n]}$ as

$$1 + \sum_{1}^{\infty} \theta^{[n]} \frac{s^n}{n!} = (1 - s)^{-\theta}.$$

We recover $\theta^{[n]}$ as the coefficient of $s^n / n!$ of the righthand side:

$$n! [s^n] (1 - s)^{-\theta} = \binom{-\theta}{n} (-1)^n.$$

Here we use a convention of extracting the coefficient of s^n by $[s^n]$.

To derive algebraically the recursion formula satisfied by the Stirling numbers of the second kind, note the identity for the difference operation

$$\Delta^k x^{n+1} = (x + k) \Delta^k x^n + k \Delta^{k-1} x^n.$$

By dividing this relation by $k!$ and recalling the definition in terms of the Newton series expansion, we deduce the recursion

$$S(n + 1, k) = S(n, k - 1) + k S(n, k). \tag{A.5}$$

Alternatively, we use (A.2) to express x^{n+1} as

$$x^{n+1} = \sum S(n + 1, k)(x)_k = (x - k + k) \sum S(n, k)(x)_k,$$

which is the sum of $\sum S(n, k)(x)_{k+1}$ and $k \sum S(n, k)(x)_k$. Comparison of like terms gives the recursion.

Multiplying both sides of the above by $x^n / n!$ and summing over n, we obtain

$$e^{xt} = \sum_{n} (xt)^n / n! = \sum_{n,k} S(n, k)(x)_k t^n / n!.$$

Exercise. Use this expression to find a closed-form expression for the coefficient $\sum(n; a_1, a_2, \ldots, a_n) = S(n, m)$ in the expression

$$\left(\sum_{k=1}^{\infty} \frac{x_k}{k} t^k \right)^m = m! \sum_{nm} \sum (n; a_1, a_2, \ldots, a_n)' x_1^{a_1} \cdots x_n^{a_n},$$

where $(n; a_1, \ldots, a_n)'$ denotes the number of ways of partitioning n subject to $\sum i a_i = n$, and $\sum a_i = m$.

Multiplying both sides of (A.1) by $t^n/n!$ and summing over n from zero to infinity, we obtain the exponetial generating function for the descending factorials as

$$\sum_n (x)_n t^n/n! = (1+t)^x = \sum_n \sum_{k=0}^{n} s(n, k) x^k t^n/n!.$$

More on the generating functions later.

These definitions do not reveal how these numbers are related to combinatorial problems in random maps and random permutations, but are useful in deriving the recursion relations they satisfy. These two kinds of numbers are also reciprocals of each other in that

$$\sum_k S(n, k) s(k, m) = \delta_{n,m}, \tag{A.6}$$

as can be seen easily from the definitions. See Riordan (1958, p. 33) or Greene and Knuth (1990, p. 7).

A.5.3 Relations with combinatorics

Here, we give combinatorial derivations of the recursion relations. Stirling numbers of the first kind are related to cycle structures of permutations. Since the set $S = \{1, 2, \ldots, n\}$ is finite, any permutation applied repeatedly to any element of S will eventually return to it. So there is a smallest number r of repeated applications of the same permutation π that yield the identity for any element of the set. The sequence $\{x, \pi(x), \ldots, \pi^{r-1}x\}$ is called a cycle of π of length r. We do not distinguish any cyclical rearrangement of it, e.g., $\{\pi^i(x), \pi^{i+1}, \ldots \pi^{r-1}x, x, \pi(x), \ldots, \pi^{i-1}(x)\}$ is the same as the original cycle, for any $i \leq r$.

Let $p(n, k)$ be the number of permutations of n objects with exactly k cycles. Then a permutation of $\{1, 2, \ldots, n-1\}$ into k cycles can be made into a permutation with k cycles by inserting the object n after any of the symbols $1, 2, \ldots, n-1$, that is, in $n-1$ ways. Additionally, symbol n can be made a cycle of length one, and attached to any of the $p(n-1, k-1)$ permutations to make them permutations of n objects with k cycles. We thus have

$$p(n, k) = (n - 1)p(n - 1, k) + p(n - 1, k - 1),$$

with the boundary conditions that $p(0, 0) = 1$ and that $p(n, k) = 0$ for negative integers n or k or for k greater than a positive n. In view of (A.4), this recursion relation and the boundary condition are identical with those for the unsigned Stirling numbers of the first kind; hence

$$p(n, k) = c(n, k)$$

for all values of the arguments.

A **partition** of a finite set $[n] := \{1, 2, \ldots, n\}$ into k parts is a collection of k subsets of S such that none of the subsets is empty, all are pairwise disjoint, and their union is the original set S. We may think of it as a single-valued map from S into k points (cells, boxes, or types). The number of such partitions is $S(n, k)$, since it satisfies the same recursion as (A.5) and the same boundary conditions as the Stirling numbers of the second kind, because we can partition $n - 1$ points of S into k subsets and place n into any of these subsets in $k \times S(n - 1, k)$ ways, or we can put n by itself as one subset and put the remaining $n - 1$ points into $k - 1$ subsets.

van Lint and Wilson (1992) define a Stirling number of the second kind as the cardinality of the set of all partitions of an n-set into k nonempty subsets.

Stanley (1983, Sec. 1.4) uses a random map construction. Consider a set of arbitrary maps of an n-set S into a set X with x elements. There are x^n such maps. Define $S(n, k)$ to be the number of partitons of $[n]$ into k blocks $B_1, B_2, \ldots, B_k$. Then $k!S(n, k)$ is the number of linearly ordered maps, as we see by making the correspondence $f(i) = b_j$ if $i \in B_j$.

Therefore,

$$x^n = \sum k!S(n, k)\binom{x}{k}.$$

The binomial coefficient is present because there are this many ways of choosing a subset Y of X with k elements. The recursions are used to show that these alternative definitions are equivalent.

A.5.4   *Explicit expressions and asymptotic relations*

Jordan (1947, p. 201) notes that

$$\Delta^k D^{-k} f(0) = \sum \frac{k!}{(n + k)!} D^n f(0) S(n + k, k),$$

which can be verified directly by noting that $(\Delta D^{-1})^k = \Delta^k D^{-k}$ even though

Δ and D do not commute.[2] When this formula is applied to $f(x) = e^x$, we derive a relation

$$\frac{(e^x - 1)^k}{k!} = \sum_{j \geq k} \frac{1}{j!} S(j, k) x^j,$$

after we note that $D^n f(0) = t^n$, $D^{-m} f(x) = e^{xt}/t^m$, and $\Delta^m (e^{xt} - 1)^m / t^m = e^{xt}(e^t - 1)^m / t^m$. Invert this relation by using the inverse relation (A.6) between the two kinds of the Stirling numbers, after changing variables by $z = e^t - 1$, to express the above as

$$z^k = \sum \frac{k!}{j!} S(j, k) \{\ln(1 + z)\}^k.$$

We obtain

$$\{\ln(1 + z)\}^k = \sum_{j \geq k} \frac{k!}{j!} s(j, k) z^j,$$

a relation used by Harris (1960) in discussing random maps.

Exercise. Use this relation to show that $\sum (n; a_1, a_2, \ldots, a_n)^* = c(n, m)$, where

$$\left(\sum_{k=1}^{\infty} \frac{x_k}{k} t^k \right)^m = m! \sum_{n=m}^{\infty} \frac{t^n}{n!} \sum (n; a_1, \ldots a_n)^* x_1^{a_1} \cdots x_n^{a_n},$$

where $(n; a_1, \ldots, a_n)^*$ denotes the number of permutations of n subject to $\sum i a_i = n$, and $\sum a_i = m$.

The roots of the descending factorial $(x)_n$ are $r_i = i$, $i = 0, 1, \ldots, n - 1$. Therefore, the coefficients of x^k is given by

$$c(n, k) = \sum{}^* r_{i_1} r_{i_2} \cdots r_{i_{n_k}},$$

where the factorial is written out, the signless version is used instead of $s(n, k)$, and $1 \leq r_{i_1} \leq \cdots \leq r_{i_{n_k}} \leq n - 1$. The symbol $\sum^*$ means the summation over all combinations of order $n - k$ of numbers subject to the constraints above. Since the product of r_1 through r_{n-1} is $(n - 1)!$, we can rewrite the above expression as

$$c(n, k) = (n - 1)! \sum{}^* \frac{1}{r_{i_1} r_{i_2} \cdots r_{i_{k-1}}},$$

---

[2] Expanding $Ef(x) = f(x + 1)$ in Taylor series, we note that $E = e^D$ and $\Delta = e^D - 1$.

with $1 \le r_{i_1} \le \cdots \le r_{i_k} \le n - 1$. If we allow for repetitions and permutations subject only to

$$r_{i_1} + r_{i_2} + \cdots + r_{i_k} = n,$$

then it becomes

$$s(n, k) = (-1)^{n-k} \frac{n!}{k!} \sum \frac{1}{r_{i_1} \cdots r_{i_k}}.$$

A.5.5   *Asymptotics*

Since we will be modeling situations with a large number of agents, and possibly a large number of types, we list here some asymptotic expressions for Stirling numbers for easy reference. See Jordan (1947, p. 173) or Abramovitz and Stegun (1968, p. 825).

We have

$$s(n + k, k)/k^{2n} \to \frac{(-1)^n}{n!2^n}$$

for $k = o(\ln n)$,

$$S(n + k, k)/k^{2n} \to \frac{1}{n!2^n}$$

for $n = o(\sqrt{k})$.

For $k = o(\ln n)$, there is the Jordan formula

$$c(n, k) = \frac{(n-1)!}{(k-1)!} (\gamma + \ln n)^{k-1} (1 + o(1)),$$

where γ is the Euler constant. See Sachkov (1996, pp. 146, 157) who also shows that

$$\frac{s(n+1, k)}{n s(n, k)} \to -1,$$

and

$$\frac{S(n+1, k)}{S(n, k)} \to k$$

as n goes to infinity.

A.6   Order statistics

Let $X_1, X_2, \ldots, X_n$ be independent samples of size n of a random variable with a cumulative distribution function $F(\cdot)$. Arrange the sample values in nonincreasing order as $Y_1 \geq Y_2 \geq \cdots \geq Y_n$. These are called order statistics. The relation $Y_i \leq y$ implies that $Y_{i+1} \leq y$. So the order statistics are not independent.

Observe that if the αth order statistic is not less than y, then the number of X not less than y is greater than or equal to α, and conversely. For fixed y, let

$$Z_i := I_{(y,\infty)}(X_i), \qquad i = 1, 2, \ldots, n.$$

Then, $\sum_{i=1}^{n} Z_i$ denotes the number of X not smaller than y. Consequently,

$$1 - F_\alpha(y) = \Pr(Y_\alpha \geq y) = \Pr\left(\sum_i Z_i \geq y\right).$$

This last expression is binomial with parameter $F(y)$. Alternatively, we can write

$$F_\alpha(y) = \sum_{j=0}^{\alpha-1} C_{n,j}[F(y)]^{n-j}[1 - F(y)]^j,$$

where F_α is the cumulative distribution function of Y_α. For example, we have

$$F_1(y) = [F(y)]^n,$$

and

$$F_n(y) = 1 - [1 - F(y)]^n,$$

by noting that the sum from $j = 0$ to $n - 1$ is the same as the sum from $j = 0$ to n, which is one minus the nth term.

Suppose that $F(\cdot)$ has density function $f(\cdot)$. Then, we have

$$f_\alpha = \lim_{\Delta y \to 0} \frac{F_\alpha(y + \Delta y) - F_\alpha(y)}{\Delta y}$$

$$= \frac{n!}{(\alpha - 1)!(n - \alpha)!}[F(y)]^{n-\alpha}[1 - F(y)]^{\alpha-1} f(y).$$

Example.   Consider a logistic distribution function $F(x) = (1 + e^{-x})^{-1}$. Let X_i, $i = 1, 2, \ldots, n$, be i.i.d. samples of size n. Define $Z_i = F(X_i)$, $i = 1, 2, \ldots, n$. These are random samples from the uniform distribution over $(0, 1)$. Let $Y_1^{(n)}$ be the largest of the order statistics Z. Noting that

$$f_1(y) = n[F(y)]^{n-1} f(y) = ny^{n-1},$$

where $F(Y_1^{(n)}) = y = F(y)^n = y^n$, we have

$$E[F(Y_1^{(n)})] = \int_0^1 ny^n \, dy = \frac{n}{n+1}.$$

Note that

$$F(E(Y_1^{(n)})) = (1 + e^{-n/(n+1)})^{-1} \sim n/(n+1),$$

and that $E[F(Y_1^{(n)})] \approx F[E(Y_1^{(n)})]$, or $E(Y_1^{(n)}) = n$, that is, the mean of $Y_1^{(n)}$ is approximately equal to $\ln(n)$. Thus, using $\ln(n)$ as a centering constant, we note that

$$\lim_{n \to \infty} \Pr(Y_1^{(n)} - \ln(n) \leq y) = \lim[1 + e^{-y - \ln(n)}]^{-n}.$$

This limit is given by the double exponential function $\exp(-e^{-y})$.

This shows an interesting fact: that a centered largest order statistic of a logistic distribution has a double exponential distribution. This is related to our discussion on assessing alternative choices and to Appendix A.14 on slow variations. What is essential in the above is the fact that

$$n[1 - F(y + \ln(n))] \to e^{-y}.$$

See Bingham et al. (1987) or Galambos (1987).

A.7   Poisson random variables and the Ewens sampling formula

A.7.1   *Approximations by Poisson random variables*

A large body of probability and statistics literature exists on approximating sums of nonnegative integer-valued random variables as Poisson variables if the summands have sufficiently high probability of taking 0 value and sufficiently weak mutual dependence: Arratia and Tavaré (1992), Arratia, Barbour and Tavaré (1992, 1999), Galambos (1987), Steele (1994), and Chen (1975), among others.

In economic modeling, there exist many situations where approximations by Poisson random variables are appropriate. We summarize here some relevant facts that are deemed useful for economic applications. In particular, random combinatorial structures such as Poisson–Dirichlet limits seem to be applicable to problems in industrial organization, such as market shares and entry and exit phenomena, to name just two. Kaplan (1977) discusses Poisson approximation for urn schemes.

In the area of industrial organization, suppose that $X_i = 1$ when firm i is in the market and $X_i = 0$ otherwise. Then, $S_n = X_1 + \cdots + X_n$ is the total number of firms in the market. Define $T_n = Z_1 + \cdots + Z_n$, where

$$Z_i = f_i(X_i, X_{i-1}, \ldots, X_1).$$

Let X_i be independent, and

$$p_i = \Pr(X_i = 1)$$

be much smaller than 1. Let $\lambda = \sum_1^n p_i$, and suppose

$$d(P_S, Q_\lambda) \le \sum_1^n p_i^2,$$

where Q_λ is the Poisson distribution with mean λ.

Next replace X_i with an independent Bernoulli random variable X_i^* with parameter p_i^*, and define Z_i^* using X_i^*. Do likewise with T_n^*. Then, we have

$$d(T_n, T_n^*) \le \Pr(T_n \ne T_n^*) \le \sum_1^n E|p_i - p_i^*|.$$

Let $U_1, U_2, \ldots, U_n$ be uniform random variables on $[0, 1]$. Define $X_i^* = 1$ if $U_i \le p_i^*$, and zero otherwise. Do likewise with the Xs, that is, X_i is 1 if $U_i \le p_i(X_{i-1}, \ldots, X_1)$, $i = 1, \ldots, n$. We have

$$\Pr(X_1 \ne X_1^*) = |p_1 - p_1^*|,$$

and

$$\Pr(X_i \ne X_i^*| = E|P_i - p_i^*|.$$

Then,

$$d(P_S, Q_\lambda) \le d(P_S, P_S^*) + d(P_S^*, Q_\lambda) \le E|p_i - p_i^*| + \sum (p_i^*)^2.$$

Let $c_i(n)$ be the number of components of size i in the structure of size n, that is, $\sum_i i c_i(n) = n$. Arratia et al. (1999), have shown that the joint distribution $\mathcal{L}(c_1(n), c_2(n), \ldots, c_n(n)) = \mathcal{L}(Z_1, Z_2, \ldots, Z_n | T_n = n)$, where Z_i are independent such that

$$E(iZ_i) \to \theta,$$

$$\Pr(Z_i = 1) \approx \theta/i,$$

and $T_n = \sum_i i Z_i$. They have also shown that $n \Pr(T_n = m) \approx g_\theta(y)$, where $g_\theta(y)$ is given by $e^{-\gamma\theta} y^{\theta-1} / \Gamma(\theta)$, and where $m/n \to y$. They find Z such that

$$\Pr\left(C^{(n)} = a\right) = \Pr(Z = a | T_n = n),$$

where $C^{(n)} = \{c_1(n), \ldots c_n(n)\}$.

Let π be a permutation of n symbols, $\{1, 2, \ldots, n\}$, say. Denote by $|\pi|$ the number of cycles in π. Assign probability to π by

$$\Pr\left(c^{(n)} = a\right) = I_{\sum_i ia_i = n} \frac{n!}{\theta^{[n]}} \prod_i \left(\frac{\theta}{i}\right)^{a_j} \frac{1}{a_j!},$$

where $\theta^{[n]} = \theta(\theta + 1) \cdots (\theta + n - 1)$ is called an **ascending factorial**. This is the Ewens sampling formula.

A.7.2　Conditional Poisson random variables

We have observed that Poisson random variables play important roles in describing random combinatorial structures in patterns formed by agents. Following Shepp and Lloyd (1966) and Arratia and Tavaré (1994), we assume that $Z_i, i = 1, 2, \ldots, n$, are independent Poisson-distributed random variables with rate x^i/j, where x is between 0 and 1:

$$\Pr(Z_i = a) = \left(\frac{x^i}{i}\right)^a \frac{e^{-x^i/i}}{a!}.$$

Next, conditional on the weighted sum $\sum_j ja_j = n$, we calculate the joint probability

$$\Pr\left(Z_1 = a_1, Z_2 = a_2, \ldots, Z_n = a_n \,\Big|\, \sum_j jZ_j = n\right)$$
$$= \frac{\Pr(Z_1 = a_1, \ldots Z_n = a_n)}{\Pr(T_n = n)},$$

where $T_n := \sum_{j=1}^n jZ_j$.

The probability of the sum, T_n, is obtained simply by calculating the probability generating function for it,

$$\Pr\left(\sum_j ja_j\right) = \sum_{W(\mathbf{a})} \Pr(Z_j = a_j, j = 1, 2, \ldots n)$$
$$= x^n \exp\left(-\sum \frac{x^j}{j}\right),$$

where $W(\mathbf{a}) = \{\mathbf{a}; \sum_j ja_j = n\}$. This expression follows from the Cauchy formula, since

$$\sum_{W(\mathbf{a})} I_{(\sum ja_j = n)} \prod_j \left(\frac{1}{j}\right)^{a_j} \frac{1}{a_j!} = 1,$$

where $I_{(\cdot)}$ is the indicator function. Therefore, the expression for the conditional probability is the same as $\Pr(\mathbf{a})$, suitably setting the values for ν and λ/μ to one, respectively. Note that this conditional probability is independent of the means of the Poisson distributions.

As an example of unequal assignments of probabilities to combinatorial structures, we consider permutations. Instead of treating each permutation as equally probable, we can twist the distribution, as is done in large-deviation theory. See Shwartz and Weiss (1995) or Arratia and Tavaré (1994) for examples. Here we explain the simplest case, where we posit mutually independent Poisson random variables Z_i having mean $\theta x^i / i$, where θ is nonnegative. We show that this one parameter generates the Ewens sampling formula.

First, note that the joint distribution is

$$\Pr(Z_1 = a_1, \ldots, Z_n = a_n)$$
$$= \exp\left(-\theta \sum \frac{x^i}{i}\right) \theta^{K_n} x^n \prod \left(\frac{1}{j}\right)^{a_j} \frac{1}{a_j!},$$

where

$$K_n = \sum a_j,$$

and

$$\sum j a_j = n.$$

The weighted sum of Zs has the probability

$$\Pr(Z_1 + 2Z_2 + \cdots + nZ_n = n) = \exp\left(-\theta \sum x^i / i\right) \theta^{K_n} x^n.$$

This follows as before from the Cauchy formula. Therefore, the probability of the Zs, conditional on the weighted sum $T_n = n$, still gives the probability of $\mathbf{a}$.

Next, introduce a new measure P_θ under which the Zs are mutually independent:

$$P_\theta(Z_i = a) = \frac{\theta^a}{E(\theta^{Z_i})} P(Z_i = a).$$

We have

$$P_\theta(Z_i = a_i, i = 1, \ldots, n) = (E\theta^{K_n})^{-1} \theta^{K_n} P(Z_i = a_i, i = 1, \ldots, n),$$

where the joint probability of the Zs is equal to

$$P\left(\mathbf{Z} = \mathbf{a} \,\middle|\, \sum_j j Z_j = n\right) = P\left(\sum j Z_j = n\right)^{-1} I_{(\sum j Z_j = n)} P(\mathbf{Z} = \mathbf{a}).$$

On the other hand, we have

$$P_\theta(\mathbf{Z} = \mathbf{a}) = \left(E\theta^{\sum j Z_j}\right)^{-1} \theta^{K_n} P(\mathbf{Z} = \mathbf{a}),$$

and hence

$$P_\theta\left(\mathbf{Z} = \mathbf{a} \,\middle|\, \sum_j Z_j = n\right)$$

$$= \left(E\theta^{\sum j Z_j}\right)^{-1} P_\theta\left(\sum_j Z_j = n\right)^{-1} \theta^{\sum Z_j} I_{(\sum j Z_j = n)} P(\mathbf{Z} = \mathbf{a}).$$

These two expressions are both proportional to the same expression $P(\mathbf{Z} = \mathbf{a})$, and both are probability densities on Z_+^n. Hence, the two normalizing constants are equal to each other:

$$E\left(\theta^{K_n}\right) = E\left(\theta^{\sum Z_j}\right) \frac{P_\theta\left(\sum_j Z_j = n\right)}{P\left(\sum_j Z_j = n\right)}.$$

With parameter θ, we weight each permutation unequally. The probability is

$$P_n(\mathbf{a}, \theta) = \frac{\prod \left(\frac{\theta}{j}\right)^{a_j} \frac{1}{a_j!}}{\sum_{W(\mathbf{a})} \prod \left(\frac{\theta}{j}\right)^{a_j} \frac{1}{a_j!}},$$

as explained above.

Equate the coefficient of x^n of both sides in the identity (Kelly 1979, Kendall 1975)

$$(1 - x)^{-\theta} = \exp\left(\theta \sum \frac{x^i}{i}\right).$$

The left-hand side yields,

$$\binom{-\theta}{n}(-1)^n = \binom{\theta + n - 1}{n} = \frac{\theta^{[n]}}{n!},$$

where

$$x^{[n]} = x(x + 1) \cdots (x + n - 1)$$

to denote ascending factorials. The right-hand side yields

$$\sum_{W(\mathbf{a})} \theta^{K_n} \left(\frac{1}{i}\right)^{a_i} \frac{1}{a_i!}.$$

Recalling the Cauchy formula, we obtain

$$P_n(\mathbf{a}, \theta) = \frac{n!}{\theta^{[n]}} \theta^{K_n} \sum_{W(\mathbf{a})} \left(\frac{1}{i}\right)^{a_i} \frac{1}{a_i!}.$$

Arratia et al. (1992) have established that by assigning probabilities, not equally to all permutations of n symbols, but according to

$$\Pr(\pi) = \frac{\theta^{|\pi|}}{\theta^{[n]}},$$

where $|\pi|$ is the total number of cycles in the product representation of the permutation π, the Ewens distribution can be expressed by

$$\Pr(\mathbf{a}) = \Pr(\mathbf{Z} = \mathbf{a} \mid T_n = n),$$

where $T_n = \sum_{i=1}^{n} i Z_i$, and where $Z_i, i = 1, 2, \ldots, n$, are independent Poisson random variables with mean θ / i, but constrained by $\sum i Z_i = n$. They show, among other things that

$$k \Pr(T_n = k) = (\theta + k - 1) \Pr(T_n = k - 1).$$

Iterating this relation, we derive

$$\Pr(T_n = k) = \frac{\theta^{[k]}}{k!} \Pr(T_n = 0) = \frac{\theta^{[k]}}{k!} e^{-\theta \sum_{j=1}^{n} 1/j}.$$

This leads to the density of the limit T_n/n, denoted by T. It is given by

$$g_\theta(x) = \frac{e^{-\gamma\theta} x^{\theta-1}}{\Gamma(\theta)}$$

for $0 < x < 1$.

A.8   Exchangeable random partitions

To discuss a large number of agents forming clusters of various sizes, the notion of exchangeable random partitions, which is due to Kingman (1978a,b), is useful. We follow Zabell (1992) in describing the notion. We begin by reviewing the notion of exchangebility of random sequences and the de Finetti representation theorem for random sequences, because exchangeable random partitions are a generalization of exchangeable random sequences.

A.8.1   Exchangeable random sequences

Let $X_1, X_2, \ldots$ be an infinite sequence of random variables taking on k discrete values, $c_1, c_2, \ldots, c_K$, say. These are possible categories or types of decisions or choices by agents (or cells, in the literature on occupancy numbers in probability theory) into which the outcomes or realizations of the sequence are classified.

The sequence is said to be **exchangeable** if for every n, the cylinder set probabilities

$$\Pr(X_1 = e_1, X_2 = e_2, \ldots, X_N = e_N) = \Pr(e_1, e_2, \ldots, e_N)$$

are invariant under all possible permutations of the subscripts of Xs.[3] In other words, two sequences have the same probability if one is a rearrangement of the other.

Let n_i denote the number of times the ith type occurs in the sequence. The vector $\mathbf{n} = (n_1, n_2, \ldots, n_k)$ is called the **frequency vector**. The vector $\mathbf{n}/N$ is known as the empirical distribution in statistics. Note that given any two sequences, one can be obtained from the other if and only if the two sequences have the same frequency vector or empirical distribution.

The observed frequency counts $n_j = n_j(X_1, X_2, \ldots, X_N)$ are sufficient statistics, in the language of statistics, for the sequence $\{X_1, X_2, \ldots, X_N\}$, because probabilities conditional on the frequency counts depend only on $\mathbf{n}$, and are independent of the choice of the exchangeable probability Pr.

By exchangeablity, each of the sequences having the same frequency vector is equally probable. There are $N!/n_1!n_2! \cdots n_k!$ such sequences, and consequently

$$\Pr(X_1, X_2, \ldots, X_N | \mathbf{n}) = \frac{n_1!n_2! \cdots n_K!}{N!}.$$

We have the de Finetti representation theorem for exchangeable sequences (de Finetti 1974, 1975): if an infinite sequence of k-valued random variables $X_1, X_2, \ldots$ is exchangeable, then the infinite limiting frequency

$$Z := \lim_{N \to \infty} \left(\frac{n_1}{N}, \frac{n_2}{N}, \ldots, \frac{n_K}{N} \right)$$

exists almost surely; and if

$$\mu(A) = \Pr(Z \in A)$$

denotes the distribution of this limiting frequency, then

$$\Pr(X_1 = e_1, X_2 = e_2, \ldots, X_N = e_N)$$

$$= \int_{\Delta_K} p_1^{n_1} p_2^{n_2} \cdots p_K^{n_K} \, d\mu(p_1, p_2, \ldots, p_{K-1}).$$

To apply the de Finetti theorem, we must choose a specific **prior** or mixing measure, $d\mu$. One way is to follow Johnson et al. (1997) and postulate that all

---

[3] These subscripts may be thought of as time indices or as giving the order in which samples are taken.

ordered k-partitions of N are equally likely. This postulate uniquely determines $d\mu$ to be

$$d\mu(p_1, p_2, \ldots p_K) = dp_1\, dp_2 \cdots dp_{K-1},$$

a flat prior.

Less arbitrary is Johnson's sufficientness postulate[4]

$$\Pr(X_{N+1} = c_i|X_1, X_2, \ldots, X_N) = \Pr(X_{N+1} = c_i|\mathbf{n}) = f(n_i, n),$$

if $\Pr(X_1 = c_1, \ldots, X_N = c_N) > 0$ for all c's. This formula states that in predicting that the next outcome is c_i, n_i is the only relevant information contained in the sample. Zabell shows that Johnson's sufficientness postulate implies that

$$\Pr(X_{N+1} = c_i|\mathbf{n}) = \frac{n_i + \alpha_i}{N + K\alpha},$$

where $\alpha = \sum \alpha_j$ is the parameter of the symmetrical Dirichlet prior, which is the mixing measure $d\mu$. Note that the Pólya urn model (Feller 1968, pp. 119–121) can produce the same conditional probability.

A.8.2   Partition exchangeability

In economic applications such as multiple-agent models of stock markets, groups of agents of different types interact. We face exactly the same problem that confronted statisticians in dealing with the so-called sampling-of-species problem. Sometimes this problem is referred to as the ecological problem in the emerging literature on multiagent or agent-based modeling in economics.

Suppose we take a snapshot of all the agents in the market – a sample of size n at a point in time and observe all the different trading strategies in use. Some or most strategies (types of agents) have been seen in such snapshots or samples taken earlier. There may be new ones not so far observed, however. As Zabell clearly explains, this is not the problem of observing an event to which we assign 0 probability, that is, an event whose probability we judge to be 0. Rather, the problem is observing an event whose existence we did not even previously suspect. A new strategy is invented, or new type of agents are born, and so on. Zabell calls it the problem of unanticipated knowledge. To deal with this problem we need Kingman's construction of exchangeable partition.

A probability function P is partition-exchangeable if the cylinder-set probabilities $P(X_1 = e_1, X_2 = e_2, \ldots, X_N = e_N)$ are invariant with respect to permutations of the time index *and* the category index. For example, suppose

---

[4] This term is adopted to avoid confusion with the usual meaning of sufficiency in statistics (see Good (1965, p. 26)).

you roll a die, and you obtain a sample $\{5, 2, 1, 5, 4, 4, 6, 4, 6\}$. Here, $K = 6$. Rearrange the time indices, i.e., the samples, into a standard descending order of observed frequency of each face of the die, $\{4, 4, 4, 5, 5, 6, 6, 1, 2\}$, and then perform the category permutation $(1, 2)(3, 5)(4, 6)$, that is, $1 \to 2 \to 1, 3 \to 5 \to 3, 4 \to 6 \to 4$. By definition, if P is partition-exchangeable we have

$$P(5, 2, 1, 5, 4, 4, 6, 4, 6) = P(6, 6, 6, 3, 3, 4, 4, 2, 1).$$

Define the frequencies of the frequencies (called abundances in the population-genetics or sampling-of-species literature) by what Zabell calls the partition vector $\mathbf{a} = (a_1, a_2, \ldots a_N)$, where a_r is the number of n_j that are exactly equal to r.[5] In the above example, the original sample has the frequencies $n_1 = 1, n_2 = 1, n_3 = 0, n_4 = 3, n_5 = 2, n_6 = 2$:

$$\mathbf{n} = (1, 1, 0, 3, 2, 2) = 0^1 1^2 2^2 3^1,$$

where the last expression is the notation of Andrews (1971) used to indicate cyclic products of permutations with a_i cycles of size i. In this example $[a_1 = 2, a_2 = 2, a_3 = 1, a_4 = a_5 = \cdots = a_{10} = 0$. Note also that $a_0 = 1$.

The partition vector plays the same role relative to partition-exchangeable sequences that the frequency vector plays for exchangeable sequences. Two sequences are equivalent, in the sense that one can be obtained from the other by a permutation of the time set and a permutation of the category set, if and only if the two sequences have the same partition vector. We can thus alternatively characterize partition exchangeability by the fact that all sequences having the same partition vector have the same probability. Probabilities conditional on the partition vector are independent of P.

We formally define that a random partition is exchangeable if any two partitions π_1 and π_2 having the same partition vector have the same probability:

$$\mathbf{a}(\pi_1) = \mathbf{a}(\pi_2) \quad \Rightarrow \quad P(\pi_1) = P(\pi_2).$$

Since partition-exchangeable sequences are exchangeable, they can be represented by $d\mu$ on the K-simplex Δ_K. To prepare our way for letting K become infinite, we use the order statistics. Denote by Δ_K^* the simplex of the ordered probabilities

$$\Delta_K^* := \left\{ (p_1^*, p_2^*, \ldots, p_K^*); p_1^* \geq p_2^* \geq \cdots \geq p_K^* \geq 0, \sum_{i=1}^{K} p_i^* = 1 \right\}.$$

In the case of the partition-exchangeable sequences, the conditional probability

---

[5] Kingman named it differently because he was working in population genetics. We use Zabell's more neutral name. In Sachkov (1996, p. 82) it is called the state vector of second specification.

becomes

$$P(X_{N+1} = c_i \mid X_1, X_2, \ldots, X_N) = f(n_i; \mathbf{a}).$$

There are $K!$ permutations of the integers $\{1, 2, \ldots, K\}$. To every permutation there corresponds the set defined by

$$\Delta_{K,\sigma} := \{(p_1, p_2, \ldots, p_K) \in \Delta_K; p_{\sigma(1)} \geq p_{\sigma(2)} \geq \cdots \geq p_{\sigma(K)}\}.$$

The map of the probability vector into the vector of probabilities with permuted indices defines a homeomorphism of $\Delta_{K,\sigma}$ onto Δ_K^*. This map can be used to transfer $d\mu$ on Δ_K^* to the subsimplex $\Delta_{K,\sigma}$.

When K is finite, $\Pr(X_1 = c_1) = \Pr(X_2 = c_2) = \cdots = \Pr(X_K = c_K) = 1/K$. When K is not finite, we cannot use this relation. In that case, instead of focusing on the probability of sequences of outcomes or the probability of a frequency vector, we focus on the partition vector and its probability.

In taking the snapshots of a market situation and counting the numbers of agents by the types of strategies they are using at that point in time, the relevant information is an exchangeable random partition of the set $\mathbf{N} := \{1, 2, \ldots, N\}$, where N is the total numbers of agents in the market at that time. We observe the first type, then possibly later the second type and so on. We need not identify what the first type is, for example. We have merely a partition of $\mathbf{N}$,

$$\mathbf{N} = A_1 \cup A_2 \cup \cdots,$$

where $A_i \cap A_j = \emptyset$, $i \neq j$, and where

$$A_1 := \{t_1^1, t_1^2, \ldots; 1 = t_1^1 < t_1^2 < \cdots\}.$$

This means that the type of the first agent observed (sampled) is called type 1. An agent of the same type may be observed (sampled) at later times t_1^2, t_1^3, and so on. An agent of a different type, called type 2, is first observed (sampled) at t_2^1. We construct a set

$$A_2 := \{t_2^1, t_2^2, \ldots; t_2^1 < t_2^2 < \cdots\},$$

where t_2^1 is the first positive integer not in the set A_1.

Example. Given a sample of size 10, taken in the order 6, 3, 4, 2, 3, 1, 6, 2, 2, 3, we have a partition

$$\{1, 2, \ldots, 10\} = \{1, 7\} \cup \{2, 5, 10\} \cup \{3\} \cup \{4, 8, 9\}.$$

Its partition vector is $\mathbf{a} = (2, 1, 2, 0, 0, \ldots, 0)$. This indicates that there are two singletons, one cluster with two numbers, and two clusters with three elements each, and the others are empty. The sum $\sum_i a_i = 5$ gives the total number of clusters, that is, five different groupings have been observed in this sample.

Take the symmetric Dirichlet distribution with parameter α, $\mathcal{D}(\alpha)$ on Δ_K. Map it onto Δ_K^* by associating $(p_1, \ldots, p_K)$ with its ordered rearrangement $(p_1^*, \ldots, p_K^*)$. The Dirichlet distribution on Δ_K induces a probability distribution on Δ_K^*. Kingman shows that this distribution converges to the Poisson–Dirichlet distribution with parameter $\theta = \lim K\alpha$ on letting K go to infinity and α to zero.

By the exchangeability of the underlying sequence, permuting time indices produces a new sequence with the same frequency vector **n**, hence the same partition vector **a**.

We state the Kingman representation theorem for the record. There is a unique $d\mu$ on ∇, the infinite simplex of all ordered defective probability vectors, such that

$$\pi(A) = \int_\nabla \pi_\mathbf{p} \, d\mu(\mathbf{p}),$$

where $d\mu(\mathbf{p})$ is a Poisson–Dirichlet process.

Instead of the Pólya urn, the generalized Pólya urn with one ball of special color (black in Hoppe, and called a mutator by Zabell) generates the correct conditional expectation when the Pólya urn is modified by the device that when the black ball is drawn, the black ball and a ball of new type are returned to the urn. See Hoppe (1987).

Explicitly, the distribution given by

$$\Pr(\mathbf{a}|N) = \frac{N!}{[\theta]_N} \prod_{j=1}^N \frac{\theta^{a_j}}{j^{a_j} a_j!},$$

known as the Ewens sampling formula or multivariate Ewens distribution (MED), governs the partition vector **a**. See Ewens (1972) or Johnson et al. (1997).

Given that we have observed a number of types of agents so far, summarized by the empirical distribution, and given the Poisson–Dirichlet prior, we obtain

$$\Pr(X_{N+1} = c_k|\mathbf{n}) = \frac{n_k}{N + \theta}.$$

Unfortunately, the Poisson–Dirichlet distribution is not easily manipulated. There is a simpler distribution, called the size-biased version, from which it can be derived. See Kingman (1993, Chap. 9) or Hoppe (1987).

A.9   Random partitions and permutations

A.9.1   Permutations

Denote the set $\{1, 2, \ldots, n\}$ by $[n]$. A permutation of $[n]$ is a one-to-one map of $[n]$ onto itself. The number of permutations is $n!$. Permutations are not distinct either because all cycles containing the same elements in the same cyclic order are the same or because relative positions of cycles is immaterial. Among $n!$ permutations the number of distinct cycle classes with a_1 of cycles of length 1, a_2 cycles of length 2, ..., and a_n of cycles of length n is given by

$$\frac{n!}{1^{a_1} 2^{a_2} \cdots n^{a_n} a_1! a_2! \cdots a_n!},$$

where $\sum_j a_j$ is the total number of cycles and $\sum_j j a_j = n$ is the total number of elements being permuted. See Riordan (1958, p. 67). The vector with these a's as components is a partition vector.

Assuming that each of the $n!$ permutations is equally likely, the Cauchy formula is

$$\Pr(a_1, a_2, \ldots, a_n) = \prod_{1}^{n} \left(\frac{1}{j}\right)^{a_j} \frac{1}{a_j!} I_{(\sum j a_j = n)},$$

where I is the indicator function, i.e., 1 when the indicated condition holds, and zero otherwise.

A.9.2 Random partitions

Denote by π a partition of an n-set, $[n] = \{1, 2, \ldots, n\}$, into parts. For example, partition into k parts means that $[n] = \{1, 2, \ldots, n\}$ is partitioned into k blocks or k subgroups, $\pi = \{B_1, B_2, \ldots, B_k\}$, such that $B_i \cap B_j = \emptyset$ when $i \neq j$, and $\cup B_j = [n]$. We may think of it as a single-valued map from $[n]$ into k points (cells, boxes, or types). In partitions, the components are the blocks $\{a_1, a_2, \ldots, a_n\}$ such that

$$n = 1^{a_1} 2^{a_2} \cdots n^{a_n},$$

which is the notation in Andrews (1971) for the partition of n into a_1 ones, a_2 twos, etc.: $n = 1 + 1 + \cdots + 1 + 2 + 2 + \cdots + n$, i.e., $\sum a_i$ is the number of blocks, and

$$\sum_{k=1}^{n} i a_i = n.$$

For example, in $10 = 1 + 1 + 3 + 5 = 1^2 3^1 5^1$, we have $a_1 = 2$, $a_3 = 1$, $a_5 = 1$ and all other as are zero.

We call the partition π type $\mathbf{a}$, or say π has partition vector $\mathbf{a}$, when the partition vector associated with the blocks is $\mathbf{a}$. That is, a_i of the blocks have exactly i elements each. We denote by $|\pi|$ the number of blocks in π. We then have $|\pi| = \sum a_i$ and $n = \sum i a_i$.

The number of such partitions is denoted by $S(n, k)$, called a Stirling number of the second kind. It satisfies the recursion relation

$$S(n + 1, k) = S(n, k - 1) + k S(n, k).$$

We can understand this relation by considering partitions of $n + 1$ points into k subsets as resulting from partitioning n points into $k - 1$ subsets and assigning the $n + 1$th point to the kth subset, or from partitioning n points into k subsets and assigning the $n + 1$th point to any one of the k subsets. The boundary condition is $S(n, 1) = 1$ for any positive integer n. Set $S(n, 0) = 0$ for $n \geq 1$, and $S(n, k) = 0$ for $k \geq n + 1$. Further details on Stirling numbers are found in Appendix A.5.

Suppose that subsets or blocks of size i can be in one of m_i distinct configurations or structures. Then we say that blocks have **structure M**, with the exponential generating function

$$M(x) := \sum_{i \geq 1}^{\infty} m_i x^i / i!.$$

An n-set has a **compound structure**, $S(M)$, when it is split into parts and each part has structure M. We count the number of internal structures of the n-set, following van Lint and Wilson (1992).

At the end of this section we discuss an example of Stirling numbers of the second kind.

For some integer-valued function $f(i)$, such as $f(i) = m_i$, where m_i is the number of labeled (that is, distinguishable) structures on a set of size i, let its generating function be denoted by

$$h(n) = \sum_{\pi} f(1)^{a_1} f(2)^{a_2} \cdots f(n)^{a_n},$$

where the summation is over all partitions with the same partition vector $\mathbf{a}$, and define the exponential generating function of this sequence as

$$H(x) = \sum_{1}^{\infty} h(n) x^n / n!.$$

Finally, let

$$G(x) = \sum_{1}^{\infty} \frac{x^i}{i!} = \exp x - 1.$$

Then, we have

Proposition. $H[M(x)] = \exp M(x) - 1.$

This is in van Lint and Wilson (1992, Theorem 14.2), and can also be proved by direct calculation of $G[M(x)]$:

$$\cdot \ G[M(x)] = \sum_{k \geq 1} \left[\sum_{i \geq 1} \frac{m_i x^i}{i!} \right]^k \frac{1}{k!}.$$

By comparing the coefficients of $x^n/n!$ we can express $h(n)$ in terms of the ms:

$$N(n, \mathbf{a}) = I_{\sum i a_i} n! \frac{m_i^{a_i}}{(i!)^{a_i} a_i!}.$$

The right-hand side of the expression for $G[M(x)]$ is

$$\sum_{k \geq 1} \frac{1}{k!} \sum \frac{m(b_1)m(b_2)\cdots m(b_k)}{b_1! b_2! \cdots b_k!} x^{b_1+b_2+\cdots b_k},$$

where we write for convenience $m(i) = m_i$, and the inner summation is over the k-tuple $(b_1, b_2, \ldots, b_k)$ with the same partition vector. Noting that $\sum_1^k b_i = \sum_1^n i a_i = n$, the inner sum becomes

$$x^n \frac{c(\mathbf{a})}{(1!)^{a_1}(2!)^{a_2}\cdots(n!)^{a_n}} m(1)^{a_1} m(2)^{a_2} \cdots m(n)^{a_n},$$

where $c(\mathbf{a})$ is the number of distinct k-tuples $(b_1, \ldots b_k)$ with exactly the same partition vector $\mathbf{a}$, that is,

$$c(a_1, \ldots, a_n) = \frac{k!}{a_1! a_2! \cdots a_n!}.$$

Therefore, the coefficient of $x^n/n!$ is given by $N(n, \mathbf{a})$ of the theorem.

Example. Let the structure M be $m_i = \gamma$ for all i. Recall that the number of k-part unordered partitions of n is given by the Stirling number of the second kind, $S(n, k)$. Therefore, we have $h(n) = \sum_{k \geq 1} S(n, k) \gamma^k$. The theorem of van Lint and Wilson says that

$$1 + \sum_{n \geq 1} \frac{S(n, k) x^n \gamma^k}{n!} = \exp\left[\gamma \sum_{n \geq 1} \frac{x^n}{n!} \right].$$

Set γ to 1; then we obtain

$$1 + \sum_{n \geq 1} \sum_{k \geq 1} S(n, k) x^n / n! = \exp(e^x - 1),$$

or

$$\frac{(e^x - 1)^k}{k!} = \sum_{n \geq k} S(n, k) x^n / n!.$$

This recursion relation is obtained in another way in Appendix A.5.

Let $\{X_1, X_2, \ldots\}$ be a sample, finite or infinite, taken from a population of agents whose characteristics, states, or choices are any one of an at most countably infinite number of types, or categories, labeled by positive integers. Let π be a random discrete probability distribution on the real line, and $X_1, X_2, \ldots$

be i.i.d. random variables with distribution π. Let K_n be the number of distinct values observed in the random sample $\{X_1, X_2, \ldots, X_n\}$. Set K_n to zero if less than n distinct values are in the sample, i.e., K_n is the almost sure limiting frequency in the sequence of samples of value n.

The atoms of π are interpreted as the frequencies in empirical distributions, or fractions of the various types or categoies of agents in an infinite population. The vector $\mathbf{P} = (P_1, P_2, \ldots)$, where P_i is the proportion or fraction of the agents of type i in the population, describes the **abundance** of type i, in the language of the sampling-of-species literature. Note that

$$\Pr(X_1 = i | \mathbf{P}) = P_i$$

by definition.

A partition of a set consisting of positive integers $1, 2, \ldots, n$ is an unordered collection of positive integers that sum to n. Alternatively, it is a collection of subsets B_j of $[n]$ such that $B_i \cap B_k = \emptyset$, $i \neq k$, and $[n] = \bigcup B_j$. Let n_i be the number of times i is observed in the first n samples $\{X_1, X_2, \ldots, X_n\}$, that is, $n_i = |B_i|$, $i = 1, 2, \ldots, n$.

One representation of the sample is to use the order statistics

$$n_{(1)} \geq n_{(2)} \geq \cdots \geq n_{(k)},$$

with $\sum n_{(i)} = n$. Another is to use the partition vector $\mathbf{a} = (a_1, a_2, \ldots, a_n)$, with $\sum_i a_i = k$ and $\sum_i i a_i = n$, where

$$a_i = |\{j : n_j = i\}|.$$

A **random partition** is a random variable π_n that assigns the same probability to all partitions of n, i.e., each partition is equiprobable under π_n. For each n, the finite sample $(X_1, X_2, \ldots, X_n)$ defines a random partition of $[n]$ described by a partition vector $\mathbf{a} = (a_1, \ldots, a_n)$, where a_i is the number of types with i agents in the sample. Partition vectors collect these components. See Zabell (1992).

A.9.3   Noninterference of partitions

Kingman discusses two properties associated with partition structures: non-interference and consistency. This subsection describes the first property. Let $P_n(\mathbf{a}) = \Pr(\pi_n = \mathbf{a})$ denote the probability distribution of the partition vector. Kingman (1978b) noted a natural consistency relation between P_n and P_{n+1}: deleting one agent from the sample of size $n + 1$ at random should be consistent with the sample of size n, i.e.,

$$\frac{i a_i}{n} P_n(\mathbf{a}) = c(n, i) P_{n-i}(a_1, \ldots, a_i - 1, \ldots, a_n),$$

where $c(n, i)$ is some constant: if an agent chosen at random is of a type with i representatives in the sample, then the probability distribution of the remaining $n - i$ agents in the sample has distribution P_{n-i} independent of the fraction of agents of type i.

Think of n as the number of shoppers on a particular day in an open-air market, for example, in some large city. Kirman's fish-market example (1995) may be thought of in this light. Each day a random number of shoppers show up in the market. Shoppers are classified or typed by the stores they shop at or the goods they buy.

It is easy to verify that the Ewens sampling formula satisfies this noninterference property.

A.9.4 *Consistency*

Another property of random partitions is consistency. For example, a sample of size n may be created by first taking a sample of size $n + 1$ and dropping one sample randomly. Thus the probabilities $P_n(a_1, a_2, \ldots, a_n)$ and $P_{n+1}(a_1, a_2, \ldots, a_{n+1})$ should satisfy

$$
P_n(\mathbf{a}) = \frac{a_1 + 1}{n + 1} P_{n+1}(a_1 + 1, a_2, \ldots, a_n, 0)
$$
$$
+ \sum_{k=2}^{n} \frac{k(a_k + 1)}{n + 1} P_{n+1}(a_1, \ldots, a_{k-1} - 1, a_k + 1, \ldots, a_n, 0)
$$
$$
+ \frac{n + 1}{n + 1} P_{n+1}(a_1, \ldots, a_n - 1, 1).
$$

The first term is the probability that a sample is dropped or lost from a collection of singletons. The last term is for the case where there are $n + 1$ agents of the same type and one of them is lost. In between, the partition vector $\mathbf{a}$ is arrived at by dropping a sample from the kth component of the partition vector, that is, there are $a_{k-1} - 1$ types, each containing $k - 1$ agents of the same type, and there are $a_k + 1$ types of k agents each. One agent of the latter type is lost, causing the number of types represented by $k - 1$ agents to be a_{k-1}, and the number with k agents to be a_k.

A.10 Dirichlet distributions

A.10.1 *Beta distribution*

Suppose we have a collection of agents of various types in a model, and we know the total number of types, K. Then, we often describe the "demography" by types of collections of agents by empirical distributions, that is, by a

K-dimensional vector of fractions of agents. The fractions are distributed on a finite-dimensional simplex. The simplest nontrivial probability distribution is the Dirichlet distribution. This distribution arises naturally every time we deal with models of agents of several types or with a finite number of choices.[6] Here, we proceed without going into the reasons.

With only two types or choices, the distribution is particularly simple because the fraction is $(p, 1 - p)$, where p has a Beta distribution,

$$B(a, b) := \frac{\Gamma(a + b)}{\Gamma(a)\Gamma(b)} p^{a-1}(1 - p)^{b-1},$$

for p in the unit interval $(0, 1)$.

A special case $B(1, \theta) = \theta(1 - p)^{\theta-1}$ is called the GEM distribution in the population-genetics literature see Johnson et al. (1997). We encounter this distribution when we discuss size-biased sampling.

A.10.2   Dirichlet distribution

With $K \geq 2$ the probability distribution on Δ_K with a simple structure is defined on the simplex Δ_K by the density

$$\frac{\Gamma\left(\sum_{i=1}^{K} a_i\right)}{\prod_{i=1}^{K} \Gamma(a_i)} \prod_{i=1}^{K} p_i^{a_i-1},$$

where $1 \geq p_i \geq 0, i = 1, 2, \ldots, K - 1$, and p_K is substituted out by $1 - p_1 - p_2 - \cdots - p_{K-1}$, so that the density is defined for $K - 1$ variables, $p_1, p_2, \ldots, p_{K-1}$. This is called the **Dirichlet distribution**. We denote the distribution with this density by $\mathcal{D}(a_1, a_2, \ldots, a_K)$.

Since we deal with exchangeable strategies, we use symmetric Dirichlet distributions with all parameters the same, rather than these more general ones. When all a_i are the same a, we use $\mathcal{D}(a, K)$ to denote the distribution.

Kingman (1975, 1993) derives the Dirichlet distribution from i.i.d. Gamma random variables as follows. Suppose $Y_1, \ldots, Y_K$ are i.i.d. with density

$$g_\alpha(y) = y^{\alpha-1}e^{-y}/\Gamma(\alpha), \qquad y > 0,$$

for some positive parameter α. Let $S = Y_1 + \cdots + Y_K$, and normalize the Ys by the sum

$$p_j = Y_j/S, \qquad 1 \leq j \leq K.$$

Now change the variables from $(Y_1, \ldots, Y_K)$ to $(S, p_1, \ldots, p_{K-1})$.

---

[6] There are actually deeper reasons than technical convenience to use the Dirichlet distributions, as discussed in Zabell (1992), for example, in the case of exchangeable partitions induced by agents.

We can directly manipulate the joint density expression as follows: First write the product of the density for $Y_j = y_j$, $j = 1, \ldots, K$, $S = s = y_1 + \cdots + y_K$,

$$p(y_1, \ldots, y_K) = \frac{(y_1 \cdots y_K)^{\alpha-1} e^{-s}}{\Gamma(\alpha)^K},$$

write the product of the y's in terms of the p's and s, and note that the expression separates into the product of two expressions in terms of s and the ps. Then, making use of the Jacobian of the transformation, we end up with

$$f(s)g(p_1, \ldots, p_K) = \frac{s^{K\alpha-1} e^{-s}}{\Gamma(K\alpha)} \frac{\Gamma(K\alpha)}{\Gamma(\alpha)^K} (p_1 \cdots p_K)^{\alpha-1}.$$

This factored form shows that the sum S of K i.i.d. Gamma random variables is also a Gamma random variable with parameter $K\alpha$, and that the fractions p_j are independent of S, and have the density called the symmetric Dirichlet disstribution $\mathcal{D}(\alpha, K)$, where the first arguments denotes the parameter, and the second indicates that it is the density for $p_1, \ldots p_K$, and where we use $p_K = 1 - p_1 - \cdots - p_{K-1}$.

We also note that the Laplace transform (or the moment generating function) of the gamma distribution is

$$\int_0^\infty g_\alpha(y) e^{-\theta y} \, dy = (1 + \theta)^\alpha$$

for $\theta > -1$. This shows that the Gamma distribution is infinitely divisible, because $(1 + \theta)^{-\alpha t}$ is the Laplace transform of the Gamma distribution with parameter αt for every positive t.

Hence, we have the Lévy–Khinchin representation

$$(1 + \theta)^{-\alpha} = \exp\left[-\alpha \int_0^\infty (1 - e^{-\theta z}) z^{-1} e^{-z} \, dz \right].$$

This identifies $\gamma(dz) = z^{-1} e^{-z} \, dz$ as the measure for the gamma process.

Let Π be a Poisson process on the real half line $S = (0, \infty)$. The count function is defined as

$$N(A) = |\Pi \cap A|$$

for every A in S. This function is such that

$$N\left(\bigcup_{j=1}^\infty A_j \right) = \sum_{j=1}^\infty N(A_j)$$

for disjoint A_j in S. This is a completely random measure with integer values.

We define $\phi(t) = N(0, t]$ for $t > 0$, and $\phi(t) = -N(t, 0]$ for $t < 0$, where $N(\cdots)$ is the counting measure on $(0, \infty)$ of the Poisson process with mean measure dx, $\gamma(dz)$. See Kingman (1993, pp. 12, 88).

The Gamma distribution $g_{\alpha(t-s)}(y)$ corresponds to $\phi(t) - \phi(s)$. For α positive, define $t_0 = 0, t_j = j\alpha$ for $j = 1, \ldots K$. Define

$$Y_j = \phi(t_j) - \phi(t_{j-1}),$$

$j = 1, \ldots, K$, It has the density $g_\alpha(y)$. The ratio

$$p_j = \frac{\phi(t_j) - \phi(t_{j-1})}{\phi(t_K)},$$

$j = 1, \ldots, K$, defines K components of a random vector in Δ_K that has the density of the Dirichlet distribution $\mathcal{D}(\alpha, K)$.

A.10.3 Marginal Dirichlet distributions

The joint density for $p_1, p_2, \ldots, p_{K-2}$ is obtained by integrating p_{K-1} out from the joint density for $x_1, \ldots, x_{K-1}$ of the Dirichlet distribution $\mathcal{D}(a_1, \ldots, a_K)$. Rewrite the expression $1 - \sum_{i=1}^{K-1} p_i$ by factoring out $1 - \sum_{i=1}^{K-2} p_i$. Change the variable to

$$q_{K-1} = \frac{p_{K-1}}{1 - \sum_{j=1}^{K-2} p_j},$$

and integrate q_{K-1} out. What is left is the Dirichlet distribution

$$\mathcal{D}(a_1, a_2, \ldots, a_{K-2}, a_{K-1} + a_K).$$

We can continue this reduction process. We see that the marginal distribution for p_j is Beta$(a_j, \sum_{k \neq j} a_k)$, with $E(p_j) = a_j / \sum_{k \neq i} a_i$.

A.10.4 Poisson–Dirichlet distribution

This distribution is for an infinite sequence $\xi = (\xi_1, \xi_2, \ldots)$ with nonincreasing elements $\xi_1 \geq \xi_2 \geq \cdots$, which sum to one: $\sum_i \xi_i = 1$.

Such a sequence with this distribution can be generated by

$$\xi_i = J_i(\lambda) / \phi(\lambda),$$

where J_i is the height of the ith largest jump in $[0 ; \lambda]$ of the counting process $\phi(\cdot)$. The heights of the jumps form a Poisson process on $(0, \infty)$ with rate $\lambda z^{-1} e^{-z}$.

Given a Poisson process with the above rate function, the Poisson–Dirichlet process can be constructed as shown by Kingman (1993, Chap. 9).

A.10.5 Size-biased sampling

We follow Kingman (1993, p. 98) to show that size-biased samples of Dirichlet distributions have the same distribution as those due to the residual allocation process. See also Pitman (1996).

Suppose that a vector $\mathbf{p} = (p_1, p_2, \ldots, p_K)$ with exchangeable components has the symmetric Dirichlet distribution $\mathcal{D}(a, K)$. Let v be a random variable on $\{1, 2, \ldots, K\}$ with probability given by

$$\Pr(v = j \mid \mathbf{p}) = p_j.$$

In sampling from a population of agents of K types with fractions p_j, $j = 1, \ldots, K$, type j will be drawn with probability p_j, that is, the first sample is of type j with probability p_j. For this reason p_v is said to be obtained by size-biased sampling. If all agents of the same type are removed, then the remaining agents have fractions $p_1, \ldots, p_{v-1}, p_{v+1}, \ldots, p_K$. We can renormalize the fractions by dividing the components of this vector by $1 - p_j$. Denote this vector by $\mathbf{q}^{(1)}$.

The joint density for $(p_v, p_1, \ldots, p_{v-1}, p_{v+1}, \ldots, p_K)$ is $\mathcal{D}(a + 1, a, a, \ldots, a)$. This can be seen by noting that by symmetry the vector $(p_j, p_1, \ldots, p_{j-1}, p_{j+1}, \ldots, p_K)$ has the same density as the original Dirichlet distribution. This occurs with probability p_j. Hence, the density of $(p_v, p_1, \ldots, p_{v-1}, p_{v+1}, \ldots, p_K)$ is $K p_1$ times the density of the original Dirichlet distribution, which is the density for the distribution $\mathcal{D}(a + 1, a, \ldots, a)$, where a is repeated $K - 1$ times. From this, the marginal density for p_v is seen to be

$$\frac{\Gamma(Ka + 1)}{\Gamma(a + 1)\Gamma(Ka - a)} p^a (1 - p)^{(K-1)a - 1}.$$

If we let a go to zero, while letting Ka approach θ, then the marginal density approaches Beta$(1, \theta)$.

Also, given p_v, the sum of the remaining components is $p_1 + \cdots p_{v-1} + p_{v+1} + \cdots + p_K = 1 - p_v$. Let $\mathbf{q}^{(1)}$ be the renormalized vector, that is, the vector in which the conditional joint distribution for the remaining components has the same distribution as that of $(1 - p_v)p^{(1)}$, where $p^{(1)}$ has the $(K - 1)$-dimensional Dirichlet distribution, $D(a, K - 1)$. Now, apply size-biased sampling to $\mathbf{q}^{(1)}$ to produce $\mathbf{q}^{(2)}$, and so on.

At the end of this process, we obtain the rearranged vector $\mathbf{q}$ of $\mathbf{p}$, such that

$$q_1 = v_1, \qquad q_2 = (1 - v_1)v_2 \ldots, \qquad q_K = v_K \prod_{j=1}^{K-1} (1 - v_j),$$

where the vs are independent, and v_j has the density of $B(a + 1, (K - j)a)$. This density approaches $B(1, \theta)$ as a approaches zero and K infinity in such as way that Ka approaches θ.

This is the reverse of starting from the random variables distributed as $B(1, \theta)$ and denoting the kth largest of the q's as p_k. This process produces $(p_1, p_2, \ldots)$, which has the Poisson–Dirichlet distribution with parameter θ as its limiting distribution. See Kingman (1993).

A.11   Residual allocation models

A population of agents of at most countably many types is called a **residual allocation model**, after the model introduced by Halmos (1944), if the fractions of all types can be expressed in the form

$$Q_1 = P_1, \qquad Q_i = P_i \prod_{j=1}^{i-1}(1 - P_j), \quad i \geq 2,$$

with a sequence of independent random variables $\{P_i\}$ defined in the interval $[0, 1]$.

Engen (1975) shows that when the P's have a Dirichlet distribution $\mathcal{D}(\epsilon, K)$, the distribution of the fractions tends to that of the residual allocation model in distriution, as ϵ approaches zero and K goes to infinity in such a way that $K\epsilon$ approaches a constant θ, when the distribution of P has the density $\theta(1 - p)^{\theta-1}$. This is called the GEM distribution by Ewens (1990, Sec. 13).

To establish this, we use a theorem of Wilks (1962, Sec. 5) to the effect that for a bounded random variable all the moments determine the distribution uniquely. We thus compare the limiting forms of the moments of the fractions and of the residual allocation models. Accordingly, suppose that P_i, $i = 1, 2, \ldots, K$, is distributed according to

$$\frac{\Gamma(K\epsilon)}{\Gamma(\epsilon)^K}(P_1 P_2 \cdots P_K)^{\epsilon-1}.$$

Let X be the fraction of the type it represents. Then, noting that the probability that $X = P_i$ (that is, the probability that the sample is of type i is P_i), we calculate its rth moment as

$$E(X^r) = E[E(X^r | P_i, i = 1, 2, \ldots, K)]$$

$$= E\left(\sum_{i=1}^{K} P_i^{r+1}\right) = \frac{\Gamma(K\epsilon + 1)\Gamma(r + \epsilon + 1)}{\Gamma(\epsilon + 1)\Gamma(K\epsilon + r + 1)}.$$

In the limit as ϵ approaches zero and $K\epsilon \to \theta$,

$$\lim E(X^r) = \frac{\Gamma(\theta + 1)\Gamma(r + 1)}{\Gamma(\theta + r + 1)}.$$

On the other hand, since $\sum_{i=1}^{k} Q_i = 1 - \prod_{i=1}^{k}(1 - P_j)$, we have $\sum_{i=1}^{j} Q_i \le$ 1, but it approaches 1 as j goes to infinity. Hence, in the limit we may interpret Q_i as the fraction of type i agents in the group of agents. We note that when the P's have density $\theta(1 - p)^{\theta-1}$,

$$\sum_{i=1}^{\infty} E\left(Q_i^{r+1}\right) = \frac{\Gamma(\theta + 1)\Gamma(r + 1)}{\Gamma(\theta + r + 1)}, \text{ which is the same as the displayed equation above.}$$

We thus conclude that the sequences of fractions given by the Dirichlet distribution specified above tend in distribution to that specified by the residual allocation model. The converse has been established by McCloskey (1965).

A.12   GEM and size-biased distributions

Ewens (1990, Sec. 13) has defined a distribution for random variables $x_1, x_2, \ldots,$ x_{n-1} that is a special case of the residual allocation model introduced by Halmos (1944) and called the GEM distribution, after Griffiths, Engen, and McCloskey. It is defined by $x_1 = z_1, x_i = z_i(1 - z_{i-1}) \cdots (1 - z_1), i = 2, 3, \ldots,$ where the z's are i.i.d. with desnity $\theta(1 - z)^{\theta-1}, 0 < z < 1, 0 < \theta < \infty$. A finite version is for $x_1, \ldots, x_n$ with z_j having density

$$f_j(z) = \frac{\Gamma((n - j + 1)\epsilon + 1)}{\Gamma(\epsilon + 1)\Gamma((n - j)\epsilon)} z^{\epsilon}(1 - z)^{(n-j)\epsilon-1}.$$

See Donnelly and Joyce (1989). As n goes to infinity while $n\epsilon$ goes to θ, this density converges to Beta$(1, \theta)$.

Let $\mathbf{x}$ have the GEM distribution, and Let $\mathbf{y}$ be defined as follows: $y_1 = x_i$ with probability x_i, and given y_1, y_2 is defined to be x_j with $x_j/(1 - x_i), i \ne j$, and so on. Then, $\mathbf{y}$ has the same distribution as $\mathbf{x}$. We say that the GEM distribution is invariant under size biasing. Since this notion is important, we summarize the steps involved in size-biasing in a context of sampling. First, pick one agent at random out of n agents. Label his type i_1, and remove from the sample of all agents of the same type. Second, choose randomly an agent from the remaining agents, and label his type i_2. Remove all agents of this second type from the remaining agents, and continue.

Fix the number of the types of agents in the sample of size n at K. The size biasing permutes the types $\{1, 2, \ldots, K\}$ into $\pi^* = \{i_1, i_2, \ldots, i_K\}$.

We have, letting n_j denote the number of agents of type j,

$$\Pr(\pi^* = (i_1, i_2, \ldots, i_K) \mid n_1, n_2, \ldots, n_K) = \frac{n_{i_1}}{n} \frac{n_{i_2}}{n - n_{i_1}} \cdots \frac{n_{i_K}}{n_{i_K}}.$$

Note that the denominator can be expressed as $n_{i_K}(n_{i_K} + n_{i_{K-1}}) \cdots (n_{i_K} + n_{i_{K-1}} \cdots)(n_{i_1} + \cdots + n_{i_K})$.

Average this probability with the Ewens sampling formula expressed in terms of the number of each types as

$$P_E(n_1, n_2, \ldots, n_K) = \frac{\theta^K}{\theta^{[n]}} \frac{n!}{n_1 n_2 \cdots n_K}.$$

The result is the sized-biased partition probability

$$P_S(n_1^*, n_2^*, \ldots, n_K^*) = \frac{\theta^K}{\theta^{[n]}} \frac{n!}{n_K^*(n_K^* + n_{K-1}^*) \cdots (n_1^* + n_2^* + \cdots + n_K^*)}.$$

Here, we use the lemma in Donnelly and Joyce (1989):

$$\sum_{\pi} \frac{1}{n_{\pi(1)}(n_{\pi(1)} + n_{\pi(2)}) \cdots (n_{\pi(1)} + \cdots + n_{\pi(k)})} = \frac{1}{n_1 n_2 \cdots n_k}.$$

Kingman (1993, Sec. 9.6) illustrates the process of size biasing on the Dirichlet distribution and shows that the size-biased version of the Dirichlet distribution is the GEM distribution. As n goes to infinity while $n\epsilon$ goes to θ, this shows that the Poisson–Dirichlet distribution has the GEM distribution as its size-biased version. We give a heuristic derivation here. For rigorous demonstration of this fact see Donnelly and Joyce (1989, Theorem 5).

Start with a vector $\mathbf{x} = (x_1, x_2, \ldots, x_n)$ whose components are all positive and sum to one. The components are distributed as the symmetric Dirichlet distribution, $\mathcal{D}(\epsilon, n)$. A random variable ν picks an integer out of $\{1, 2, \ldots, n\}$ with

$$\Pr(\nu = j) = x_j, \qquad 1 \le j \le n.$$

Define a new vector $\mathbf{x}'$ by rearranging the components of $\mathbf{x}$ by putting x_ν as the first component. The components of this new vector are distributed as the Dirichlet distribution $\mathcal{D}(\epsilon + 1, \epsilon, \ldots, \epsilon)$. By integrating the variables from the second to the nth, we see that x_ν has the density

$$\frac{\Gamma(n\epsilon + 1)}{\Gamma(\epsilon + 1)\Gamma((n-1)\epsilon)} z^\epsilon (1 - z)^{(n-1)\epsilon - 1}.$$

Name this random variable z_1, that is, z_1 has the density displayed above.

The remaining $n - 1$ components of $\mathbf{x}$ sum to $1 - x_\nu$, i.e., $1 - z_1$. Renormalize these components by dividing them by $1 - z_1$, and name the resultant vector $\mathbf{x}^{(1)}$. The components of this new vector are positive and sum to one. Their joint distribution is $\mathcal{D}(\epsilon, n - 1)$. We repeat the above process of selecting randomly a component from this new vector, $x_k^{(1)}$, say. It has the density

$$\frac{\Gamma((n-1)\epsilon + 1)}{\Gamma(\epsilon + 1)\Gamma((n-2)\epsilon)} z^\epsilon (1 - z)^{(n-2)\epsilon - 1}.$$

Name this random variable z_2.

By repeating the above process the components of the original vector **x** are rearranged into $(y_1, y_2, \ldots)$ with

$$y_1 = z_1, \, y_j = z_j(1 - z_1)(1 - z_2) \cdots (1 - z_{j-1}),$$

$j = 1, 2, \ldots$, where z_j has exactly the density shown at the beginning of this section.

Hoppe (1987) establishes the relationship between the residual allocation model and the size-biased sampling as follows. If P_i is distributed as Beta(a_i, b_i), then $\{Q_n\}$ has the generalized Dirichlet distribution. When $b_k = \sum_{j=k+1}^{n} a_j$ for some $n \geq 2$, then $\{Q_1, Q_2, \ldots, Q_n\}$ has the $\mathcal{D}(a_1, a_2, \ldots, a_n)$ distribution.

If $(P_1, P_2, \ldots, P_n)$ are $\mathcal{D}(\alpha, n)$, then the size-biased permutation of $(P_1, \ldots, P_n)$ is known to be a residual allocation model that has the generalized Dirichlet distribution with the residual fraction distributed as Beta$(1 + \alpha, (n - i)\alpha), i = 1, 2, \ldots, n$.[7] Hoppe (1986) has shown that if a type is randomly deleted and the remaining population is rescaled so that the rescaled fractions sum to one, and the rescaled population is the same as the original one except for the numbering of the types, then the population is Poisson–Dirichlet, and conversely, if a type is randomly deleted from a Poisson–Dirichlet distribution, then the distribution of the rescaled residual population is the same as the Poisson–Dirichlet distribution except for the numbering.

Pitman (1996) has allowed the residual allocation models to have dependent residual fractions. We next describe his characterizations of residual allocation models that are invariant with respect to size-biased permutations.

Construct a sequence Π_n of random partitions of $[n]$ as follows. We think of them in terms of sequential sampling without replacement of n agents from a large population of agents. Given a sequence of random variables $(P_1, P_2, \ldots)$ such that $\sum P_i = 1$, with $P_n \geq 0$, Π_1 consists of the first agent sampled. With probability P_1 the next agent sampled is of the same type as the first, and with probability $R_1 = 1 - P_1$ he is of a new type and is put in a new block. Thus the probability that the block containing the first agent, A_1, is of size n_1 is $P_1^{n_1-1}$, i.e.,

$$\Pr(\Pi_1 = \{A_1\}) = E\left(P_1^{n_1-1}\right).$$

---

[7] See Pitman (1995) for the characterization of the set of fractions in ∇ to be invariant under size-biased permutation. See p. 231 for the definitions of Δ and ∇. Since labeling of agents is for convenience and labels carry no special meaning in economic models for the agents (i.e., agents are exchangeable in the technical sense of the probability literature), we delabel the agents, or we deem two vectors of fractions to describe the same population if they differ only in the ways the types are numbered.

With two types of agents in the sample, and with the size of A_i being n_i, $i = 1, 2$, we have

$$\Pr(\Pi_2 = \{A_1, A_2\}) = E\left(P_1^{n_1-1} P_2^{n_2-1} R_1\right).$$

Given $\Pi_n = \{A_i\}_1^n$ with $|A_i| = n_i$, $\sum_i n_i = n$, the next agent sampled is of type i, i.e., belongs to block A_i, with probability P_i, and with probability $R_i = 1 - P_1 - \cdots - P_i$ he belongs to a new type, i.e., starts a new block. Therefore,

$$\Pr\left(\Pi_n = \{A_i\}_1^k\right) = E\left(\prod_{i=1}^{k} P_i^{n_i-1} \prod_{j=1}^{n-1} R_j\right).$$

This probability depends on the blocks A_j, $j = 1, \ldots, n$, only through their sizes n_j, $j = 1, \ldots, n$. Pitman (1996, Theorem 4) shows that if the probability is symmetric in these arguments, then this construction is invariant under size-biased permutation.

Denote the infinite-dimensional cube by

$$Q = [0, 1] \times [0, 1] \times \cdots,$$

and denote the infinite-dimensional simplex by

$$\Delta = \left\{\mathbf{x}; x_i \geq 0, \sum_{i=1}^{\infty} x_i \leq 1\right\}.$$

Define its subset

$$\nabla = \left\{\mathbf{x}; x_i \geq 0, \sum_{i=1}^{\infty} x_i = 1\right\}.$$

Denoting a point in the cube by $\mathbf{y}$, we define a map T from Q into Δ by $x_1 = y_1$, and for $i \geq 2$ by

$$x_i = (T\mathbf{y})_i = y_i \prod_{k=1}^{i-1}(1 - y_k).$$

We use λ^m to denote the Lebesgue measure on the m-dimensional cube. The m-dimensional version of T, denoted by T_m, maps this m-dimensional cube into the m-dimensional $\Delta_m = \{(x_i)_{i=1}^m; x_i \geq 0, \sum_i x_i \leq 1\}$.

If $\prod_j(1 - y_j) = 0$, then $T\mathbf{y} \in \nabla$, because $1 - \sum x_j = \prod(1 - y_j)$.

For $\mathbf{x} \in \nabla$ such that x_i is positive for all i, the inverse map T^{-1} exists and is such that

$$(T^{-1}\mathbf{x})_i = \frac{x_i}{1 - x_1 - x_2 - \cdots x_{i-1}}.$$

The Jacobian matrix $\partial(x_1, x_2, \ldots, x_m)/\partial(y_1, y_2, \ldots, y_m)$ has zeros below the diagonal and $1, 1 - y_1, (1 - y_1)(1 - y_2), \ldots, \prod_1^{m-1}(1 - y_k)$ along the main diagonal; hence, its determinant is given by

$$J = \prod_{k=1}^{m-1}(1 - y_k)^{m-k} = \prod_{k=1}^{m-1}\left(1 - \sum_{i=1}^{k} x_i\right).$$

Therefore, the measure κ_m on Δ_m induced by the map T_m is such that

$$\frac{d\kappa_m}{dx_1 \, dx_2 \cdots dx_m} = \frac{1}{(1 - x_1)(1 - x_1 - x_2) \cdots \left(1 - \sum_1^{m-1} x_i\right)}.$$

When we rewrite it with

$$d\kappa_m = dx_1 \frac{dx_2}{1 - x_1} \frac{dx_3}{1 - x_1 - x_2} \cdots \frac{dx_m}{1 - x_1 \cdots x_{m-1}},$$

we recognize that the measure κ_m is constructed by size-biased sampling as follows: first pick x_1, which is uniformly distributed on $[0,1]$. Next, pick x_2, which is uniformly distributed on $[0, 1 - x_1]$. Point x_i is thus uniformly distributed on the residual interval $[0, 1 - x_1 - x_2 \cdots - x_{i-1}]$.

Next, we follow Ignatov (1982) and introduce a one-to-one continuous map of Q into itself by[8]

$$(L_\theta(\mathbf{y}))_i = 1 - y_i^{1/\theta}$$

for some positive θ. For simpler notation we drop θ from L from now on. Then the transformation $T(L(\mathbf{y}))$ is such that

$$x_1 = 1 - y_1^{1/\theta},$$

and

$$x_i = \left(1 - y_i^{1/\theta}\right) \prod_{j=1}^{i-1} y_j^{1/\theta}$$

for $i \geq 2$. Then κ_θ^m is defined by

$$\frac{d\kappa_\theta^m}{dx_1 \, dx_2 \cdots dx_m} = \theta^m \left(\prod_{j=1}^{m-1}\left(1 - \sum_{k=1}^{j} x_k\right)\right)^{-1} (1 - x_1 - x_2 - \cdots - x_m)^{\theta-1}$$

on Δ, and its infinite-dimensional version κ_α is such that $\kappa_\alpha(\nabla) = 1$.

Next, we consider rearranging the elements of $\mathbf{x} \in \nabla$ in nonincreasing order. Denote this operation by ρ.[9] Define

$$\nu = \rho\kappa,$$

---

[8] Note that the variable $z = 1 - y^{1/\theta}$ has the density $\theta(1 - z)^{\theta-1}$.

[9] This is called the ranking function by Donnelly and Joyce (1989).

where we drop the subscript θ. We examine the first coordinate of v and denote it by h:

$$h([0, a]) = v^1(u : u \leq a) = \kappa(\mathbf{x} \in \Delta_1; \max_i x_i \leq a)$$

$$= \lambda \left(\mathbf{y} \in Q; 1 - y_1^{1/\theta} \leq a, \ 1 - y_i^{1/\theta} \leq a \prod_{k=1}^{i-1} y_k^{-1/\theta}, \ i \geq 2 \right).$$

Noting that y_1 and $\{y_j\}_2^\infty$ are independent of λ, we have the infinite-dimensional version

$$h([0, a]) = \int_0^a h\left([0, a(1-u)^{-1})\theta(1-u)^{\theta-1} du,\right.$$

by putting $u = 1 - y_1^{1/\theta}$.

To proceed further we note that h is absolutely continaous with respect to the Lebesgue measure on $[0, 1]$. Denote the density by $g(u)$. The integral equation can be expressed conveniently as

$$g(u) = \theta u^{-1}(1-u)^{\theta-1} \left\{ 1 - \int_{u/(1-u)}^\infty g(v)\,dv \right\}.$$

In the range of $u \in [1/2, 1]$, the integral above on the right-hand side is zero, since $g(v)$ is. Therefore, we obtain

$$g(u) = \theta u^{-1}(1-u)^{\theta-1}$$

for u in $[1/2, 1]$. This result has also been obtained by Watterson (1976) and Watterson and Guess (1977).

A.13   Stochastic difference equations

Stochastic difference equations with random coefficients arise in studying price differences or returns of an asset. The asymptotic behavior of the solutions of these equations for large time, called the tail behavior, may exhibit the so-called power laws, and is important for that reason.

In studying stationary solutions of stochastic linear difference equations

$$x_{n+1} = A_n x_n + B_{n+1},$$

which are of the form

$$x_n = \sum_{k=1}^n \phi_{n,k} B_k + \phi_{n,0} x_0,$$

with $\phi_{n,k} = \prod_{j=k+1}^n A_j$, where $(A_k, B_k)_{k=1}^n$ are two-dimensional i.i.d. random vectors, de Haan et al. (1989) quote Kesten (1973) as providing a motivation for approximating sums by maximal terms. Kesten shows that the expression

$\sum_k \phi_{k,1} B_{k+1}$ has a tail comparable to $\max_K (\phi_{k,1} B_{k+1})$ (and that the tail of the latter is determined by $\max_j \ln A_j$). See Goldie (1991) for more readable discussions of these relations. See also Bingham et al. (1987, Sec. 8.15) or Pruitt (1987) for more recent treatments of the relations between sums and maxima. See Vervaat (1979), Letac (1986), and Chamayou and Letac (1991) on stationary distributions as sollutions of stochastic difference equations.

As the first and easy entry to the subject we describe the work of Darling (1952), who showed that for i.i.d X's, $E(Z_n)$ approaches 1, where $Z_n = S_n / X_n^*$, with $X_n^* = \max(X_1, \ldots, X_n)$, and $S_n = \sum X_i$. Bingham et al. (1987) have shown that this is equivalent to $1 - F$ being slowly varying. See their Theorem 8.15.2. Feller (1971, VIII.8, Example (b)) shows that for a distribution function $F(x)$ that is strictly less than one for all x, there are scale factors a_n such that X_n^*/a_n has a nondegenerate distribution (i.e., not concentrated at 0) if and only if $1 - F(x)$ varies regularly with a negative exponent.

Let the distribution function F of X have density ϕ, and define

$$G(x) = 1 - F(x) = \int_x^\infty \phi(u)\, du.$$

The characteristic function of Z_n is

$$E(e^{it Z_n}) = \int_0^\infty \phi(\beta)\, d\beta$$
$$\times \int_0^\beta \cdots \int_0^\beta e^{it(\beta+\beta_2+\cdots+\beta_n)/\beta} n\phi(\beta_2) \cdots \phi(\beta_n)\, d\beta_2 \cdots d\beta_n,$$

because there is no loss of generality in assuming that $X_n^* = X_1$. Thus, we have

$$E(e^{it Z_n}) = n e^{it} \int_0^\infty \left\{ \int_0^\beta e^{it\alpha} \phi(\alpha) d\alpha \right\}^{n-1} d\beta.$$

Differentiating the characteristic function with respect to it and setting t to 0, we obtain the mean of Z_n as

$$E(Z_n) = 1 + n(n-1) \int_0^\infty F(\beta)^{n-2} [1 - F(\beta)] \int_0^1 \left[\frac{1 - F(\beta u)}{1 - F(\beta)} - 1 \right] dF(\beta).$$

Darling then shows that the expression in the large square bracket goes to zero as β goes to infinity if the tail of the distribution is slowly varying.

The distribution function for X_n^*/a_n is $F^n(a_n x)$. Suppose that $F^n(a_n x) \to H(x)$ as n goes to infinity. Writing $F = 1 - (1 - F)$ and taking logarithms, this amounts to $n[1 - F(a_n x)] \to -\ln H(x)$. If $1 - F(x)$ varies regularly, then determine a_n so that $n[1 - F(a_n)] \to 1$; then $n[1 - F(a_n x)] \to x^{-\rho}$, with a positive ρ.

A.14   Random growth processes

Consider a discrete-time stochastic process

$$S_{t+1} = \lambda_{t+1} S_t, \tag{A.7}$$

where $\{\lambda_t\}$ is a sequence of i.i.d. positive-valued random variables. On considering λ_t as a growth factor, and S as the size or share of some economic variable (such as share of markets, size of firms, etc.), this equation describes a random growth process in which the product of random variables rather than the more common sum of random variables is involved.[10]

Suppose that $S_t \to S_\infty$, where

$$S_\infty \overset{d}{=} \lambda S_\infty,$$

where λ has the same distribution as λ_1, and the equality is in distribution. Proceeding informally, suppose $f(\cdot)$ is the density function for the λ's. Suppose that

$$E\left(\lambda_1^\kappa\right) = 1,$$

i.e.,

$$\int_0^\infty a^\kappa f(a)\, da = 1.$$

Let

$$H_t(S) := \Pr(S_t > S).$$

Then,

$$H_{t+1}(S) = \Pr(S_{t+1} > S) = \Pr(S_t > S/\lambda_{t+1})$$

$$= E\left[E\left(S_t > \frac{S}{\lambda_{t+1}}\middle|\lambda_{t+1}\right)\right] = E[H_t(S/\lambda_{t+1})]$$

$$= \int_0^\infty H_t(S/a) f(a)\, da.$$

In steady state, we arrive at

$$H_\infty = \int_0^\infty H_\infty(S/a) f(a)\, da.$$

---

[10] Differences between the product and the sum of random variables are sometimes striking.

This equation has a solution

$$H_\infty(S) = cS^{-\kappa},$$

with some constant c. This is a power-law distribution.

When the mean of A is one, i.e., when $\kappa = 1$, we have Zipf's distribution, which has been discussed in a number of cases. See Woodroofe and Hill (1975), Chen (1980), and the more recent Gabaix (1998).

Equation (A.7) is a special case of

$$S_{t+1} = \lambda_{t+1} S_t + B_{t+1}, \tag{A.8}$$

which is discussed in Vervaat (1979), de Haan et al. (1989), and Goldie (1991), for example. We discuss scalar cases. See Kesten (1973) for vector-valued processes.

In the case of (A.7) Verwaat has shown that if $E\lambda_1^\kappa = 1$, $E[\lambda_1^\kappa \ln^+ \lambda_1] < \infty$, and $E|B_1|^\kappa < \infty$, then there exists a constant c such that

$$\Pr(S_\infty > S) \sim cS^{-\kappa}.$$

A.15　Diffusion approximation to growth processes

Suppose a process $\{S_t\}$ has a density $p(S, t)$ that is governed by a forward Chapman–Kolmogorov equation

$$\frac{\partial}{\partial t} p(S, t) = -\frac{\partial}{\partial S}[\mu(S)Sp(S, t)] + \frac{1}{2}\frac{\partial^2}{\partial S^2}[\sigma S^2 p(S, t)],$$

where μ and σ are in general functions of S. When μ and σ are constant, its stationary solution satisfies

$$0 = \mu[Sp_e(S)] + \frac{\sigma^2}{2}[S^2 p_e(S)]'.$$

The form $p_e(S) = S^{-\kappa-1}$ is a solution of this equation with $\kappa = 1 - 2\mu/\sigma^2$. The distribution is of the form $\Pr(S > s) = cs^{-\kappa}$. When μ/σ^2 is small, this is close to the Zipf distribution.

References

Abramovitz, M., and I. A. Stegun (1968). *Handbook of Mathematical Functions* (Dover Publications, Inc., New York).

Aghion, P., and P. Howitt (1992). A model of growth through creative destruction, *Econometrica* **60**, 323–351.

Akerlof, G. A. (1980). A theory of social custom, of which unemployment may be one consequence, *Quart. J. Econ.* **94**, 74–775.

Akerlof, G. A., and R. D. Milbourne (1980). The short run demand for money, *Econ. J.* **90**, 885–900.

Aldous, D. J. (1985). Exchangeability and related topics, in *Lecture Notes in Mathematics*, **1117**, edited by A. Dold and B. Eckmann (Springer-Verlag, Berlin).

——— (1998). Tree-valued Markovian and Poisson-Galton-Watson distributions, *DIAMACS Series in Discrete Mathematics* **41**, 1–20 (American Mathematic Society, Providence).

Amaral, L. A., S. V. Buldyrev, S. Havlin, P. Maas, M. A. Salinger, H. E. Stanley, and M. H. R. Stanley (1997). Scaling behavior in economics: The problem of quantifying company growth, *Physica A* **244**, 1–24.

Amemiya, T. (1985). *Advanced Econometrics* (Harvard University Press, Cambridge, MA).

Anderson, S. P., A. de Palma, and J.-F. Thisse (1993). *Discrete Choice Theory of Product Differentiation* (MIT Press, Cambridge, MA).

Andrews, G. (1971). *Theory of Partitions* (Addison-Wesley Publishing Co., Reading, MA).

Aoki, M. (1976). *Optimal Control and System Theory in Dynamic Economic Analysis* (North-Holland, New York).

——— (1995). Economic fluctuations with interactive agents: Dynamic and stochastic externalities, *Jpn. Econ. Rev.* **46**, 148–65.

——— (1996a). *New Approaches to Macroeconomic Modeling: Evolutionary Stochastic Dynamics, Multiple Equilibria, and Externalities as Field Effects* (Cambridge University Press, New York).

——— (1996b). "Multiple Equilibria, Uncertainty, and Degeneracy: An Example of Stochastic Interactive Dynamics with Social Influences," Mimeograph, EU CompEcs Working Paper No. 34, Dept. Pol. Econ. Univ. Siena.

——— (1997). Shares in emergent markets: Dynamics and statistical properties of equilibrium classification of agents in evolutionary models, in *Statistical Methods in Control and Signal Processing*, edited by T. Katayama and S. Sugimoto (Marcel Dekker, New York).

(1998a), "A Stochastic Model of Prices and Volumes in a Share Market with Two Types of Participants," Mimeograph, Department of Economics, University California, Los Angeles; paper presented at the 1998 Annual Meeting, Society for Economic Dynamics, University of Pennsylvania, Philadelphia.

(1998b). A simple model of asymmetrical business cycles: Interactive dynamics of a large number of agents with discrete choices. *Macroecon. Dynam.* **2**, 427–442.

(2000a). Respecifications of the Kiyotaki–Wright model, Paper presented at the 2000 Wehia Workshop, Marseille.

(2000b). Cluster size distributions of economic agents of many types in a market, *J. Math. Anal. Appl.* **249**, 32–52.

(2000c). Open models of share markets with two dominant types of participants, *J. Econ. Behav. Org.* **49**, 199–216.

(2000d). Herd behavior and return dynamics in a share market with many types of agents, in *Statistical Physics*, edited by M. Tokuyama and H. E. Stanley (American Institute of Physics, Melville, New York).

Aoki, M., and Y. Miyahara (1993). Stochastic aggregation and dynamic field effects, Working Paper No. 3, Center for Computable Economics, University of California, Los Angeles.

Aoki, M., and Y. Shirai (2000). A New Look at the Diamond Search Model: Stochastic Cycles and Equilibrium-Selection in Search Equilibrium, *Macroeconomic Dynamics* **4**, No. 4, 487–505.

Aoki, M., and H. Yoshikawa (2002). Demand saturation-creation and economic growth, *J. of Econ. Behav. and Org.* **48**, 127–154.

Arratia, R., and S. Tavaré (1992). The cycle structure of random permutations, *Ann. Probab.* **20**, 1567–91.

(1994). Independent process approximations for random combinatorial structures, *Adv. Math.* **104**, 90–154.

Arratia, R., A. D. Barbour, and S. Tavaré (1992). Poisson process approximations for the Ewens sampling formula, *Ann. Appl. Probab.* **2**, 519–35.

(1999). On Poisson-Dirichlet limits for random decomposable combinatorial structures, *Comb. Probab. Comput.* **8**, 193–208.

Becker, G. S. (1974). A theory of social interactions, *J. Pol. Econ.* **82**, 1063–1093.

(1990). A note on restaurant pricing and other examples of social influences on prices, *J. Pol. Econ.* **99**, 11-9-16,

Bellman, R. (1949). *Dynamic Programming* (Princeton University Press, Princeton, NJ).

Bingham, N. H., C. M. Goldie, and J. L. Teugels (1987). *Regular Variation, Encyclopedia of Mathematics* **27** (Cambridge University Press, New York).

Blank, A., and S. Solomon (2000). Power laws in cities' population, financial markets and internet sites (scaling in systems with a variable number of components), *Physica A* **287**, 279–88.

Bollobas, B. (1985). *Random Graphs* (Academic Press, Orlando, FL).

Brandt, A. (1986). The stochastic equation $Y_{n+1} = A_n Y_n + B_n$ with stationary coefficients, *Adv. Appl. Probab.* **18**, 211–20.

Brémaud, P. (1999). *Markov Chains: Gibbs Fields, Monte Carlo Simulation, and Queues* (Springer-Verlag, New York).

Chamayou, J.-F., and G. Letac (1991). Explicit stationary distributions for compositions of random functions and products of random matrices, *J. Theor. Probab.* **4**, 3–36.

Chen, L. H. Y. (1995). Poisson approximation for dependent trials, *Ann. Probab.* **3**, 534–45.

Chen, W. (1980). "On Weak Form of Zipf's Law" Ph.D. dissertation, University of Michigan, Ann Arbor, MI.

Çinlar, E. (1975). *Introduction to Stochastic Processes* (Prentice Hall, Englewood Cliffs, NJ).

Clower, R. (1965). The Keynesian counter revolution: A theoretical appraisal in *The Theory of Interest Rates*, edited by F. Hahn and F. Brechling, (Macmillan, London).

Costantini, D., and U. Garibaldi (1979). A probabilistic foundation of elementary particle statistics. Part I, *Stud. Hist. Phil. Mod. Phys.* **28**, 483–506.

(1989), Classical and quantum statistics as finite random processes, *Found. Phys.* **19**, 743–54.

(1999). "A Finitary Characterization of the Ewens Sampling Formula," Mimeograph, Department of Statistics, University of Bologna.

(2000). A probability theory for macroeconomic modelling, Mimeograph, Department of Statistics, University of Bologna.

Cox, D. R., and H. D. Miller (1965). *The Theory of Stochastic Processes* (Chapman & Hall, London).

Darling, D. A. (1952). The influence of the maximum term in the addition of independent random variables, *Trans. Am. Math. Soc.* **73**, 95–107.

David, F. N., and D. E. Barton (1962). *Combinatorial Chance* (C. Griffin, London).

Davis, S. J., R. Haltiwanger, and S. Schuh (1996). *Job Creations and Destructions* (MIT Press, Cambridge, MA).

Day, R., and W. Huang (1990). Bulls, bears and market sheep, *J. Econ. Behav. Org.* **14**, 299–330.

De Finetti, B. (1974, 1975). *Theory of Probability, Vols. 1, 2* (John Wiley & Sons, London).

de Haan, L., S. I. Resnick, H. Rootzén, and C. de Vries (1989). Exremal behavior of solutions to a stochastic difference equation with applications to arch processes, *Stoch. Proc. Appl.* **32**, 213–24.

Derrida, B., and H. Flyvbjerg (1987). The random map model: A Disordered model with deterministic dynamics, *J. Physique* **48**, 971–78.

Derrida, B., and L. Peliti (1991). Evolution in a flat fitness landscape, *Bull. Math. Biol.* **53**, 355–82.

Diamond, P. (1982). Aggregate demand management in search equilibrium, *J. Polit. Econ.* **90**, 881–94.

Diamond, P., and D. Fudenberg (1989). Rational expectations business cycles in search equilibrium, *J. Polit. Econ.* **97**, 606–20.

Dixit, A. (1989). Entry and exit decisions of firms under fluctuating real exchange rates, *J. Pol. Econ.* **97**, 620–637.

Donnelly, P. J., and P. Joyce (1989). Continuity and weak convergence of ranked and size-biased permutations on the infinite simplex, *Stoch. Proc. Appl.* **31**, 89–103.

Donnelly, P. J., and S. Tavaré (1987). The population genealogy of the infinitely-many neutral alleles model, *J. Math. Biol.* **25**, 381–91.

Donnelly, P. J., W. J. Ewens, and S. Padmadisastra (1991). Functionals of random mappings: Exact and asymptotic results, *Adv. Appl. Probab.* **25**, 437–55.

Doyle, P. G., and J. L. Snell (1984). *Random Walks and Electric Networks*, Washington D. C.

Dréze, J. H. (1992). *Money and Uncertainty: Inflation, Interest, Indexation*, Edizioni del'elefante, Rome.

Dupuis, P. A., and R. S. Ellis (1997). *A Weak Convergence Approach to the Theory of Large Deviations* (John Wiley & Sons, New York).

Durrett, D. (1991). *Probability: Theory and Examples* (Wadsworth & Brooks/Cole, Pacific Grove, CA).

Engen, S. (1975). A note on the geometric series as a species frequency model, *Biometrika* **62**, 694–99.

Ewens, W. J. (1972). The sampling theory of selectively neutral alleles, *Theor. Pop. Biol.* **3**, 87–112.

——— (1979). *Mathematical Population Genetics* (Springer-Verlag, Berlin).

——— (1990). Population genetics theory – The past and the future, in *Mathematical and Statistical Problems in Evolution*, edited by S. Lessard (Kluwer Academic Publishers, Boston).

Feller, W. (1939). Die grundlagen der volterraschen theorie des kamphes ums dasein in wahrscheinlichkeitstheoretischer behandlung, *Acta Biotheoretica* **3**, 87–112.

——— (1968). *An Introduction to Probability Theory and Its Applications, Vol. I*, 3rd ed. (John Wiley & Sons, New York).

——— (1971). *An Introduction to Probability Theory and Its Applications, Vol. II*, 2nd ed. (John Wiley & Sons, New York).

Gabaix, X. (1998). "Zipf's Law for Cities: An Explanation," Ph.D. dissertation, Department of Economics, Harvard University, Cambridge, MA.

Galambos, J. (1987). *Asymptotic Theory of Extreme Order Statistics*, 2nd ed. (Krieger, Malabar, FL).

Gardiner, C. W. (1990). *Handbook of Stochastic Methods*, 2nd ed. (Springer-Verlag, Berlin).

Goldie, C. M. (1991). Implicit renewal theory and tails of solutions of random equations, *Ann. Appl. Probab.* **1**, 126–66.

Good, I. J. (1965). *The Estimation of Probabilities: An Essay on Modern Bayesian Methods* (MIT Press, Cambridge, MA).

Grasman, J., and O. A. van Herwaarden (1999). *Asymptotic Methods for the Fokker–Planck Equation and the Exit Problem in Applications* (Springer-Verlag, Berlin).

Greene, D. H., and D. E. Knuth (1990). *Mathematics for the Analysis of Algorithms* (Birkhauser, Boston).

Grimmett, G. R., and D. R. Stirzaker (1992). *Probability and Random Processes* (Oxford University Press, Oxford).

Guess, H. A., and W. J. Ewens (1972). Theoretical and simulation results relating to the neutral allele theory, *Theor. Pop. Biol.* **3**, 434–47.

Halmos, P. (1944). Random alms, *Ann. Math. Statist.* **15**, 182–89.

Hansen, J. C. (1990). A functional central limit theorem for the Ewens sampling formula, *J. Appl. Probab.* **27**, 28–43.

Harris, B. (1960). Probability distributions related to random mappings, *Ann. Math. Statist.* **31**, 1045–62.

Hildebrand, F. B. (1976). *Advanced Calculus for Applications* (Prentice Hall, Englewood Cliffs, NJ).

Hirabayashi, T., H. Takayasu, H. Miura, and K. Hamada, The behavior of a threshold model of market price in stock exchange, *Fractals* **1**, 29–40.

Hirsch, M. W., and S. Smale (1974). *Differential Equations, Dynamical Systems, and Linear Algebra* (Academic Press, New York).

Hoppe, F. M. (1984). Pólya-like urns and the Ewens sampling formula, *J. Math. Biol.* **20**, 91–94.

——— (1986). Size-biased filtering of Poisson–Dirichlet samples with an application to partition structures in genetics, *J. Appl. Probab.* **23**, 1008–12.

——— (1987). The sampling theory of neutral alleles and an urn model in population genetics, *J. Math. Biol.* **25**, 123–59.

Horowitz, A., and E. Lai (1996). Patent length and the rate of innovation, *Int. Econ. Rev.* **37**, 785–801.

Ignatov, T. (1982). A constant raising in the asymptotic theory of symmetric grops, and Poisson-Dirichlet measure, *Theoy Probab. Appl.* **27**, 136–47.

Ingber, L. (1982). Statistical mechanics of neocortical interactions, *Physica A* **5**, 83–107.

Iwai, K. (1984a). Schumpeterian dynamics: An evolutionary model of innovation and imitation, *J. Econ. Behav. Org.* **5**, 159–90.

(1984b). Schumpeterian dynamics, Part II: Technological progress, firm growth and economic selection, *J. Econ. Behav. Org.* **5**, 321–51.

(1996). The bootstrap theory of money: A search-theoretic foundation of monetary economics, *Struct. Change Econ. Dyn.* **7**, 451–77.

Johnson, N. L., S. Kotz, and N. Balakrishnan (1997). *Discrete Multivariate Distributions* (John Wiley & Sons, New York).

Jones, C. I. (1995). R & D based models of economic growth, *J. Polit. Econ.* **103**, 759–784.

Jones, C. I., and J. C. Williams (1998). Measuring the social return to R & D, *Q. J. Econ.* **113**, 1119–35.

Jordan, C. (1947). *Calculus of Finite Differences*, 2nd ed. (Chelsea Publishing Co., New York).

Jovanovic, B. (1987). Micro shocks and aggregate risk, *Q. J. Econ.* **102**, 395–409.

Kaplan, N. (1977). Two applications of a Poisson approximation for dependent events, *Ann. Probab.* **5**, 787–94.

Karlin, S., and H. Taylor (1981). *A Second Course in Stochastic Processes* (Academic Press, New York).

Katz, L. (1955). Probability of indecomposability of a random mapping function, *Ann. Math. Statist.* **26**, 512–17.

Kelly, F. (1977). Exact results for the Moran neutral allele model, *Adv. Appl. Probab.* **9**, 197–99.

(1979). *Reversibility and Stochastic Networks* (John Wiley & Sons, New York).

(1983). Invariant measures and the *Q*-matrix, in *Probability, Statistics, and Analysis*, edited by J. F. C. Kingman and G. E. H. Reuter (Cambridge University Press, Cambridge, England).

Kendall, D. G. (1948a). On the generalized "birth-and-death" process, *Ann. Math. Statist.* **19**, 1–15.

(1948b). On some modes of population growth leading to R. A. Fisher's logarithmic series distribution, *Biometrika* **35**, 6–15.

(1949). Stochastic processes and population growth, *J. Roy. Statist. Soc. Ser. B* **11**, 230–264.

(1967). On finite and infinite sequences of exchangeable events, *Stud. Sci. Math. Hungar.* **2**, 319–27.

(1975). Some problems in mathematical genealogy, in *Perspective in Probability and Statistics*, edited by J. Gani (Academic Press, New York).

Kesten, H. (1973). Random difference equations and renewal theory for products of random matrices, *Acta Math.* **131**, 208–48.

(1974). Renewal theory for functionals of a Markov chain with general state space, *Ann. Probab.* **2**, 355–86.

Keynes, J. M. (1973). *A Treatise on Probability* (Macmillan for Royal Economic Society, Cambridge, England).

Kimura, M. (1955). Solution of a process of random genetic drift with a continuous model, *Proc. Nat. Acad. Sci. U.S.A.* **41**, 144–50.

Kingman, J. F. C. (1969). Markov population processes, *J. Appl. Probab.* **6**, 1–18.

(1975). Random discrete distributions, *J. R. Statist. Soc. B* **37**, 1–22.

(1978a). Random partitions in population genetics, *Proc. R. Soc.* **361**, 1–20.

(1978b). Representation of partition structures, *J. London Math. Soc.* **18**, 374–80.

(1980). *Mathematics of Genetic Diversity* (SIAM, Philadelphia).

(1982). The coalescent, *Stoch. Process. Appl.*, **13**, 235–48.

(1993). *Poisson Processes* (Oxford University Press, Oxford, England).

Kirman, A. (1993). Ants, rationality and recruitment, *Q. J. Econ.* **108**, 137–56.

(1995). "Economies with Interacting Agents," Discussion Paper No. A-500, Rheinische Friedrich-Wilhelms-Universität, Bonn.

Kirman, A., and N. J. Vriend (1995). "Evolving market structure: A model of price dispersion and loyalty," Mimeograph, the European University Inst. San Domenico, It.

Kiyotaki, N., and R. Wright (1993). A search-theoretic approach to monetary economy, *Am. Econ. Rev.* **83**, 63–77.

Kullback, S., and R. A. Leibler (1956). On information and sufficiency, *Ann. Math. Stat.* **22**, 79–86.

Kupka, J. G. (1990). The distribution and moments of the number of components of a random mapping function. *J. Appl. Probab.* **27**, 202–7.

Kuznets, S. (1953). *Economic Change* (Norton, New York).

Kydland, F. E., and E. C. Prescott (1982). Time to build and aggregate fluctuations, *Econometrica* **50**, 1345–70.

Lawler, G. (1995). *Introduction to Stochastic Processes* (Chapman & Hall, London).

Leadbetter, M. R., G. Lindgren, and H. Rootzén (1983). *Extremes and Related Properties of Random Sequences and Processes* (Springer-Verlag, New York).

Leijonhufvud, A. (1968). *Keynesian Economics and Economics of Keyens* (Oxford University, Oxford).

(1974). "The Varieties of Price Theory: What Microfoundations for Macrotheory," Discussion Paper No. 44, Department of Economics, University of California, Los Angeles.

(1993). Towards not-too-rational macroeconomics, *Southern Econ. J.* **60**, 1–13.

Letac, G. (1986). A contraction principle for certain Markov chains and its applications, *Contemp. Math.* **50**, 263–73.

Levy, M., and S. Solomon (1996). Power laws are logarithmic Boltzmann laws, *Int. J. Mod. Phys.* **7**, 595–601.

Malinvaud, E. (1977). *Theory of Unemployment Reconsidered*, Wiley & Sons, New York.

Mantegna, R., and H. E. Stanley (1994). Stochastic process with ultraslow convergence to a Gaussian: The truncated Lévy flight, *Phys. Rev. Lett.* **73**, 2946–49.

(1995). Scaling behavior in the dynamics of an economic index, *Nature* **376**, 46–49.

Matsuyama, K. (1995). Complementarities and cumulative processes in models of monopolistic competition, *J. Econ. Lit.* **23**, 701–729.

McCloskey, J. W. (1965). "A Model for the Distribution of Individuals by Species in an Environment, Ph.D. thesis, Michigan State University.

McFadden, D. (1972). Conditional logit analysis of qualitative choice behavior, pp. 105–142 in *Frontiers in Econometrics* edited by P. Zarembka (Academic Press, New York; also Institute of Urban & Regional Development, University of California, Berkeley).

(1974). *The Measurement of Urban Travel Demand* (Institute of Urban & Regional Development, University of California, Berkeley).

Mekjian, A. Z. (1991). Cluster distributions in physics and genetic diversity, *Phys. Rev. A* **44**, 8361–75.

Morse, P. M., and H. Feshbach (1953). *Methods of Mathematical Physics* (McGraw-Hill, New York).

Murphy, K., A. Schleifer, and R. W. Vishny (1989). Industrialization and the big push, *J. Pol. Econ.* **97**, 1003–75.

Norris, J. R. (1997). *Markov Chains* (Cambridge University Press, New York).

Orszak, J. M. (1997). Review of new approaches to macroeconomic modeling by Masanao Aoki, *Economica* **64**, 367–368.

Pitman, J. (1995). Exchangeable and partially exchangeable random partitions, *Probab. Theory Rel. Fields*, **102**, 145–58.

(1996). Random distributions invariant under size-biased permutation, *Adv. Appl. Probab.* **28**, 525–39.

Pollett, P. K. (1986). Connecting reversible Markov processes, *Adv. Appl. Probab.* **18**, 880–900.

Pruitt, W. (1987). The contribution to the sum of the summand of maximum modulus, *Ann. Probab.* **15**, 885–96.

Riordan, J. (1958). *An Introduction to Combinatorial Analysis* (John Wiley & Sons, New York).

Risken, H. (1989). *The Fokker–Planck Equation: Methods of Solution and Applications*, 2nd ed. (Springer-Verlag, Berlin).

Sachkov, V. (1996). *Combinatorial Methods in Discrete Mathematics* (Cambridge University Press, New York).

Scherer, F. M. (1980). *Industrial Market Structure and Economic Performance*, 2nd ed. (Houghton Mifflin Co., Boston).

Schmookler, J. (1966). *Invention and Ecoonomic Growth* (Harvard University Press, Cambridge).

Segerstrom, P. S. (1998). Endogenous growth without scale effects, *Amer. Econ. Rev.* **88**, 1290–1310.

Shepp, L. A., and S. P. Lloyd (1966). Ordered cycle lengths in a random permutation, *Trans. Am. Math. Soc.* **121**, 340–57.

Shwartz, A., and A. Weiss (1995). *Large deviations for performance analysis*, Chapman & Hall, London.

Slutzky, E. (1937). The summation of random causes as the source of cyclic processes, *Econometrica*, **5**, 105–46.

Smith, K. (1969). The effects of uncertainty on monopoly price, capital stock and utilization of capital, *J. Econ. Theory* **1**, 48–59.

Sommerfeld, A. (1949). *Partial Differential Equations in Physics* (Academic Press, New York).

Soize, C. (1994). *The Fokker–Planck equation for stochastic dynamical systems and its explicit steady state solutions* (World Scientific, Singapore).

Solomon, S., and M. Levy (1996). Spontaneous scaling emergence in generic stochastic systems, *Int. J. Mod. Phys.* **7**, 745–51.

Solow, R. M. (1994). Perspectives on growth theory, *J. Econ. Perspectives* **8**, 45–54.

Sornette, D., and R. Cont (1997). Convergent multiplicative processes repelled from zero: Power laws and truncated power laws, *J. Phys. I France* **7**, 431–44.

Stanley, R. P. (1983). *Enumerative Combinatorics* (Birkhauser, Boston).

Steele, J. M. (1994). Le Cam's inequality and Poisson approximations, *Am. Math. Monthly*, Jan., 48–54.

Sutton, J. (1997). Gibrat's legacy, *J. Econ. Lit.* **35**, 40–59.

Takayasu, H., and A. Sato (1997). Stable infinite variance fluctuations in randomly amplified Langevin systems, *Phys. Rev. Lett.* **79**, 966–67.

Takayasu, H., A. Sato, and M. Takayasu (1997). Stable infinite variance fluctuations in randomly amplified Langevin systems, *Phys. Rev. Lett.* **79**, 966–69.

Tavaré, S. (1984). Line of descent and genealogical processes and their application in population genetics models, *Theor. Pop. Biol.* **26**, 119–64.

Tiago de Oliveira, J. (1973). An extreme Markovian stationary processes, *Proc. 4th Conf. Probability Theory, pp. 217–225* (Academy of Romania, Brasov).

Tobin, J. (1972). "Inflation and Unemployment," Cowles Foundation Paper No. 361, Cowles Foundation for Research in Economics at Yale, New Haven, CT.

Todorovic, P. (1992). *An Introduction to Stochastic Processes and Their Applications* (Springer-Verlag, New York).

Uzawa, H. (1969). Time preference, and the Penrose effect in a two-class model of economic growth, Part II, *J. Polit. Econ.* **77**, 628–52.

van Kampen, N. G. (1992). *Stochastic Processes in Physics and Chemistry*, rev. ed. (North Holland, Amsterdam).

van Lint, J., and R. M. Wilson (1992). *A Course in Combinatorics* (Cambridge University Press, New York).

Vershik, A. M., and A. A. Shmidt (1981). Limit measures arising in the asymptotic theory of symmetric groups, I, *Theory Probab. Appl.* **16**, 70–85.

Vervaat, W. (1979). On a stochastic difference equation and a representation of non-negative infinitely divisible random variables, *Adv. Appl. Probab.* **11**, 750–83.

Watson, G. N. (1952). *Treatise on the Theory of Bessell Functions*, 2nd ed. (Cambridge University Press).

Watterson, G. A. (1976). The stationary distribution of the infinitely-many neutral alleles diffusion model, *J. Appl. Probab.* **13**, 639–51.

(1984). Lines of descent and the coalescent, *Theor. Pop. Biol.* **26**, 77–92

Watterson, G. A., and H. A. Guess (1977). Is the most frequent allele the oldest? *Theor. Pop. Biol.* **11**, 141–60.

Wilks, S. (1962). *Mathematical Statistics* (John Wiley & Sons, New York).

Willmot, P., J. Dewynee, and S. Howison (1993). *Option Pricing: Mathematical Models and Computation* (Oxford Financial Press, Oxford, England).

Woodroofe, M., and B. M. Hill (1975). On Zipf's law, *J. Appl. Probab.* **12**, 181–206.

Wright, R. (1995). Search, evolution, and money, *J. Econ. Dyn. Control* **19**, 181–206.

Yoshikawa, H. (1995). *Macroeconomics and the Japanese Economy* (Oxford University Press, Oxford).

(2000). *Macroeconomics* in Japanese (Sobunsha, Tokyo).

Young, A. (1998). Growth without scale effects, *J. Pol. Econ.* **106**, 41–63.

Zabell, S. L. (1982). W. E. Johnson's sufficientness postulate, *Ann. Stat.* **10**, 1090–1099.

(1992). Predicting the unpredictable, *Synthese* **90**, 205–32.

Author Index

Subject Index

Printed in the United States
By Bookmasters